Charles L. Whitfield, MD, FASAM
Joyanna Silberg, PhD
Paul Jay Fink, MD
Editors

Misinformation Concerning Child Sexual Abuse and Adult Survivors

Misinformation Concerning Child Sexual Abuse and Adult Survivors has been co-published simultaneously as *Journal of Child Sexual Abuse,* Volume 9, Numbers 3/4 2001.

Pre-publication REVIEWS, COMMENTARIES, EVALUATIONS . . .

"A THOROUGH, INTELLECTUALLY STIMULATING, AND COMPELLING PRIMER. . . . This collection of scholarly articles represents a comprehensive view of the issues. This is a must for everyone's bookshelf."

Ann Wolbert Burgess, RN, DNSc, CS
Professor of Psychiatric Nursing
School of Nursing
Boston College

Misinformation Concerning Child Sexual Abuse and Adult Survivors

Misinformation Concerning Child Sexual Abuse and Adult Survivors has been co-published simultaneously as *Journal of Child Sexual Abuse,* Volume 9, Numbers 3/4 2001.

The *Journal of Child Sexual Abuse* Monographic "Separates"

Below is a list of " separates," which in serials librarianship means a special issue simultaneously published as a special journal issue or double-issue *and* as a "separate" hardbound monograph. (This is a format which we also call a "DocuSerial.")

"Separates" are published because specialized libraries or professionals may wish to purchase a specific thematic issue by itself in a format which can be separately cataloged and shelved, as opposed to purchasing the journal on an on-going basis. Faculty members may also more easily consider a "separate" for classroom adoption.

"Separates" are carefully classified separately with the major book jobbers so that the journal tie-in can be noted on new book order slips to avoid duplicate purchasing.

You may wish to visit Haworth's Website at . . .

http://www.HaworthPress.com

. . . to search our online catalog for complete tables of contents of these separates and related publications.

You may also call 1-800-HAWORTH (outside US/Canada: 607-722-5857), or Fax 1-800-895-0582 (outside US/Canada: 607-771-0012), or e-mail at:

getinfo@haworthpressinc.com

Misinformation Concerning Child Sexual Abuse and Adult Survivors, edited by Charles L. Whitfield, MD, FASAM, Joyanna Silberg, PhD, and Paul J. Fink, MD (Vol. 9, No. 3/4, 2001). *"A THOROUGH, INTELLECTUALLY STIMULATING, AND COMPELLING PRIMER. . . . This collection of scholarly articles represents a comprehensive view of the issues. This is a must for everyone's bookshelf." (Ann Wolbert Burgess, RN, DNSc, CS, Professor of Psychiatric Nursing, School of Nursing, Boston College)*

Misinformation Concerning Child Sexual Abuse and Adult Survivors

Charles L. Whitfield, MD, FASAM
Joyanna Silberg, PhD
Paul Jay Fink, MD
Editors

Misinformation Concerning Child Sexual Abuse and Adult Survivors has been co-published simultaneously as *Journal of Child Sexual Abuse,* Volume 9, Numbers 3/4 2001.

HMTP

The Haworth Maltreatment & Trauma Press
An Imprint of
The Haworth Press, Inc.
New York • London • Oxford

Published by

The Haworth Maltreatment & Trauma Press, 10 Alice Street, Binghamton, NY 13904-1580 USA

The Haworth Maltreatment & Trauma Press is an imprint of The Haworth Press, Inc., 10 Alice Street, Binghamton, NY 13904-1580 USA.

Misinformation Concerning Child Sexual Abuse and Adult Survivors has been co-published simultaneously as *Journal of Child Sexual Abuse*, Volume 9, Numbers 3/4 2001.

The development, preparation, and publication of this work has been undertaken with great care. However, the publisher, employees, editors, and agents of The Haworth Press and all imprints of The Haworth Press, Inc., including The Haworth Medical Press® and The Pharmaceutical Products Press®, are not responsible for any errors contained herein or for consequences that may ensue from use of materials or information contained in this work. Opinions expressed by the author(s) are not necessarily those of The Haworth Press, Inc.

Cover design by Thomas J. Mayshock Jr.

Library of Congress Cataloging-in-Publication Data

Misinformation concerning child sexual abuse / Charles L. Whitfield, Joyanna Silberg, and Paul Jay Fink, editors.
     p. cm.
    Includes bibliographical references and index.
    ISBN 0-7890-1900-0 (alk. paper)–ISBN 0-7890-1901-9 (pbk : alk. paper)
    1. Child sexual abuse. 2. False memory syndrome. 3. Medical misconceptions. I. Whitfield, Charles L. II. Silberg, Joyanna L. III. Fink, Paul Jay.
RC560.C46 M54 2002
616.85′822390651–dc21
                                                 2002001750

Indexing, Abstracting & Website/Internet Coverage

This section provides you with a list of major indexing & abstracting services. That is to say, each service began covering this periodical during the year noted in the right column. Most Websites which are listed below have indicated that they will either post, disseminate, compile, archive, cite or alert their own Website users with research-based content from this work. (This list is as current as the copyright date of this publication.)

Abstracting, Website/Indexing Coverage . . . . Year When Coverage Began

- *Academic Search Elite (EBSCO)* **1996**
- *Applied Social Sciences Index & Abstracts (ASSIA)
  (Online: ASSI via Data-Star) (CDRom: ASSIA Plus)
  <www.csa.com>* **1992**
- *Behavioral Medicine Abstracts* **1992**
- *BUBL Information Service, an Internet-based Information
  Service for the UK higher education community
  <URL: http://bubl.ac.uk/>* **1995**
- *Cambridge Scientific Abstracts (Health & Safety Science
  Abstracts/Risk Abstracts) <www.csa.com>* **1992**
- *caredata CD: the social & community care database
  <www.scie.org.uk>* **1994**
- *Child Development Abstracts & Bibliography (in print & online)
  <www.ukans.edu>*. **1994**
- *CINAHL (Cumulative Index to Nursing & Allied Health
  Literature), in print, EBSCO, and SilverPlatter, Data Star,
  and Paper Chase. (support materials include Subject Heading List,
  Database Search Guide, and instructional video) <www.cinahl.com>* . . **1993**
- *CNPIEC Reference Guide: Chinese National Directory
  of Foreign Periodicals* **1995**
- *Criminal Justice Abstracts* **1992**
- *Criminal Justice Periodical Index* **1995**
- *Educational Administration Abstracts (EAA)* **1992**

(continued)

(continued)

Special Bibliographic Notes related to special journal issues (separates) and indexing/abstracting:

- indexing/abstracting services in this list will also cover material in any "separate" that is co-published simultaneously with Haworth's special thematic journal issue or DocuSerial. Indexing/abstracting usually covers material at the article/chapter level.
- monographic co-editions are intended for either non-subscribers or libraries which intend to purchase a second copy for their circulating collections.
- monographic co-editions are reported to all jobbers/wholesalers/approval plans. The source journal is listed as the "series" to assist the prevention of duplicate purchasing in the same manner utilized for books-in-series.
- to facilitate user/access services all indexing/abstracting services are encouraged to utilize the co-indexing entry note indicated at the bottom of the first page of each article/chapter/contribution.
- this is intended to assist a library user of any reference tool (whether print, electronic, online, or CD-ROM) to locate the monographic version if the library has purchased this version but not a subscription to the source journal.
- individual articles/chapters in any Haworth publication are also available through the Haworth Document Delivery Service (HDDS).

Misinformation Concerning Child Sexual Abuse and Adult Survivors

CONTENTS

LONG TERM SEQUELAE OF CHILD SEXUAL ABUSE AND CLINICAL IMPLICATIONS

ABOUT THE EDITORS

Charles L. Whitfield, MD, FASAM, is in private practice in Atlanta, Georgia. He is a member of the Leadership Council on Mental Health, Justice, and the Media, and on the faculty of the Rutgers Institute on Alcohol Studies at Rutgers University in New Brunswick, New Jersey.

Joyanna Silberg, PhD, is a clinician at Sheppard Pratt Health System in Baltimore, Maryland, and is Executive Vice President of the Leadership Council for Mental Health, Justice, and the Media. She is also President of the International Society for the Study of Dissociation.

Paul Jay Fink, MD, a psychiatrist in private practice in Philadelphia, Pennsylvania, is President of the Leadership Council for Mental Health, Justice, and the Media, and is a past president of the American Psychiatric Association.

Foreword

This special volume focuses on important topics that are relevant to all those who work with victims, offenders or families in which sexual abuse has occurred, those who conduct research in the field, and those who work with these cases in the legal arena. I am quite pleased that the Leadership Council for Mental Health, Justice and the Media (LC) has compiled and edited this collection. This scientific nonprofit organization has been on the forefront in an attempt to combat misinformation concerning child sexual maltreatment and the long-term effects experienced by adult survivors of such abuse.

In recent years, there has been more media attention and journal articles that have misrepresented the state-of-knowledge in this field. A backlash movement has attracted the attention of the media, advocacy organizations, and the courts. This movement has attempted to minimize the effects of child sexual abuse in several arenas. Too often, the public and some professionals have been misled by media publicity and articles published in other journals that appear scientific, but in reality, are biased opinions or overgeneralized research. The field of child sexual abuse has made significant strides in the past decade in dealing more objectively with what we know and what we have yet to learn. Unfortunately, forensic cases are being decided in many courts based upon the recommendations and conclusions of so called "expert witnesses" who do not actually know the clinical research or understand the dynamics of such abusive relationships.

This volume attempts to correct some of this misinformation. The Board and members of the LC have graciously taken on the task of organizing and editing this peer reviewed volume to provide the state-of-the-science information concerning some of the current topics. They have assembled an impressive group of articles and professionals from the scientific, forensic, and clinical fields to address such myths as "false memory syndrome," "recovered memory therapy," and the "lack of harm" to certain boys due to child sexual abuse. We hope this publication will shed light on areas which are in need of more re-

[Haworth co-indexing entry note]: "Foreword." Geffner, Robert. Co-published simultaneously in *Journal of Child Sexual Abuse* (The Haworth Maltreatment & Trauma Press, an imprint of The Haworth Press, Inc.) Vol. 9, No. 3/4, 2001, pp. xvii-xviii; and: *Misinformation Concerning Child Sexual Abuse and Adult Survivors* (ed: Charles L. Whitfield, Joyanna Silberg, and Paul J. Fink) The Haworth Maltreatment & Trauma Press, an imprint of The Haworth Press, Inc., 2001, pp. xiii-xiv. Single or multiple copies of this article are available for a fee from The Haworth Document Delivery Service [1-800-HAWORTH, 9:00 a.m. - 5:00 p.m. (EST). E-mail address: getinfo@haworthpressinc.com].

xiii

search, provide suggestions to clinicians treating clients who have been abused in childhood, and ensure that information released to the public, as well as to professionals in the field, is done in an accurate and objective manner.

Robert Geffner, PhD
Editor

Acknowledgments

The editor would like to acknowledge those professionals who served as ad-hoc reviewers for Volume 9. These people, in addition to the Editorial Board members, helped review articles and provided valuable assistance and feedback to authors. I appreciate the time and effort spent in this endeavor by:

Fred Berlin, MD, PhD, The Johns Hopkins University, Baltimore, Maryland

Sandra Bloom, MD, The Sanctuary at Northwestern, Northwestern Institute of Psychiatry, Fort Washington, Pennsylvania

Catherine Classen, PhD, Stanford University School of Medicine, Stanford, California

David L. Corwin, MD, Medical Director, Child Protection Team, Primary Children's Medical Center, Salt Lake City, Utah

Suzanne L. Davis, PhD, DecisionQuest, Kingwood, Texas

Victoria Follette, PhD, Psychology Department, University of Nevada–Reno, Reno, Nevada

Renee Frederickson, PhD, LP, Frederickson and Associates PA, St. Paul, Minnesota

Colleen Friend, LCSW, School of Public Policy and Social Research, University of California–Los Angeles, Los Angeles, California

David H. Gleaves, PhD, Department of Psychology, Texas A&M University, College Station, Texas

Steven N. Gold, PhD, Center for Psychological Studies, Nova Southeastern University, Fort Lauderdale, Florida

Seth Goldstein, JD, Child Abuse Forensic Institute, Napa, California

Michael Hertica, MS, Torrance Police Department, Torrance, California

Sam Kirschner, PhD, Independent Practice, Gwynedd Valley, Pennsylvania

Kathryn Kuehnle, PhD, Department of Mental Health Law and Policy, University of Southern Florida

Patricia Long, PhD, Department of Psychology, Oklahoma State University, Stillwater, Oklahoma

Melissa McDermott-Lane, LCSW-C, The Listening Place, Ellicot City, Maryland

Nancie Palmer, ACSW, PhD, Department of Social Work, Washburn University, Topeka, Kansas

Mary Beth Williams, PhD, Independent Practice, Warrenton, Virginia

I would also like to acknowledge the contributions of and thank those members who are rotating off of the board. Holly Ramsey-Klawsnik, PhD, of Klawsnik & Klawsnik Psychotherapy Associates in Canton, Massachusetts, and Mindy Rosenberg, PhD, in private practice in Sausalito, California, have been an asset to the journal and have provided invaluable input.

Introduction:
Exposing Misinformation
Concerning Child Sexual Abuse
and Adult Survivors

Charles L. Whitfield
Joyanna Silberg
Paul Jay Fink

SUMMARY. This article introduces a special volume on misinformation about child sexual abuse. Despite extensive research findings on the

---

Charles L. Whitfield, MD, FASAM is in private practice in Atlanta, GA, a member of the Leadership Council on Mental Health, Justice and the Media, and on the faculty of the Rutgers Institute on Alcohol Studies, Rutgers University, New Brunswick, NJ. Joyanna Silberg, PhD, is a clinician at Sheppard Pratt Health System, Baltimore, MD, Executive Vice-President of the Leadership Council for Mental Health Justice and the Media, and President of the International Society for the Study of Dissociation. Paul Jay Fink, MD, is a psychiatrist in Private Practice in Philadelphia, PA, President of the Leadership Council for Mental Health, Justice, and the Media, and Past President of the American Psychiatric Association.

Address correspondence to: Paul Jay Fink, MD, 191 Presidential Boulevard, Suite C-132, Bala Cynwyd, PA 19004.

This publication has been edited by the Leadership Council for Mental Health, Justice, and the Media (LC). The LC is a nonprofit, multidisciplinary group dedicated to promoting ethical applications of psychological science to human welfare. The Council's mission includes correcting misinformation used to serve vested interests in the area of mental health. The organization came into being because it was observed that the press, the legal system, and even scientific journals were increasingly misrepresenting scientific findings about many important issues that relate to the health and welfare of children and other victims of interpersonal violence.

[Haworth co-indexing entry note]: "Introduction: Exposing Misinformation Concerning Child Sexual Abuse and Adult Survivors." Whitfield, Charles L., Joyanna Silberg, and Paul Jay Fink. Co-published simultaneously in *Journal of Child Sexual Abuse* (The Haworth Maltreatment & Trauma Press, an imprint of The Haworth Press, Inc.) Vol. 9, No. 3/4, 2001, pp. 1-8; and: *Misinformation Concerning Child Sexual Abuse and Adult Survivors* (ed: Charles L. Whitfield, Joyanna Silberg, and Paul Jay Fink) The Haworth Maltreatment & Trauma Press, an imprint of The Haworth Press, Inc., 2001, pp. 1-8. Single or multiple copies of this article are available for a fee from The Haworth Document Delivery Service [1-800-HAWORTH, 9:00 a.m. - 5:00 p.m. (EST). E-mail address: getinfo@haworthpressinc.com].

1

long-term effects and consequences of child sexual abuse, misinformation on this topic is widespread. Several forces have worked to support and disseminate this erroneous information. Because it is difficult to comprehend the horror of sexual crimes against children, society's denial and disbelief have often unwittingly supported the agendas of those who want to discount or minimize the impact of these crimes. The media has also contributed to the aura of skepticism surrounding claims of sexual abuse and its mental health impact, and has reported favorably on controversial and unproven claims such as the "false memory syndrome." In the hope of countering misinformation and thus raising the level of discourse to the engagement of real scientific issues, a number of well known and respected researchers and clinicians examine various facets of the problem. *[Article copies available for a fee from The Haworth Document Delivery Service: 1-800-HAWORTH. E-mail address: <getinfo@haworthpressinc.com> Website: <http://www.HaworthPress.com> © 2001 by The Haworth Press, Inc. All rights reserved.]*

KEYWORDS. Child sexual abuse, misinformation, pedophile advocacy, "false memory syndrome," denial

Child maltreatment, along with its pervasive personal, relational, and societal effects, has been identified as a major public health issue. There is an increasingly well developed database on the long term impact of child sexual abuse (CSA) and its cost to society (Dallam, 2001; Franey, Geffner, & Falconer, 2001). Research has repeatedly shown CSA to be a major contributor to long term, disabling mental health outcomes across the life span, including depression and suicidality (Bensley, Van Eenwyk, Spieker, & Schoder, 1999; Peters & Range, 1995), post traumatic stress disorder (McLeer, Deblinger, Henry, & Orvaschel, 1992; Schaaf & McCann, 1998), truancy, delinquency (Chandy, Blum, & Resnick, 1996), and substance abuse (Bensley et al., 1999; Johnsen & Harlow, 1996). It can also be significantly associated with somatization and serious physical problems, from heart disease to cancer (Felitti et al., 1998; McCauley et al., 1997). However, issues having to do with CSA often remain controversial, and misinformation about the effects of CSA is common. In the hope of countering misinformation and thus raising the level of discourse to the engagement of real scientific issues, the Leadership Council is editing this special collection. To this end, we have brought together a number of original articles that examine this problem in detail. The authors, many of whom are respected researchers and/or clinicians, examine the problem of CSA from various angles. Each author addresses a different facet of the problem, and the combined result provides a comprehensive overview of the methods and arguments by those who seek to misinform the public on issues related to the sexual abuse of children.

There is no single source or cause for the misinformation about CSA exposed here. Numerous social, cultural, and political forces have contributed to this problem. In many cases these forces have worked in synchrony to deny the often destructive impact of sexual abuse on children's lives, and to interfere with programs developed to prevent and treat the problem. More recently, special interest groups have sought to silence the voices of writers, teachers, scientists and researchers knowledgeable about effects of CSA. In fact, it is currently acceptable, even fashionable, to doubt the victims, those who prosecute for them, and those who treat their post-traumatic illness (Benatar, 1995). Since CSA was first reported on by the media 30 years ago, extremists on both sides of the issue seemed to garner the most press and public attention. All of society suffers from these efforts, as both victims and the accused have a right to the best scientific information available on these topics.

The media have played an important role in enabling and disseminating the misinformation about CSA. As Kitzinger (1996) stated,

> Journalists are in the business of finding, constructing and selling 'news' in a particular way. They are looking for the 'good story'–one that will grab the reader and be seen as politically or socially important. In order to sell more of their product, many writers and reporters value what is new, different and 'newsworthy,' over what is true. Thus the increasing controversy over sexual abuse stimulated by false accusation advocates was made for a hungry press desensitized to stories about abuse. (p. 325)

Kennedy (1995) found that in the mid-1990s, four out of every five media presentations were biased in favoring "false memory" claims. Journalists who were polled claimed that they found this to be a more interesting story, that stories about abuse were "old" news, and they felt these stories were easier to tolerate and write about (Kitzinger, 1996). Thus, the media shifted the focus away from the risks and harm to children to highlight supposed "false accusations." The media have frequently oversimplified the controversy concerning the validity and impact of adult memories of CSA.

SOCIETAL DENIAL

When interviewed, confessed child molesters often describe the ease with which they fooled people in their communities by "looking good," by being so kind and responsible that no one would believe an accusation of sexual abuse or assault (e.g., Salter, 1998). This is part of the "grooming" behavior that molesters commonly use with the child and the family or others to make them all feel a false sense of safety when the child is in his or her care (Emrick, 1996). Their chief collaborators in crime, the prisoners tell Salter, are the good people who do not want to believe that CSA occurs. As a result, parents readily hand over their children to them and most molesters go undetected. If evidence of abuse comes to light, child molesters can rest assured that most adults will ignore it. Thus, these convicted felons summarized one of the biggest problems in awareness and acknowledgment of sexual abuse crimes: The public simply does not want to believe that these kinds of crimes occur, and is eager to embrace other explanations when they are offered.

The impact of societal denial is highlighted in Cheit's article in this volume, "The Legend of Robert Halsey." Cheit first lays out the overwhelming evidence against Robert Halsey, a child molester who was convicted and sentenced to two life terms in prison in 1993. Cheit then documents how this evidence has been ignored and how academic and public resources were used to generate support for the notion that Halsey was wrongly convicted. In the end, Cheit provides a cautionary tale which shows how even the clearly guilty can generate public sympathy and support, while the plight of their victims is ignored.

In Dallam's first article in this collection, "Crisis or Creation? A Systematic Examination of 'False Memory Syndrome' " she critically examines the insufficient evidence for the existence of a "false memory syndrome" (FMS) and the lack of any empirical data supporting the False Memory Syndrome Foundation's contention that it constitutes an "epidemic." She also demonstrates how statistical data was shaped to create the appearance of an epidemic and how a lack of independent research led the media to misinform the public about the extent of false memories. Her research suggests that "False Memory Syndrome" is a pseudoscientific device constructed to defend parents against civil actions by children claiming to have been abused.

MISINFORMATION AS A LEGAL DEFENSE STRATEGY

Purposeful misinformation (disinformation) is a common tactic used in court to defend people who have committed various crimes. Because sexual abuse is a serious crime, those accused of abusing children have a powerful incentive to misrepresent the prevalence and harmful effects of CSA. Disinformation has been common in other types of situations as well. For example, by denying the link between smoking and serious health problems, for decades tobacco companies were able to continue their lucrative business without being held accountable for the toxicity of their product. Similarly, it should not surprise us that people accused of molesting children, along with their attorneys and experts, may resort to disinformation in an attempt to raise doubts about the guilt of those accused of child abuse.

Whitfield describes the "false memory" defense from a clinical, legal, and political perspective in his article in this publication. He outlines 22 erroneous claims and defensive positions commonly used by false memory advocates or defense experts to cast doubt on the guilt of those accused of molesting children. He shows how many of these strategies are also routinely used by confessed or convicted child molesters. Whitfield then responds to the 22 positions or claims by drawing from both the clinical and scientific literature.

Brown's article, "(Mis)Representations of the Long-Term Effects of Childhood Sexual Abuse in the Courts," describes how defense attorneys and expert witnesses frequently misrepresent and distort the facts regarding the long-term consequences of CSA. After studying legal evidence provided in over 50 legal cases by "false memory" advocates, Brown identifies five basic pro-false memory arguments which have been used in an attempt to deny an association between CSA and adult outcomes. Brown then reviews the clinical and scientific literature which, as a whole, refutes the contention that no causal link has been demonstrated between CSA and adult symptoms.

MISINFORMATION ON THE LONG TERM SEQUELAE OF CHILD SEXUAL ABUSE

The meaning and interpretation of scientific studies can be distorted by the investigator's bias. In the early days, investigators were perhaps too quick to ascribe harm to CSA based on studies using inadequate samples and confounded variables. These problems were later resolved through better research using representative sampling and appropriate controls. Recently, a meta-analysis was published which suggested that the results of numerous methodologically sound studies have overstated the harmful effects of child sexual abuse. The article was embraced by organizations supporting pedophiles but condemned by both the public and Congress. In her second article in this volume, "Science or Propaganda? An Examination of Rind, Tromovitch, and Bauserman (1998)," Dallam carefully examines this controversial study which claimed to find that boys are not necessarily harmed by sexual relations with adults. After reviewing the sociopolitical repercussions of the article's publication, she then examines the claim that the study was based more on propaganda than scientific reasoning. After documenting numerous problems with how the study was performed and reported, Dallam examines the authors' previous professional work for evidence of bias. She shows that rather than being dispassionate scientists, two of the authors have published in a sociopolitical journal that advocates for pedophilia.

In "A Critical Appraisal of the 1998 Meta-Analytic Review of Child Sexual Abuse Outcomes Reported by Rind, Tromovitch, and Bauserman," Whittenburg, Tice, Baker, and Lemmey focus on the methodology used by Rind et al. (1998). They also provide a comprehensive review of the relevant literature, highlighting areas and populations that the authors missed. They conclude, as did Dallam, that the Rind et al. interpretations and recommendations were not based upon science due to the serious methodological flaws and the apparent bias of the authors.

In their article "The Real Controversy About Child Sexual Abuse Research: Contradictory Findings and Critical Issues Not Addressed by Rind, Tromovitch, and Bauserman in Their 1998 Outcomes Meta-Analysis," Tice et al. carefully show how and why the narrow view taken by Rind et al, which claimed that adult-child sex is not necessarily harmful to children, is invalid. This is because Rind et al. neglected to analyze all the studies published on the effects of child sexual abuse, but instead focused only on their own limited selection of the most conservative population to study–college students. This kind of error is commonly used in the generation of pseudo-scientific disinformation by some "false memory" advocates.

CLINICAL IMPLICATIONS

The hostile stance of many false memory advocates along with the threat of malpractice suits if abuse is reported has caused many mental health professionals to become apprehensive when treating patients for current or past CSA. In "Implications of the Memory Controversy for Clinical Practice: An Overview of Treatment Recommendations and Guidelines," Courtois describes how clinicians can rise above the fray and minimize their legal liability by developing scientifically-based practices. After providing an overview of the controversies concerning delayed recall of memories of childhood abuse, Courtois discusses the results of seven international professional task forces on the memory debate, and outlines areas of consensus. She concludes that clinicians must strive to neither suggest nor suppress reports of remembered or suspected abuse and trauma; instead, they must practice from a stance of supportive neutrality regarding the historical accuracy of memories of abuse, especially when memories have been recovered after a period of unavailability and/or are unclear.

CONCLUSION

Setting the record straight about the exploitation of children is an important task. Professionals have a responsibility to maintain a more objective and less polemic stance on the diagnosis and treatment of post-traumatic disorders. Too frequently the misinformation and half truths spread by special interest groups triumph over the dissemination of accurate information. It is important to examine these contentious issues from a scientific perspective. This special collection sheds more light by confronting the facts about the very important topic of CSA.

REFERENCES

Benatar, M. (1995). Running away from sexual abuse: Denial revisited. *Families in Society: The Journal of Contemporary Human Services*, *76*, 315-20.

Bensley, L. S., Van Eenwyk, J., Spieker, S. J., & Schoder, J. (1999). Self-reported abuse history and adolescent problem behaviors. I. Antisocial and suicidal behaviors. *Journal of Adolescent Health*, *24*, 163-172.

Chandy, J. M., Blum, R.W., & Resnick, M. D. (1996). Gender-specific outcomes for sexually abused adolescents. *Child Abuse & Neglect*, *20*, 1219-1231.

Dallam, S. J. (2001). The long-term medical consequences of childhood trauma. In K. Franey, R. Geffner, & R. Falconer (Eds.), *The cost of child maltreatment: Who pays? We all do*. (pp. 1-14). San Diego, CA: Family Violence & Sexual Assault Institute.

Emrick, R. L. (1996). *Sexual offenders: A provider's handbook*. Thousand Oaks, CA: Sage.

Felitti, V. J., Anda, R. F., Nordenberg, D., Williamson, D. F., Spitz, A. M., Edwards, V., Koss, M. P., & Marks, J. S. (1998). The relationship of adult health status to childhood abuse and household dysfunction. *American Journal of Preventive Medicine*, *14*(4), 245-258.

Franey, K., Geffner, R., & Falconer, R. (Eds.). (2001). *The cost of child maltreatment: Who pays? We all do*. San Diego, CA: Family Violence & Sexual Assault Institute.

Johnsen, L. W., & Harlow, L. L. (1996). Childhood sexual abuse linked with adult substance use, victimization, and AIDs-risk. *AIDS Education and Prevention*, *8*, 44-57.

Kennedy, K. (1995). Distortions in media reports about memory and sexual abuse. *Truth About Abuse*, *2*(1), 3-4, Richmond, WA.

Kitzinger, J. (1996). Media representations of sexual abuse risks. *Child Abuse Review*, *5*, 319-333.

McCauley, J., Kern, D. E., Kolodner, K., Dill, L., Schroeder, A. F., DeChant, H. K., Ryden, J., Derogatis, L., & Bass, E. B. (1997). Clinical characteristics of women with a history of childhood abuse: Unhealed wounds. *Journal of the American Medical Association*, *277*, 1362-1368.

McLeer, S. V., Deblinger, E., Henry, D., & Orvaschel, H. (1992). Sexually abused children at high risk for post-traumatic stress disorder. *Journal of the American Academy of Child and Adolescent Psychiatry, 31*, 875-879.

Peters, D. K., & Range, L. M. (1995). Childhood sexual abuse and current suicidality in college women and men. *Child Abuse & Neglect, 19*, 335-341.

Rind, B., Tromovitch, P., & Bauserman, R. (1998). A meta-analytic examination of assumed properties of child sexual abuse using college samples. *Psychological Bulletin, 124*, 22-53.

Salter, A. (1998). Truth, lies and sex offenders. PAL Video. Thousand Oaks, CA: Sage.

Schaaf, K. K., & McCann, T. R. (1998). Relationship of childhood sexual, physical, and combined sexual and physical abuse to adult victimization and posttraumatic stress disorder. *Child Abuse & Neglect, 22*, 1119-1133.

Crisis or Creation?
A Systematic Examination
of "False Memory Syndrome"

Stephanie J. Dallam

SUMMARY. In 1992, the False Memory Syndrome Foundation (FMSF), an advocacy organization for people claiming to be falsely accused of sexual abuse, announced the discovery of a new syndrome in-

Stephanie J. Dallam, RN, MSN, is a researcher and writer for the Leadership Council. Prior to working for the Council, she worked in pediatric intensive care for 10 years at University of Missouri Hospital and Clinics, and is a former nursing instructor at the University of Missouri-Columbia. She has written numerous articles on issues related to the welfare of children.

Address correspondence to: Stephanie J. Dallam, Leadership Council, 191 Presidential Boulevard., Suite C-132, Bala Cynwyd, PA 19004 (E-mail: sjd.scout@worldnet.att.net).

A portion of this article was presented at the 15th International Fall Conference International Society for the Study of Dissociation, November 1998.

An earlier version of some of the issues presented in the present article previously appeared in S. J. Dallam. (1997). Is there a false memory epidemic? *Treating Abuse Today,* 7(3), 29-37.

[Haworth co-indexing entry note]: "Crisis or Creation? A Systematic Examination of 'False Memory Syndrome.'" Dallam, Stephanie J. Co-published simultaneously in *Journal of Child Sexual Abuse* (The Haworth Maltreatment & Trauma Press, an imprint of The Haworth Press, Inc.) Vol. 9, No. 3/4, 2001, pp. 9-36; and: *Misinformation Concerning Child Sexual Abuse and Adult Survivors* (ed: Charles L. Whitfield, Joyanna Silberg, and Paul Jay Fink) The Haworth Maltreatment & Trauma Press, an imprint of The Haworth Press, Inc., 2001, pp. 9-36. Single or multiple copies of this article are available for a fee from The Haworth Document Delivery Service [1-800-HAWORTH, 9:00 a.m. - 5:00 p.m. (EST). E-mail address: getinfo@haworthpressinc.com].

volving iatrogenically created false memories of childhood sexual abuse. This article critically examines the assumptions underlying "False Memory Syndrome" to determine whether there is sufficient empirical evidence to support it as a valid diagnostic construct. Epidemiological evidence is also examined to determine whether there is data to support its advocates' claim of a public health crisis or epidemic. A review of the relevant literature demonstrates that the existence of such a syndrome lacks general acceptance in the mental health field, and that the construct is based on a series of faulty assumptions, many of which have been scientifically disproven. There is a similar lack of empirical validation for claims of a "false memory" epidemic. It is concluded that in the absence of any substantive scientific support, "False Memory Syndrome" is best characterized as a pseudoscientific syndrome that was developed to defend against claims of child abuse. *[Article copies available for a fee from The Haworth Document Delivery Service: 1-800-HAWORTH. E-mail address: <getinfo@haworthpressinc.com> Website: <http://www.HaworthPress.com> © 2001 by The Haworth Press, Inc. All rights reserved.]*

KEYWORDS. Amnesia, child sexual abuse, epidemic, false memory, incest, legislation, pseudoscience, public policy, recovered memory, syndrome evidence, suggestibility

"False Memory Syndrome" has been described as a widespread social phenomenon where misguided therapists cause patients to invent memories of sexual abuse (McCarty & Hough, 1992). The syndrome was described and named by the families and professionals who comprise the False Memory Syndrome Foundation (see Freyd, March 1993, p. 4), an organization formed by parents claiming to be falsely accused of child sexual abuse. Proponents of the syndrome claim that it is occurring at epidemic levels, and some have gone so far as to characterize it as the mental health crisis of the 1990s (e.g., Gardner, 1993, p. 370). Critics, on the other hand, have suggested that the syndrome is based on vague, unsubstantiated generalizations, which do not hold up to scientific scrutiny (e.g., Page, 1999), and that the syndrome's primary purpose is to discredit victims' testimony (e.g., Murphy, 1997). This article critically examines the assumptions underlying the concept to determine whether there is sufficient empirical evidence to support "False Memory Syndrome" as a valid diagnostic construct. Epidemiological evidence is then examined to determine whether there is data to support claims of either a public health crisis or epidemic.

THE MAKING OF A MOVEMENT:
THE HISTORY OF THE FMSF

Two consistent findings have emerged from research on child sexual abuse: The problem is widespread (e.g., Finkelhor, 1994) and child abuse is extensively undisclosed and underreported (e.g., Lawson & Chaffin, 1992; National Clearinghouse on Family Violence, 1997). Even when reported, child sexual abuse is extremely difficult to prosecute and few perpetrators are ever brought to justice (Dziech & Schudson, 1989). Despite research showing that children rarely confabulate stories of abuse (e.g., Goodwin, Sahd, & Rada, 1979; Thoennes & Tjaden, 1990), offenders often convincingly argue that their accuser has falsely accused them. In addition, the legal system has historically viewed children as the property of their parents and professionals have discounted women's reports of incestuous abuse as wishful fantasies (Haugaard & Reppucci, 1988). As a result, legal and mental health professionals have tended to be overly suspicious of and unresponsive to reports of sexual abuse (Clevenger, 1992).

In the 1980s, some incest victims attempted to hold their abusers accountable by seeking compensation in courts for abuse-related injuries. Although, many had corroboration for their abuse, most lawsuits were disallowed because the time period (i.e., statute of limitations) in which they had to raise such a claim had expired. Most state laws consider sexual abuse to be a personal injury, which tend to have short statute of limitations. Consequently, actions were generally time-barred by a victim's 19th or 20th birthday–an age where most people are still dependent on their parents.

Armed with a growing body of research and clinical literature (e.g., Herman & Schatzow, 1987; Terr, 1991) showing that many child abuse victims experience traumatic or dissociative amnesia, or for other reasons are unable to recognize the harm the abuse has caused them until they are well into adulthood, advocates lobbied state legislatures to extend the time period for filing suits. Many states responded by extending statutes of limitations for civil actions related to child sexual abuse and, for the first time, many incest perpetrators were within reach of the law. However, for the most part, only victims who claimed to have only recently remembered their abuse qualified for this exception in the statute of limitations (Brown, Scheflin, & Hammond, 1998).

Accused parents, many of whom were affluent and respected members of the community, sought out defense lawyers and psychological experts for help in defending against abuse-related claims. A new concept, "False Memory Syndrome," was advanced by parents and professionals as an alternative explanation for delayed memories of sexual abuse (see Freyd, March 1993, p. 4), and in March 1992 the False Memory Syndrome Foundation (FMSF) was founded.

The foundation's leaders, Pamela and Peter Freyd, were motivated because their adult daughter privately accused Peter of sexually abusing her as a child. They were put in touch with other parents claiming to be falsely accused by Dr. Harold Lief (Calof, 1993a), who was later revealed to be Pamela's personal psychiatrist (J. Freyd, 1993). Families were also referred by Ralph Underwager and Hollida Wakefield, a husband and wife team who are prominent advocates for people accused of molesting children. A frequent defense expert witness, Underwager's philosophy concerning the prosecution of child sexual abuse has been summed up by the statement that it is "more desirable that a thousand children in abuse situations are not discovered than for one innocent person to be convicted wrongly" (Kraft, 1985, p. 1).

Underwager and Wakefield were also instrumental in helping the Freyds organize the foundation (P. Freyd, May 21, 1992; Underwager & Wakefield, 1994). The original toll-free number for the FMSF rang at Underwager's private Institute for Psychological Therapies, and Underwager and Wakefield developed the initial questionnaire used to survey families who contacted the FMSF (P. Freyd, May 21, 1992).[1]

With the help of Harold Lief and Marin Orne,[2] the FMSF quickly gathered a respectable appearing advisory board, giving the new syndrome an aura of scientific acceptance (P. Freyd, June 1998, p. 1). Although the FMSF was billed as a scientific organization, its actions were mainly geared toward defending parents against abuse accusations and blaming them on psychotherapists. According to Pamela Freyd (1992, May 1), "This Foundation came into being because many of us believe that we have been judged guilty by therapists who have never met us . . . " (p. 1). According to Martin Gardner (1993), a prominent member of the FMSF Scientific and Professional Advisory Board, the FMSF was formed "to combat a fast-growing epidemic of dubious therapy that is ripping thousands of families apart, scarring patients for life, and breaking the hearts of innocent parents and other relatives" (p. 370).

Despite the fact that "False Memory Syndrome" remained undefined and had never been the subject of any research, the FMSF focused its early activities on influencing the media and legal system. In its first official newsletter, supporters were told that the main activities of the foundation would be: (1) "press releases with accurate information on topics such as child abuse statistics and memory"; (2) developing a resource center and database for legal cases involving repressed memories; (3) a study of beliefs of mental health professionals; and (4) "other things that you tell us need to be done to help you" ("Foundation Activities," March 1992, p. 2).

After surveying its members, the FMSF reported that most parents who joined the organization were concerned that they were going to be sued by their children ("Legal Actions," June 12, 1992, p. 2). Some had even been criminally convicted for molesting children (FMSF, 1993). An early FMSF newsletter assured these parents that "the FMS Foundation Legal Advisory Board is working with all possible speed" ("Legal News," November 1992). The FMSF immediately began to disseminate information to the media concerning this burgeoning "epidemic" of what the foundation alleged to be false memories.

EVALUATION OF "FALSE MEMORY SYNDROME" AS A DIAGNOSTIC CONSTRUCT

Definition of "False Memory Syndrome"

The definition of "False Memory Syndrome" did not evolve from clinical studies; rather the purported syndrome's description is based on the accounts of parents claiming to be falsely accused of child sexual abuse, usually by their adult daughters. As a result, more than a year after her organization was founded, Pamela Freyd, the FMSF's Executive Director, was still unable to articulate a list of the signs and symptoms that characterize the "syndrome" (Calof, 1993a). The FMSF later adopted the following definition, offered by research psychologist and then FMSF advisor John Kihlstrom[3] (1993):

> When a memory is distorted, or confabulated, the result can be what has been called the False Memory Syndrome–a condition in which a person's identity and interpersonal relationships are centered around a memory of traumatic experience which is objectively false but in which the person strongly believes. Note that the syndrome is not characterized by false memories as such. We all have memories that are inaccurate. Rather, the syndrome may be diagnosed when the memory is so deeply engrained that it orients the individual's entire personality and lifestyle, in turn disrupting all sorts of other adaptive behaviors. The analogy to personality disorder is intentional. False Memory Syndrome is especially destructive because the person assiduously avoids confrontation with any evidence that might challenge the memory. Thus it takes on a life of its own, encapsulated, and resistant to correction. The person may become so focused on the memory that he or she may be effectively distracted from coping with the real problems in his or her life. (p. 10)

According to Campbell Perry (1995), a member of the FMSF Scientific and Professional Advisory Board, the main distinguishing feature of "False Memory Syndrome" is that "an individual enters therapy with a 'recovered memory' therapist; one who believes that all psychic distresses are the product of repressed memories of childhood sexual abuse, and who interprets all failures to recall the incest as evidence of 'denial' " (p. 192). The therapist then uses "disguised" hypnosis (i.e., procedures such as guided imagery, relaxation, dream analysis, regression work and sodium amytal) to elicit abuse-related "memories" (p. 189). The real tragedy of "False Memory Syndrome," according to Pamela Freyd, is that afflicted patients lose their families and all their "memory of childhood happiness" (Taylor, 1992).

The FMSF's Index Case

"False Memory Syndrome" is unconventional in that it is usually "diagnosed" without any supporting clinical evaluation. The earliest publicized case of what was purported to be "False Memory Syndrome" is that of Jennifer Freyd, the daughter of FMSF founders Peter and Pamela Freyd. In December 1990, Jennifer, a respected psychologist and memory researcher, privately accused her father of sexually abusing her. Ten months later, Pamela anonymously published an article in *Issues in Child Abuse Accusations*, an obscure journal devoted to defending against child abuse accusations published by Ralph Underwager. In the article, Pamela claimed her daughter had falsely accused her father of incest and that "the accusations arose during the course of therapy in which the therapist elicited 'repressed memories' " (Doe, 1991, p. 154).

Although it appeared under the pseudonym "Jane Doe," Pamela mailed the article, and revealed both her own and her daughter's real identity, to many people including senior members of Jennifer's department, who received it at the time they were deciding whether to promote her. Hechler (1996) noted that the portrait that the article painted of Jennifer was far from flattering. "She was described during various periods of her life as sexually promiscuous, professionally unproductive, anorexic and sexually frustrated."

When Jennifer Freyd, PhD (1993) finally told her side of the story, it became apparent that her case meets few of the characteristics of "False Memory Syndrome" described in FMSF literature. First, she did not spend months in therapy for an unrelated problem before she remembered the abuse. Jennifer consulted the therapist because of intense anxiety over her parents' upcoming visit. She recalled the abuse after her second session. Second, no memory recovery techniques were utilized; Jennifer's memories emerged at home after the therapist merely asked if she had ever been abused. Third, after recovering the memories, she did not sue her parents, threaten them with public exposure, and according to Jennifer, it was never her intention to cut her parents out of her life. Jennifer reported that she broke off communication only after "repeated and intense efforts to communicate constructively" (p. 20), and in response to her parent's ongoing "obsession" with her sexuality (p. 16). Finally, although "False Memory Syndrome" is said to disrupt all sorts of "adaptive behaviors" and to distract sufferers "from coping with the real problems in her life" (Kihlstrom, 1993, p. 10), in the wake of the charges, Jennifer did not abandon her career, neglect her children, or leave her husband. Rather than organizing her life around the accusation, Jennifer Freyd has remained a respected and productive academic psychologist at the University of Oregon.

In answering her parent's charges, Jennifer Freyd (1993) also revealed information which casts doubt on their motives and the credibility of Pamela Freyd's published account of her daughter's case. For example, Jennifer revealed that Pamela introduced a number of fictional elements into what was billed as a true story of a mother's struggle with her daughter's "false accusation" of paternal sexual abuse. Throughout the story Pamela wrote, falsely, that her daughter had been denied tenure at her last job. Astonishingly, it is this fictional element that Pamela Freyd offers as a possible explanation for Jennifer's "false memories." She wrote: "Is 'violation' a feeling that comes when tenure doesn't?" (Doe, 1991, p. 162).

Jennifer Freyd (1993) also revealed that her father was a chronic alcoholic throughout her childhood,[4] and had himself been sexually abused as a boy by an older man, a fact he seemed to take pride in (according to Jennifer, he frequently described himself as having been a "kept" boy). She also noted that her abuse memories were consistent with never forgotten memories of her family's pattern of sexualized and intrusive behavior (p. 13); memories which Peter and Pam have for the most part confirmed (Fried, 1994; Hechler, 1996). Jennifer Freyd (1993) also noted that her only sibling, a sister, was already estranged from her parents at the time of the allegations. In addition, Peter Freyd's own mother (who is also Pamela's step-mother) and his only sibling, a brother, were also estranged from Pamela and Peter. It should be noted that these family members support Jennifer's side of the story. In a statement, Peter's brother William Freyd stated, "There is no doubt in my mind that there was severe abuse in the home of Peter and Pam. . . . The False Memory Syndrome Foundation is a fraud designed to deny a reality that Peter and Pam have spent most of their lives trying to escape" (W. Freyd, 1995, as cited by Whitfield, 1995, p. 7).

Lack of Empirical Validation for "False Memory Syndrome"

To date, no empirical validation has been offered for "False Memory Syndrome" as a diagnostic construct; nor have the symptoms that characterize this putative syndrome ever been systematically described and studied. As a result, "False Memory Syndrome" has never been accepted as a valid diagnosis by any professional organization, and usage of the term has been the subject of heated criticism in peer reviewed scientific journals. For example, 17 behavioral scientists coauthored a statement objecting to the term "False Memory Syndrome" as "a non-psychological term originated by a private foundation whose stated purpose is to support accused parents" (Carstensen et al., 1993, p. 23). Critics have suggested that the syndrome is based on vague, unsubstantiated generalizations, which do not hold up to scientific scrutiny. For example, Page (1999) noted, "FMSF members paradoxically claim to place great value on scientific inquiry, while permitting their syndrome to remain so vaguely defined that it is virtually impossible not only to study it, but to determine who suffers from it" (http://www.feminista.com/v2n10/cutlerpage. html).

The FMSF has responded to such criticism by admitting that it does not have any evidence for its syndrome besides the stories that it hears from those who call the foundation seeking help:

> We wish to emphasize the existence of a condition that needs to be considered and then confirmed or rejected when further information emerges. For that aim, the term "false memory syndrome" is satisfactory. ("Our Critics," April 1993, p. 3)

Examination of the Assumptions Underlying the Construct

Due to the lack of research on "False Memory Syndrome," assumptions underlying the concept were examined. A review of the writings of, and media interviews granted by, false memory proponents reveals that their construction of the purported syndrome is, for the most part, based on six main assumptions. These assumptions are as follows: (1) A recovered memory is likely to be a false memory; (2) False/recovered memories are usually caused by incompetent therapists doing "recovered memory therapy"; (3) It is easy to implant false memories of traumatic events that never happened; (4) People who recover memories are highly suggestible; (5) "False Memory Syndrome" is common among psychotherapy patients who recover traumatic memories; and (6) Alleged perpetrators are somehow immune to developing false memories.

For "False Memory Syndrome" to be considered a valid construct, each of these assumptions must be tested and supported by scholarly research. Furthermore, to qualify as a syndrome, each assumed characteristic should be found in relation to the others. For example, a person who recovers a memory of sexual abuse should be found to be suggestible, to have recovered the memories only after undergoing extensive psychotherapy focused on finding memories, and no corroboration should be found for memories that "return" in this fashion (Brown, Scheflin, & Whitfield, 1999). A brief review of the scientific literature fails to support these assumptions, both alone, and in relation to one another.

Assumption 1: A recovered memory is likely to be false memory. The most common argument offered in support of "False Memory Syndrome" is the purported lack of evidence for repression. An early FMSF publication stated: "Psychiatrists advising the Foundation members seem to be unanimous in the belief that memories of such atrocities cannot be repressed. Horrible incidents of childhood are remembered" (FMSF, 1992, p. 2). This statement implies that any traumatic memory that is forgotten and then recalled later must be false. Some false memory proponents have admitted that traumatic amnesia can occur for a single, traumatic event such as rape. However, they argue that there is no support for the claim that individuals can be completely amnesiac for *repeated* episodes of sexual abuse or that memories of abuse can be accurately remembered years later (e.g., Underwager & Wakefield, 1995).

The assumption that delayed memories should be considered false is countered by countless studies of traumatized populations. At last count, over 68 studies have documented the reality of recovering forgotten memories of trauma (Brown et al., 1999). At the same time, research has shown that the misremembering of childhood events is more often characterized by forgetting negative experiences that actually happened than it is by remembering ones that did not (Brewin, Andrews, & Gotlib, 1995). In addition, the diagnostic manual used by mental health professionals (i.e., *Diagnostic and Statistical Manual of Mental Disorders,* 4th ed.) recognizes memory problems to be a common feature of five post-traumatic conditions: post-traumatic stress disorder, dissociative amnesia, dissociative fugue, dissociative disorder not-otherwise-specified, and dissociative identity disorder (American Psychiatric Association, 1994).

As to the reliability of recovered memories, research suggests that recovered memories are no more and no less accurate than continuous memories (Brown et al., 1999). Longitudinal studies have demonstrated that individuals with legally documented abuse histories have recovered accurate abuse-related memories after claiming to have forgotten the traumatic experience (Corwin & Olafson, 1997; Duggal & Sroufe, 1998; Weene, 1995; Williams, 1995), and substantial proportions of those who recover memories of abuse have been able to find external corroborative evidence to support their memory (e.g., Andrews et al., 1999; Chu, Frey, Ganzel, & Matthews, 1999; Dalenberg, 1996).[5] After reviewing the evidence, Scheflin and Brown (1996) suggested that if courts require an evidentiary hearing on the issue of whether repressed memories are reliable, then they "must, consistent with the science, hold either that such memories are reliable or that all memory, repressed or otherwise, is unreliable" (p. 183).

Another problem with the assumption that a recovered memory should be considered false is that, while there is abundant research demonstrating the fallibility of retrospective recall (e.g., Loftus, Korf & Schooler, 1989), there has been no systematic research documenting "False Memory Syndrome" and no professional organization has officially recognized its existence. Conversely, at least one professional body has questioned the syndrome's validity. The British Psychological Society (BPS) surveyed 108 therapists on their patients who had recovered memories. The results revealed that many patients recovered their memories prior to beginning therapy, few therapists reported using any techniques to aid recall, and some form of corroboration was reported in 41% of cases (Andrews et al., 1999). Overall, the BPS could find no convincing evidence for a specific "False Memory Syndrome" leading the Society to issue a statement asserting: "There is now consistent evidence that 'False Memory Syndrome' cannot explain all, or even most, examples of recovered memories of trauma" (Reaney, 2000).

Assumption 2: Recovered memories are usually caused by therapists practicing "recovered memory therapy." Anytime a therapy patient recovers a memory either inside or outside of therapy, false memory proponents are likely to accuse the therapist of engaging in "recovered memory therapy." Although many clinicians report that what critics call "memory recovery therapy" (e.g., hypnosis, guided imagery, sodium amytal, etc., that is focused solely on memory recovery) is not common among mainstream clinicians (e.g., Briere, 1995; Calof, 1993b), false memory proponents claim that such therapy is a nation-wide phenomenon that "has devastated thousands of lives" (Ofshe & Watters, 1993, p. 4). In fact, Underwager has asserted that when a person has no recall of abuse and they go to a therapist and recover a memory, "it's common sense to realize that the therapy caused the memory" (Morris, April 24, 1992).

The assumption that recovered memories are usually caused by therapists using suggestive techniques is countered by numerous studies reporting that a substantial proportion of those who recover memories of abuse, do so without ever having participated in therapy (e.g., Albach, Moorman, & Bermond, 1996; Andrews et al., 1999; Chu et al., 1999). For example, Albach et al. (1996) found no significant differences in amnesia, memory recovery, or other memory phenomena between abuse survivors in the Netherlands who participated in psychotherapy and those who did not. The authors concluded that therapy was not a significant contributor to the recall of abuse in a majority of Dutch patients. Further research has shown that when memories are recovered while participating in some type of therapy, most memories are recalled outside of therapy and without the prior use of recall techniques (e.g., Andrews et al., 2000; Chu et al., 1999; Dalenberg, 1996; Elliot, 1997).

Scheflin and Brown (1999) tested this assumption by examining the types of therapy received by 30 former patients who sued their therapists for implanting false memories. Scheflin and Brown reported that none of the cases fit the profile of the patient being misled in treatment and subsequently correcting their misperceptions. Instead, they found that patients tended to re-evaluate their perceptions of their therapy after pressure from their families and significant exposure to the views of false memory proponents. In addition, "*none* [italics in original] of the 30 cases could be classified narrowly as 'recovered memory therapy,' and none had a single-minded focus on recovering memories" (p. 685).

Assumption 3: It is easy to implant false memories of traumatic events. False memory proponents have asserted that it is extremely easy for therapists to inadvertently implant in their patients a set of false autobiographical memories of child abuse. Kihlstrom (1996), for example, wrote that "even a few probing questions and suggestive remarks by an authoritative figure such as a therapist may be sufficient to inculcate a belief on the part of a patient that he or she was abused . . . " There is currently mixed data on the ability of authority figures to "implant" wholly false traumatic memories; however, memory researchers agree that the creation of illusory memories requires substantial suggestive influence (e.g., Lindsay, 1998). After a comprehensive review of the literature, Lindsay and Read (1994) concluded, "There is little reason to fear that a few suggestive questions will lead psychotherapy clients to conjure up vivid and compelling illusory memories of childhood sexual abuse" (p. 294).

Empirical research indicates that two main factors influence the likelihood of a subject producing a false memory report: (1) the strength of suggestive influences, and (2) the perceived "plausibility" of the suggested event (Lindsay, 1998). For example, Porter, Yuille and Lehman (1999) reported that they have been successful in getting some research subjects to "recover" a memory for a false stressful event (e.g., dog attack) after using extensive suggestive techniques coupled with misleading participants to believe that the false scenario was witnessed and reported by a parent. After using guided imagery and repeated retrieval attempts, Porter et al. reported that 26% of participants "recovered" a complete memory for the false experience ostensibly endorsed as true by their parents, and another 30% recalled aspects of the false experience. Using similar techniques, Pezdek, Finger and Hodge (1997) tried to mislead adults to believe that they had been lost in a shopping mall as children. They also tried to convince them that they had experienced rectal enemas as children. While three out of 20 subjects erroneously claimed to have been lost in the mall (a relatively common and familiar experience), no subjects would erroneously agree that they had had a rectal enema (an event more analogous to sexual abuse).

The willingness of some research subjects to modify childhood memories in favor of their parents' recollections points to a neglected area of research on memory and suggestibility: the ability of authority figures to induce false reports of *not* having been abused (Fish, 1998). Richard Kluft, a psychiatrist at Temple University, observed that such experiments show that "a family determined to mess up a child's sense of reality has a good chance of succeeding" (Bavley, 1995).

Assumption 4: People who recover memories are highly suggestible. The assumption of suggestibility is central to the contention that therapists are rewriting the memory banks of vulnerable patients. An article in the FMSF's newsletter stated, "When a distressed client enters therapy, that person is almost by definition 'highly suggestible' " ("How Could This," November, 1993, p. 3). However, the assumption that adults who recover memories of abuse are highly suggestible has not been supported by research specifically designed to test its validity. In fact, investigators have found that the memory of patients who reported having recovered memories of childhood sexual trauma were actually *less* subject to distortion following suggestive prompts than psychiatric patients who did not report having recovered such memories (Leavitt, 1997; 1999). Clancy, McNally and Schachter (1999) compared women who had recovered memories of abuse to those who had not to see whether imagining unusual childhood events inflated their confidence that these events had happened to them. They found that although guided imagery did not significantly inflate confidence that early childhood events had occurred in either group, the control group was more likely to be confident that an imagined event had occurred than the group with a history of recovered memory.

Assumption 5: "False Memory Syndrome" is common. Within a month of the founding of the FMSF, its leaders claimed that "False Memory Syndrome" was widespread. For example, Pamela Freyd told a reporter for the *Utah County Journal* that "hundreds, perhaps thousands, of families across the country are grappling with fallout from false memories of sexual abuse brought on by psychotherapy" (Morris, April 21, 1992). In 1998, FMSF advisor Terrence W. Campbell estimated that in any given year, as many as 750,000 clients are at a risk of developing false memories due to psychotherapy (Tyroler, 1999). Clearly, claims about a new diagnostic category reaching epidemic proportions require careful analysis and substantiation (Pope, 1996). However, the FMSF has never performed any epidemiological research to support its claims.

In fact, a major problem hampering the study of the construct is that it is not being found in the clinical populations where its proponents claim the syndrome is rampant. For example, Hovdestad and Kristiansen (1996) surveyed 113 women with self-reported histories of incest, approximately half of whom reported at least one recovered memory and who could, therefore, potentially be suffering from false memories. They found that women who had recovered memories of child sexual abuse did not differ significantly from those with continuous memories. Not only did the criteria described by the FMSF fail to discriminate between the two groups, there was also no evidence to suggest that recovered memories were associated with certain types of therapy.

Assumption 6: Alleged perpetrators are immune to FMS. FMSF advisory board member Campbell Perry (1995) has acknowledged the lack of empirical underpinnings for "False Memory Syndrome" noting that, "FMS is not a syndrome in the conventional sense." Instead, he insisted on a "looser" meaning of this term, suggesting that "False Memory Syndrome" qualifies as a syndrome in terms of "a set of behaviors believed to have a common cause or basis" (pp. 191-2). According to Perry, "The False Memory Syndrome fits comfortably into this alternative formulation, which conceptualizes a syndrome in terms of a process that led to a particular outcome" (p. 192).

Critics, however, point out that in the case of "False Memory Syndrome" the "outcome" (i.e., a false memory) proceeds *a priori* from the assumption that the disputed memories are in fact false (e.g., Calof, 1993a). The FMSF has never tested this assumption as it does not investigate the backgrounds of those claiming to be falsely accused (P. Freyd, March 1994) and professionals rarely evaluate those said to be afflicted with the disorder (Pope, 1996). Consequently, in absentia "diagnoses" of the syndrome are often made by untrained lay people based solely on the denials of the alleged perpetrator.

The assumption that memories of parents are more accurate or truthful than those of their children has led many to criticize the FMSF's lack of objectivity in their syndrome's conceptualization and application (e.g., Courtois, 1995; Hoult, 1998; Whitfield, 1995).[6] Not only is there no empirical support for such a biased assumption, the results of numerous studies have shown the direct opposite. After reviewing the literature on retrospective recall of childhood experiences, Brewin et al. (1995) found that parents often recall a happier childhood for their offspring than collateral data would account for, while adults recall their own childhood with greater accuracy. Moreover, Brewin et al. found that memory distortion occurred more often to inhibit recall, and that parents may play a significant role in distorting reality and determining the family mythology concerning earlier events.

The FMSF's noncritical acceptance of the denials of those accused of child abuse is particularly problematic given that offenders who molest children have been found to have an extraordinary capacity for denial and minimization. In a study of sex offenders, Nugent and Kroner (1996) found that child molesters tend to be particularly skilled at impression management, and that denial is so ingrained and pervasive of a response that it has little relation to whether or not offenders committed the offense. They cautioned that in evaluating allegations of sexual abuse, clinicians should rely on independent corroboration as opposed to denials of those accused of molestation. After reviewing the research and clinical literature on sex offenders, forensic psychologist Richard Lanyon wrote the following:

> Clinical evidence suggests that in denying an actual molestation, it is not uncommon for the man to vigorously denigrate and vilify the child and other accusers, to loudly proclaim his innocence, to present unsolicited evidence of a frame-up, and to actively seek to influence the examiner and others with statements about the unfairness of the accusation, the financial burden, and the amount of personal suffering that is being forced on him. (Lanyon, 1993, p. 38)

Despite ample evidence of sex offenders strong defenses against admitting or recognizing their problem, the only time false memory proponents have "diagnosed" "False Memory Syndrome" in those accused of abuse, has been *after* they confessed to molesting children. In these instances the diagnosis has been used to counter the confessions of men now claiming to be innocent. For example, a defense psychiatrist argued that a Canadian minister's confession to sexually assaulting his daughter was based on a false memory that spontaneously developed during marital therapy with his wife. The psychiatrist testified that the man was emotionally unstable because of his daughter's allegations of abuse and his marital difficulties. In this emotionally charged atmosphere, the man experienced "spontaneous" hypnosis, which caused him to create false memories. His daughter, who moved out of the house at age 16, was not called to testify and the man was acquitted (Tyler, 1997).[7]

INCIDENCE DATA ON A "FALSE MEMORY SYNDROME"

To date, the only statistical evidence offered to support claims of a false memory epidemic is the telephone contacts to and/or membership figures of the FMSF. Because no other data exist, FMSF advisor Campell Perry (1995) has suggested that the FMSF's figures must be considered "crude estimates" of the phenomenon (p. 191). To determine whether the FMSF has collected data suggestive of a mental health crisis, a systematic study of their data collection and reporting practices was undertaken.

Examination of FMSF Membership and Contact Figures

Method. A number of leading databases (e.g., Lexis-Nexis, NewsBank, Index to Legal Periodicals, PsychLit, Medline, etc.) were searched to find both professional and lay articles reporting statistical information on the FMSF's contacts and membership. Transcripts from television programs and the complete archive of FMSF newsletters were also reviewed for similar information. To be included in this study, the article or transcript had to include a precise numerical figure that was explicitly identified as either FMSF membership or contacts. In addition, the article must have attributed the number to an FMSF member or publication, or indicated that a member of the FMSF was interviewed while researching the article. A total of 92 media reports (primarily newspaper articles), eight journal articles, and 36 FMSF newsletter references met inclusion criteria.

FMSF tax forms filed with the Internal Revenue Service (IRS) were obtained to provide a standard of comparison and were assumed to contain correct information. As a nonprofit charity, the FMSF is required to file a tax form every year (IRS 990), and the forms are available to the public. Although membership figures are not required by these forms, the foundation's accountant reported current membership figures on two of the forms–1995 and 1996.[8]

Results. Careful examination of the FMSF's reporting practices revealed that contact and membership figures reported to the public were unaccountably variable (see Table 1). In addition, membership figures quoted to the public often were highly inflated over the actual figures reported to the IRS during the same time period. For example, in early 1994, the *Sacramento Bee* reported that Pamela Freyd "said her Foundation has 11,000 members, including health professionals and lawyers" (Dobbin, March 9, 1994). In an article ironically titled, "Ethical Issues in the Search for Repressed Memories," FMSF advisor Harold Merskey (1996) reported, "The FMSF has grown rapidly with over 12,000 members by early 1995 and with more than 21,000 listed inquiries" (pp. 328-9). In April 1995, Ofra Bikel's Frontline documentary "Divided Memories" (which relied heavily on the FMSF for information) reported that the foundation had 15,000 members.[9] Toward the end of 1995, the FMSF's newsletter suggested that the organization was "over 17,000 strong" ("Make a Difference," 1995).[10] These figures are significantly larger than those reported to the IRS for 1995. The FMSF reported that by the end of 1995, they had 2,385 members, a portion of who were professionals rather than families.

Although the problem of inaccurate membership figures being reported to the public was brought to Pamela Freyd's attention in 1995 (see Lawrence, 1995), inflated figures continued to be a problem. As Table 1 demonstrates, in 1996 the average membership figure reported to the public was approximately six times higher than the figure reported to the IRS.

Figure 1 displays reported membership figures in relation to reported contacts. This graph demonstrates that while both contacts and membership figures appear to rise rapidly, actual membership levels remained relatively flat. Figure

TABLE 1. Comparison between numbers reported in FMSF literature or by media and actual membership figures reported to IRS.

Year	Membership Figures Reported to Public			Figures Reported to IRS*
	N	Range	Average	
1992	3	300-2,000	1,133	NA
1993	17	1,500-7,000	3,724	NA
1994	12	2,300-12,000	7,858	NA
1995	12	2,500-17,000	11,375	2,385
1996	4	11,000-18,000	15,250	2,500
1997	2	3,000-18,000	10,500	NA

*Obtained from 990 tax forms filed with the IRS. Membership figures were only documented on IRS tax forms for 2 years: 1995 and 1996.

1 also reveals a pattern of what appears to be the intermixing of cumulative contact figures (usually phone calls to the organization) with membership figures. The FMSF stopped reporting membership figures in 1997. Although it is not possible to say for certain why the FMSF stopped this practice, it did so right after Mike Stanton, a Pulitzer Prize winning investigative reporter, reported that the FMSF's true membership was "about 3,000." in July of 1997 (p. 45). Several months prior to the publication of Stanton's article, a member of the FMSF reported in testimony before a Georgia Senate Judiciary Subcommittee that the organization had 18,000 members (Renaud, March 6, 1997).[11] The last membership figure found in the print media was in the *Los Angeles Daily Journal*. Citing Pamela Freyd, the article reported that the FMSF has "some 3,000 dues-paying members" and has been contacted by 18,000 adults (Romo, September 22, 1997). No further mention of FMSF membership figures was found.

By January of 1999, Pamela Freyd announced that the epidemic of false memories was winding down. Phone calls to the organization had declined steadily since 1995 and "the vast majority" of families which had called in 1998 were concerned about accusations by young children, not accusations based on recovered memories (P. Freyd, January 1999, p. 1). According to Freyd, "The number of families newly accused on the basis of recovered memories is now no more than a trickle" (p. 1).

An Example of the FMSF's Mishandling of Its Statistical Data

Examination of the FMSF's reporting practices in early 1994 provide an intriguing case-study in how FMSF statistics were at times mislabeled to support the perception of a growing epidemic. In the January 1994 newsletter, Pamela Freyd states:

FIGURE 1. Comparison of average FMSF contact and membership figures reported to the media versus actual membership figures reported to the IRS.*

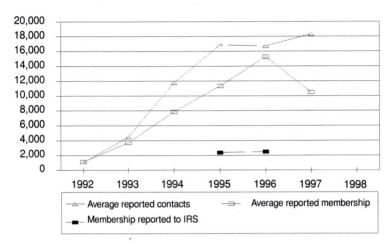

*Obtained from 990 tax forms filed with the IRS. Membership figures were only documented on IRS tax form for 2 years: 1995 and 1996.

We start the new year with almost 10,000 families. Imagine, 10,000 families *who have contacted* the foundation to say that they are *worried* about someone in their family who entered therapy and who then claimed to have recovered repressed memories of abuse taking place 10, 20, 30, even 40 years ago [italics added]. (P. Freyd, January 1994, p. 1)

In the next newsletter, these same "worried" contacts were presented with a different spin: "There are now over 10,000 families who have complained that someone they love has received radical therapy for a condition that did not exist" (P. Freyd, February 1994, p. 3).

The following newsletter (March 1994) implied that 11,000 "worried" contacts now represented both "documented cases" and members of the organization. The front page of the March 1994 newsletter featured a bar graph titled: "Number of Cases Documented." The graph shows 11,000 documented cases of false memory during the preceding two years. However, a close examination of the accompanying text revealed that the FMSF had been contacted by 11,000 people. Thus, "documented cases" were actually phone calls asking for information. The text also reveals that in over a third of these 11,000 calls, the "callers or writers have said they had a family problem, but we do not yet have the details" (P. Freyd, March 1994, p. 1).[12] It should also be noted that FMSF's phones are answered by lay volunteers rather than mental health professionals ("Who's Who," 1992). These volunteers do not investigate the story of the person on the other end of the line, and Pamela Freyd has admitted that "we do not know the truth or falsity of any of the reports that we receive" (P. Freyd, March 1994, p. 1). Thus, rather than 11,000 cases, in actuality the FMSF had *no* documented cases of "False Memory Syndrome." Despite this lack of data, Pamela Freyd concluded that "False Memory Syndrome" is now at "crisis" levels (p. 1).

The same issue of the FMSF newsletter included a letter written by an anonymous FMSF volunteer. The volunteer wrote: "Can you conceive of an organization that grew from 250 families in March 1992, to 11,000 in February 1994?" (p. 8). This letter implied that contacts (phone calls and letters with questions and concerns, along with 4,000 cases of "family problems" of which the organization has no details) were now members of the foundation. The next day, the transformation of phone queries into FMSF membership was completed when an article in the *Sacramento Bee* reported that Pamela Freyd "said her Foundation has 11,000 members, including health professionals and lawyers" (Dobbin, March 9, 1994).

These erroneous statistics later found their way into professional journals. For example, citing the March 1994 issue of the FMSF newsletter, an article in the *Journal of Family Law* reported that the FMSF claims "over 11,000 members" (Ahrens, 1996, p. 389). Figure 1 demonstrates that rather than having over 11,000 members in 1994, the FMSF's actual membership would have been less than 2,385.[13]

DISCUSSION:
THE SOCIAL CONSEQUENCES OF FALSE MEMORY RHETORIC

Pamela Freyd has frequently broadcast her organization's commitment to accurate reporting of information to the public. In the FMSF's newsletter she stated: "We are alarmed about the misconceptions about memory that are being relayed in the media and in the incest-survivor movement and we are trying to get the most accurate and most scientific information about memory available to the public" (P. Freyd, March 1993, p. 4). Pamela Freyd has also criticized those who misuse science for political purposes:

> Perhaps the most disturbing aspect of the current phenomenon [repressed memories], is the misuse of science to promote a political end. It

is the scientific issues that are the focus of the False Memory Syndrome Foundation. (P. Freyd, January 1994, p. 1)

Noting that statistics can have social consequences, the FMSF has also criticized incest activists who misuse their statistical data to promote their own agenda:

> Activists inevitably present themselves as knowledgeable enough about some social condition to bring it to our attention. . . . [T]his putative knowledge seems to give the crusaders' estimates the weight of authority. The activists seek to emphasize the problem's magnitude and importance; they have nothing to lose by providing big numbers. ("Thoughts on Sex Abuse," April 1993, p. 6)

The current review reveals that the FMSF has acted like the special interest groups it frequently criticizes. Specifically, the FMSF has emphasized the magnitude and importance of "False Memory Syndrome" and yet failed to publish any empirically based research supporting the existence of an identifiable syndrome or an epidemic. It has also participated in the dissemination of inaccurate statistical data which misled the public about the extent of the alleged problem. This lack of scholarly activities coupled with advocacy activities on behalf of those accused of sexually abusing children run counter to the FMSF's claim to be an objective scientific organization. In sum, the FMSF has conducted itself as a partisan organization with a strong sociopolitical agenda. As such, it has been extraordinarily successful in influencing social attitudes toward child abuse and fueling the current controversy about the validity of reports by those claiming to be victims of sexual assault.

The Response of the Media. Because of the FMSF's emphasis on influencing the press (see, e.g., "I Want to Help," 1992, p. 4), the debate over false memories has largely been played out in the national media (Heaton & Wilson, 1998). Sociologist Katherine Beckett (1996) analyzed the evolution of the treatment of child sexual abuse in leading magazines and found that between 1980 and 1984 only 7% of stories focused on false accusations of child sexual abuse. With the founding of the FMSF in 1992, stories about false memories emerged; by 1994 Beckett found that 85% of the articles on child sexual abuse focused on false memories and false accusations. Mike Stanton (1997) spent a year studying the recovered memory controversy. Like Beckett, he found that false memory rhetoric had greatly influenced media reporting and that articles about false memory had been heavily slanted in favor of accepting the accused parents' stories without questioning whether they might in fact be guilty. Stanton faulted the press for neglecting to examine the motivations of the foundation and for having uncritically relied on "FMSF experts and propaganda" for their information (p. 46). Research by Kondora (1998) supported these findings. She noted that with the advent of false memory stories, "lost was any substantive concern for the women and children who had endured abuse." Instead, the media's sympathies were focused on a newly constructed victim: the accused perpetrator.

Legal and Legislative Actions. Claims of a false memory epidemic, supported by newspaper articles quoting FMSF experts and statistics, have been used by false memory proponents to lobby federal and state legislatures to enact legislation helpful to accused child molesters (e.g., Renaud, 1997). Legislation has been introduced in numerous states that would severely limit the types of treatment that therapists could do with their patients.[14] The proposed legislation would also allow third-parties (e.g., alleged sex offenders) access to a patient's confidential therapy records, and make therapists liable to third-parties who object to any aspect of the therapy being done (for a review of legislative efforts see Dallam, 1998).

The FMSF has also attempted to sway the outcome of numerous legal cases involving charges of child molestation by filing amicus briefs on behalf of the accused (e.g., *State of New Hampshire v. Hungerford,* 1997; *Wilson v. Phillips,* 1999). In addition, many false memory proponents are high priced defense experts who appear overly willing to attach the label of "False Memory Syndrome" on alleged victims in order to discredit their testimony. For example, FMSF advisor Harold Merskey testified that a woman suing Toronto doctor, Leo Pilo, for damages caused by childhood sexual abuse probably suffered from "False Memory Syndrome." He offered this opinion without any direct examination of the plaintiff, and in spite of the fact that the woman's story was corroborated by two other victims, and Pilo's medical license had been previously revoked in a separate proceeding in which he *admitted* the women's charges (Landsberg, 1995).

Treatment of Abuse Victims. False memory rhetoric has made it popular to question the credibility of those reporting childhood abuse. A study of 113 adult victims of childhood sexual abuse in Ottawa found that although many of the women had corroborative evidence for their memories, over one-half had been accused by someone of having false memories. The women reported that exposure to false memory rhetoric led to increased symptoms of anxiety and depression, increased self-doubt about their memories, and an overall slowing of the progress of therapy (Allard, Kristiansen, Hovdestad, & Felton, accepted for publication, cited in Brown et al., 1998).

The "false memory" label has also been used in an attempt to discredit victims who have won judgments against their perpetrator. Consider the experience of Jennifer Hoult as reported in the peer-reviewed professional journal *Ethics and Behavior*. Hoult (1998) won a civil suit against her father (a FMSF member) for rape. Despite the judgment against her father and his record of having admitted to molesting another child (he denied molesting his daughter), Jennifer was portrayed as suffering from "False Memory Syndrome" on promotional materials distributed at FMSF conferences. Hoult reported that false memory proponents misrepresented the facts of her case to make it appear that her therapist implanted her memories and to make her appear unstable: "They claimed I was suicidal, unemployed, estranged from my family, and a victim of therapy, and they insinuated that I was malicious and a liar" (p. 137).

False memory rhetoric has also had a chilling effect on the willingness of therapists to believe and appropriately treat abuse survivors (see the Courtois article in this volume). Because of the risk of being charged with implanting false memories, some insurance providers are advising practitioners to refuse to take clients who allege delayed recall (Brown, 1997). Those who do treat such patients have been subjected to threats, picketing, ethics complaints, and civil and criminal legal actions (Calof, 1998). Despite the fact that a memory cannot be confirmed as either true or false without some form of external corroboration, some false memory advocates have improperly suggested to patients that the abuse they allege never happened. A London newspaper recently reported that a young woman committed suicide after being told by a therapist that her memories of abuse by her father were false. The mother confirmed the abuse and lodged a formal complaint against the practitioner who treated her daughter. The bereaved mother issued the following statement:

> My daughter has been abused by her father from the age of seven until 15. She had developed psychiatric problems and was admitted voluntarily to a clinic, where she was seen by the therapist. She rang me afterwards and was in a terrible state. She had been told her abuse was part of false memory syndrome. Two weeks later she took an overdose of prescription medication and died. I believe that had my daughter been believed, she would have stayed at the unit and would be alive today. (Dobson, 1998)

CONCLUSION

The "False Memory Syndrome" is a controversial theoretical construct based entirely on the reports of parents who claim to be falsely accused of incestuous abuse. In 1993, the FMSF noted that "False Memory Syndrome" is "a condition that needs to be considered and then confirmed or rejected when further information emerges" ("Our Critics," April 1993, p. 3). The current empirical evidence suggests that the existence of such a syndrome must be rejected. False memory advocates have failed to adequately define or document the existence of a specific syndrome, and a review of the relevant literature demonstrates that the construct is based on a series of faulty assumptions, many of which have been disproven. Likewise, there are no credible data showing that the vague symptoms they ascribe to this purported syndrome are widespread or constitute a crisis or epidemic.

This does not imply, however, that memory is infallible or that all people who are accused of sexual abuse are guilty. Both continuous and delayed memories are subject to distortion, and there are valid reasons to be suspicious of memories that are recalled only after the extensive use of suggestive techniques. Nevertheless, common sense and professional practice dictates that claims about a new diagnostic category reaching epidemic proportions require scientific substantiation. The public policy issues impacted by the false memory controversy are so important that they deserve the most careful and intellectually honest scholarship that the academic and professional community has to offer. In the absence of any substantive scientific documentation, "False Memory Syndrome" must be recognized as a pseudoscientific syndrome that was developed by an advocacy group formed by people seeking to defend against claims of child abuse.

NOTES

1. Shortly before the founding of the FMSF, Underwager and Wakefield gave an interview to the editor of *Paidika: The Journal of Paedophilia,* a Dutch journal that promotes social acceptance for pedophilia. In the article, Underwager expressed his belief that choosing pedophilia can be "a responsible choice" for an individual. Underwager asserted that, "Paedophiles can boldly and courageously affirm what they choose. They can say what they want is to find the best way to love. I am also a theologian and as a theologian I believe it is God's will that there be closeness and intimacy, unity of the flesh, between people. A paedophile can say: 'This closeness is possible for me within the choices that I've made' " (Geraci, 1993, pp. 3-4). When the interview came to light in 1993, Underwager resigned from the foundation. Wakefield remains on the board (see Dallam [1997] for more information).

2. According to Jennifer Freyd (1993), both Lief and Orne treated Peter Freyd for chronic alcoholism during the 1980s.

3. Kihlstrom later resigned from the FMSF and is no longer affiliated with the foundation.

4. In an interview, Peter Freyd stated that one of the reasons he finally sought treatment for his chronic alcoholism was because "I was worried about the fact that my memory wasn't as good as it used to be" (Hechler, 1996).

5. See also the Recovered Memory Archive at Brown University. The archive is available on the Internet and has documented more than 80 corroborated cases of re-

covered traumatic memories (http://www.brown.edu/Departments/Taubman_Center/ Recovmem/Archive.html).

6. In an article titled "How Do We Know We Are Not Representing Pedophiles," Pamela Freyd (February 29, 1992) suggested that the new organization could not be harboring molesters because "we are a good-looking bunch of people, graying hair, well dressed, healthy, smiling . . . " (p. 1).

7. As one might expect, the FMSF has become popular with pedophiles. In fact, many pedophile organizations now link directly to the FMSF's website (e.g., see SafeHaven Foundation, an organization for "responsible boylovers," http://www. safet.net/info/index.html).

8. As a nonprofit charity, the FMSF's tax forms (IRS 990) are available to the public.

9. The FMSF also promoted and distributed a videotape of "Divided Memories" along with numerous other newspaper articles containing incorrect membership or contact figures for the foundation. I was not able to find any corrections either in the newspapers, or in materials distributed by the FMSF.

10. The full statement was: "Remember that three years ago, FMSF didn't exist. A group of 50 or so people found each other and today we are over 17,000. Together we have made a difference."

11. This figure was provided by a FMSF member during testimony before the Georgia Senate Judiciary Subcommittee. The testimony was supportive of H.B. 440, a bill that would allow relatives of patients to sue therapists for creating or suggesting false memories of abuse.

12. FMSF's records have never been examined by an independent scientific body; thus it is unclear if all reported telephone contacts actually represent concerned families. For example, at one point the FMSF newsletter stated, " . . . approximately 40% of our calls are from professionals requesting information" ("Who Calls," 1992). It is also unclear how repeat phone calls are handled, or how many of the situations described by callers fit the definition of False Memory Syndrome offered by Kihlstrom (1993). These questions are particularly important given the fact that when the British Psychological Society (1995) examined the files of the FMSF's counterpart in England, the British False Memory Society (BFMS), they found that many files were "sketchy, unsystematically recorded notes." About half were merely records of telephone inquires. Of the rest, only about a third contained any reference to recovered memory but did not contain any information on how the memories had returned. Despite this lack of documentation, the BFMS has represented their contacts as evidence of a false memory crisis.

13. Although membership figures were not reported to the IRS in 1994, during this time period FMSF literature reported membership figures were steadily increasing. If these reports are correct, then prior to 1995 the FMSF would have had fewer members than in 1995 when the FMSF reported to the IRS that it had 2,500 members.

14. The legislation has yet to pass in any state.

REFERENCES

Ahrens, J. G. (1996). Recovered memories: True or false? A look at false memory syndrome. *Journal of Family Law, 34*, 376-401.

Albach, F., Moormann, P., & Bermond, B. (1996). Memory recovery of childhood sexual abuse. *Dissociation, 9*, 261-273.

American Psychiatric Association. (1994). *Diagnostic and statistical manual of mental disorders* (4th ed.). Washington DC: Author.

Andrews, B., Brewin, C. R., Ochera, J., Morton, J., Bekerian, D. A., Davies, G. M., & Mollon, P. (1999). Characteristics, context and consequences of memory recovery among adults in therapy. *British Journal of Psychiatry, 75,* 141-146.

Andrews, B., Brewin, C. R., Ochera, J., Morton, J., Bekerian, D. A., Davies, G. M., & Mollon, P. (2000). The process of memory recovery among adults in therapy. *British Journal of Clinical Psychology, 39,* 11-26.

Bavley, A. (1995, April 2). The issue: Memories of sexual abuse. *Kansas City Star,* p. B1.

Beckett, K. (1996). Culture and the politics of signification: The case of child sexual abuse. *Social Problems, 43,* 57-76.

Brewin, C., Andrews, B., & Gotlib, I. (1995). Psychopathology and early experience. *Psychological Bulletin, 113,* 82-98.

Briere, J. (1995). Child abuse, memory, and recall: A commentary. *Consciousness and Cognition, 4,* 83-87.

British Psychological Society. (1995, January) *Report on recovered memories.* Leicester, UK: Author.

Brown, D., Scheflin, A. W., & Hammond, D. C. (1998). *Memory, trauma treatment, and the law.* New York: W.W. Norton.

Brown, D., Scheflin, A. W., & Whitfield, C. L. (1999). Recovered memories: The current weight of the evidence in science and in the courts. *The Journal of Psychiatry & Law, 27,* 5-156.

Brown, L. S. (1997). The private practice of subversion: Psychology as tikkun olam. *American Psychologist, 52,* 449-462.

Calof, D. (1993a). A conversation with Pamela Freyd, PhD, co-founder and Executive Director, False Memory Syndrome Foundation, Inc., Part 1. *Treating Abuse Today, 3,* 25-39.

Calof, D. (1993b). Facing the truth about false memories. *Family Therapy Networker, 17,* 39-45.

Calof, D. (1998). Notes from a practice under siege: Harassment, defamation, and intimidation in the name of science. *Ethics & Behavior, 8,* 161-187.

Carstensen, L., Gabrieli, J., Shepard, R., Levenson, R., Mason, M., Goodman, G., Bootzin, R., Ceci, S., Bronfrenbrenner, U., Edelstein, B., Schober, M., Bruck, M., Keane, T., Zimering, R., Oltmanns, T., Gotlib, I., & Ekman, P. (1993, March). Repressed objectivity. *APS Observer, 6,* 23.

Chu, J., Frey, L., Ganzel, B., & Matthews, J. (1999). Memories of childhood abuse: Dissociation, amnesia, and corroboration. *American Journal of Psychiatry, 156,* 749-755.

Clancy, S. A., McNally, R. J., & Schachter, D. (1999). Effects of guided imagery in women reporting recovered memories. *Journal of Traumatic Stress, 12,* 559-570.

Clevenger, N. (1992). Statutes of limitations: Childhood victims of sexual abuse bringing civil actions against their perpetrators after attaining the age of majority. *Journal of Family Law, 30,* 447-469.

Corwin, D. L., & Olafson, E. (1997). Videotaped discovery of a reportedly unrecallable memory of child sexual abuse: Comparison with a childhood interview videotaped 11 years before. *Child Maltreatment, 2*, 91-112.

Courtois, C. A. (1995). Recovery memory/false memory polarities: Balance and collaboration needed. *Consciousness and Cognition, 4*, 133-134.

Dalenberg, C. J. (1996). Accuracy, timing and circumstances of disclosure in therapy of recovered and continuous memories of recovered and continuous memories of abuse. *Journal of Psychiatry & Law, 24*, 229-275.

Dallam, S. J. (1997). Unsilent witness: Ralph Underwager and the FMSF. *Treating Abuse Today, 7*(1), 27-39.

Dallam, S. J. (1998). The criminalization of psychotherapy. *Treating Abuse Today, 8*, 15-27.

Dobbin, M. (1994, March 9). Jury's still out on validity of hidden memory. *Sacramento Bee*, p. E1.

Dobson, R. (1998, April 5). Abused lose out over memory scares. *The Independent* (London), p. 2.

Doe, J. [Pamela Freyd]. (1991). How could this happen? Coping with a false accusation of incest and rape. *Issues in Child Abuse Accusations, 3*, 154-165.

Duggal, S., & Sroufe, L. A. (1998). Recovered memory of childhood sexual trauma: A documented case from a longitudinal study. *Journal of Traumatic Stress, 11*(2), 301-321.

Dziech, B. W., & Schudson, C. B. (1989). On trial: America's courts and their treatment of sexually abused children. Boston, MA: Beacon Press Books.

Elliott, D. M. (1997). Traumatic events: Prevalence and delayed recall in the general population. *Journal of Consulting and Clinical Psychology, 65*, 811-820.

False Memory Syndrome Foundation. (1992). *Legal aspects of false memory syndrome*. Philadelphia: Author.

False Memory Syndrome Foundation. (1993, April 17). *Summary of legal survey data from False Memory Syndrome Foundation*. Presented at FMSF Conference "Memory and Reality: Emerging Crisis."

Finkelhor, D. (1994). The international epidemiology of child sexual abuse. *Child Abuse & Neglect, 18*, 409-417.

Fish, V. (1998). The delayed memory controversy in an epidemiological framework. *Child Maltreatment, 3*, 204-223.

Freyd, J. (1993). Personal perspectives on the delayed memory debate. *Treating Abuse Today, 3*(5), 13-20.

Freyd, P. (1992, February 29). How do we know we are not representing pedophiles? *False Memory Syndrome Newsletter, 1*, p. 1.

Freyd, P. (1992, May 1). Dear friends. *FMS Foundation Newsletter, 1*, 1.

Freyd, P. (1993, March). Our Critics. *FMS Foundation Newsletter, 2*, 2-3.

Freyd, P. (1994, January). Dear friends. *FMS Foundation Newsletter, 2*, 1-2.

Freyd, P. (1994, February). Dear Friends. *FMS Foundation Newsletter, 3*, 1-3.

Freyd, P. (1994, March). Dear friends. *FMS Foundation Newsletter, 3*, 1.

Freyd, P. (1998, June). Dear friends. *FMS Foundation Newsletter, 7*, p. 1-2.

Freyd, P. (1999, January). Dear friends. *FMS Foundation Newsletter, 8*, 1-2.

Fried, S. (1994, January). War of remembrance: How the problems of one Philadelphia family created the False Memory Syndrome Foundation. *Philadelphia Magazine*, *85*, pp. 66-71, 149-157.

Gardner, M. (1993). Notes of a fringe-watcher: The false memory syndrome. *Skeptical Inquirer*, *17*, 370-375.

Geraci, J. (1993). Interview: Hollida Wakefield and Ralph Underwager. *Paidika: The Journal of Pedophilia*, *3*, 2-12.

Goodwin, J., Sahd, D., & Rada, R. T. (1979). Incest hoax: False accusations, false denials. *Bulletin of American Academy of Psychiatry & Law*, *6*, 269-276.

Haugaard, J., & Reppucci, N. (1988). *The sexual abuse of children: A comprehensive guide to current knowledge and intervention strategies*. San Francisco: Jossey-Bass Publishers.

Heaton, J. A., & Wilson, N. L. (1998). Memory, media, and the creation of mass confusion. In S. J. Lynn & K. M. McConkey (Eds.), *Truth in Memory*. (pp. 349-371). New York: Guilford Press.

Hechler, D. (1996). *False memories or true trauma?* Unpublished manuscript.

Herman, J. L., & Schatzow, E. (1987). Recovery and verification of memories of childhood sexual trauma. *Psychoanalytic Psychology*, *4*, 1-14.

Hoult, J. (1998). Silencing the victim: The politics of discrediting child abuse survivors. *Ethics & Behavior*, *8*, 125-140.

Hovdestad, W. E., & Kristiansen, C. M. (1996). A field study of "false memory syndrome": Construct validity and incidence. *Journal of Psychiatry & Law*, *24*, 299-338.

How could this have happened to my child? Mind control. (1993, November 3). *FMS Foundation Newsletter*, *2*(10), pp. 3-4.

I want to help. (April 1, 1992). *FMS Foundation Newsletter*, *1*(2), p. 4.

Kihlstrom, J. F. (1993). *The recovery of memory in the laboratory and clinic*. Talk presented at the joint convention of the Rocky Mountain Psychological Association and the Western Psychological Association, Phoenix, April 1993.

Kihlstrom, J. F. (1996). The trauma-memory argument and recovered memory therapy. In K. Pezdek & W. P. Banks (Eds.), *The recovered memory/false memory debate* (pp. 297-311). New York: Academic Press.

Kondora, L. L. (1998, March). A textual analysis of the construction of the False Memory Syndrome: Representations in popular magazines, 1990-1995. *Dissertation Abstracts*, DAI-B 58/09, p. 4721.

Kraft, S. (1985, February 11). Careers, reputations damaged; False molestation charges scar lives of the accused. *Los Angeles Times*, p. 1.

Landsberg, M. (1995, November 25). The incredible sex abuse case of Dr. Leo Pilo. *Toronto Star*, p. K1.

Lanyon, R. I. (1993). Assessment of truthfulness in accusations of child molestation. *American Journal of Forensic Psychology*, *11*, 29-42.

Lawrence, L. R. (1995). False Memory Syndrome Foundation's membership exaggerated: Organization only has about 4,000 members. *Moving Forward*, *3*(3), 6-7.

Lawson, L., & Chaffin, M. (1992). False negatives in sexual abuse disclosure interviews. *Journal of Interpersonal Violence*, *7*, 532-542.

Leavitt, F. (1997). False attribution of suggestibility to explain recovered memory of childhood sexual abuse following extended amnesia. *Child Abuse & Neglect, 21,* 265-272.

Leavitt, F. (1999). Suggestibility and treatment as key variables in the recovered memory debate. *American Journal of Forensic Psychology, 17,* 5-18.

Legal actions against parents. (1992, June 12). *FMS Foundation Newsletter, 1,* p. 2.

Legal news. (1992, November 5). *FMS Foundation Newsletter, 1,* p. 7.

Lindsay, D. S. (1998). Depolarizing views on recovered memory experiences. In S. J. Lynn & K. M. McConkey (Eds.), *Truth in Memory* (pp. 481-494). New York: Guilford Press.

Lindsay, D. S., & Read, J. D. (1994). Incest resolution psychotherapy and memories of childhood sexual abuse. *Applied Cognitive Psychology, 8,* 281-338.

Loftus, B. F., Korf, N. L., & Schooler, I. W. (1989). Misguided memories: Sincere distortions of reality. In I. C. Yuille (Ed.), *Credibility assessment* (pp. 261-474). Dordrecht, The Netherlands: Kluwer Academic Publishers.

Make a difference. (1995, September). *FMS Foundation Newsletter [online edition], 4*(8). Retrieved March 28, 1996, from the World Wide Web: http://iquest.com/ ~fit/articles/news4_08.html.

McCarty, L., & Hough, S. (1992, October 28). Childhood trauma: Cases of false memory? *The Winchester Star* (Winchester, VA).

Merskey, H. (1996). Ethical issues in the search for repressed memories. *American Journal of Psychotherapy, 50,* 323-335.

Morris, M. (1992, April 21). "False Memory Syndrome" taking its toll on families. *Utah County Journal* (Orem, Utah), p. A8.

Morris, M. (1992, April 24). Psychologists decry "hokey" therapy. *Utah County Journal,* p. A1.

Murphy, Wendy J. (1997). Debunking "false memory" myths in sexual abuse cases. *Trial,* 54-60.

National Clearinghouse on Family Violence. (1997). Fact sheet on child sexual abuse. Ottawa, Canada: Author.

Nugent, P. M., & Kroner, D. G. (1996). Denial, response styles, and admittance of offenses among child molesters and rapists. Journal of Interpersonal Violence, 11, 475-486.

Ofshe, R., & Watters, E. (1993, March/April). Making monsters. *Society,* 4-16.

Our critics. (1993, April 6). *FMS Foundation Newsletter, 2,* 3-4.

Page, J. C. (1999). False memory syndrome: A false construct. *Feminista!, 2*(10), (online journal available at http://www.feminista.com/v2n10/cutlerpage.html).

Perry, C. (1995). The false memory syndrome (FMS) and "disguised" hypnosis. *HYPNOS: The Swedish Journal of Hypnosis in Psychotherapy and Psychosomatic Medicine, 22,* 189-197.

Pezdek, K., Finger, K., & Hodge, D. (1997). Planting childhood memories: The role of event plausibility. *Psychological Science, 8,* 437-441.

Pope, K. S. (1996). Memory, abuse, and science: Questioning claims about the false memory syndrome epidemic. *American Psychologist, 51,* 957-974.

Porter, S., Yuille, J., & Lehman, D. (1999). The nature of real, implanted, and fabricated memories for emotional childhood events: Implications for the recovered memory debate. *Law & Human Behavior, 23,* 517-537.

Reaney, P. (2000, March 13). New research casts doubts on False Memory Syndrome. *Reuters* (London).

Renaud, T. (1997, March 6). A lawmaker's brush with false memories. *Fulton County Daily Report* (GA).

Romo, C. (1997, September 22). Recovered memory faces recall. *Los Angeles Daily Journal*, pp. 1, 4.

Scheflin, A. A., & Brown, D. (1996). Repressed memory or dissociative amnesia: What the science says. *Journal of Psychiatry & Law, 24*, 143-188.

Scheflin, A. A., & Brown, D. (1999). The false litigant syndrome: "Nobody would say that unless it was the truth." *Journal of Psychiatry & Law, 27*, 649-705.

Stanton, M. (1997, July/August). U-turn on memory lane. *Columbia Journalism Review*, 44-49.

State of New Hampshire v. Hungerford, No. 95-429. (Supreme Court of New Hampshire, 1997 NH Lexis 64).

Taylor, B. (1992, May 18). True or false? *Toronto Star*, p. C1.

Terr, L. C. (1991). Childhood traumas: An outline and overview. *American Journal of Psychiatry, 148*, 10-20.

Thoennes, N., & Tjaden, P. G. (1990). The extent, nature, and validity of sexual abuse allegations in custody and visitation disputes. *Child Sexual Abuse & Neglect, 14*, 151-163.

Thoughts on sex abuse statistics. (1993, April) *FMS Foundation Newsletter, 2*, 5-6.

Tyler, T. (1997, June 8). Man acquitted of abuse in false memory twist. *The Toronto Star*, p, A1.

Tyroler, P. (1999, January). Book review: "Smoke and Mirrors: The Devastating Effect of False Sexual Abuse Claims." *FMS Foundation Newsletter, 8*(1) (E-mail edition).

Underwager, R., & Wakefield, H. (1994). *Return of the Furies: An investigation into recovered memory therapy*. Peru, IL: Open Court.

Underwager, R., & Wakefield, H. (1995). Special problems with child abuse cases. In J. Ziskin (ed.), *Coping with psychiatric and psychological testimony*, 5th Ed. (pp. 1315-1370). Los Angeles, CA: Law and Psychology Press.

Weene, K. A. (1995). Clinical note on a documented case of early childhood repression. *Journal of Psychohistory, 23*, 145-148.

Whitfield, C. (1995). *Memory and abuse: Remembering and healing the effects of trauma*. Deerfield Beach, FL: Health Communications, Inc.

Who calls the foundation? (1992, July 21). *FMS Foundation Newsletter, 2*, p. 2.

Who's who in the office? (1992, August/September). *FMS Foundation Newsletter, 2*, p. 3.

Williams, L. M. (1995). Recovered memories of abuse in women with documented child sexual victimization histories. *Journal of Traumatic Stress, 8*, 649-673.

Wilson v. Phillips, No. G019891. (Cal. Ct. App. 4th Dist., 1999).

The Legend of Robert Halsey

Ross E. Cheit

SUMMARY. This article examines the criminal conviction of Robert Halsey for sexually abusing two young boys on his school-van route near Pittsfield, Massachusetts. Mr. Halsey's name has been invoked by academics, journalists, and activists as the victim of the "witch hunt" in this country over child sexual abuse. Based on a comprehensive examination of the trial transcript, this article details the overwhelming evidence of guilt against Mr. Halsey. The credulous acceptance of the "false conviction" legend about Robert Halsey provides a case study in the techniques and tactics used to minimize and deny sexual abuse, while promoting a narrative about "ritual abuse" and "witch hunts" that apparently requires little or no factual basis. The second part of this article analyzes how the erroneous "false conviction" narrative about Robert Halsey was con-

Ross E. Cheit, JD, PhD, is Associate Professor of Political Science and Public Policy at Brown University. He directs the Recovered Memory Project, an Internet-based archive and research project, through the Taubman Center for Public Policy and American Institutions at Brown. He is currently writing a book about the law and politics of child sexual abuse cases.

Address correspondence to: <Ross_Cheit@Brown.Edu>.

The author acknowledges useful comments from the audience in New Zealand, and from fellow panelists at the Law and Society meetings. Special thanks to Jessica Dubin for outstanding research assistance. Thanks also to Tom Anton and the Taubman Center for Public Policy and American Institutions at Brown University for research support.

Earlier versions of this article were presented at the Department of Psychology, University of Auckland; Auckland, New Zealand (September 4, 1998) and at the Annual Conference of the Law and Society Association, Aspen, Colorado (June 5, 1998).

[Haworth co-indexing entry note]: "The Legend of Robert Halsey." Cheit, Ross E. Co-published simultaneously in *Journal of Child Sexual Abuse* (The Haworth Maltreatment & Trauma Press, an imprint of The Haworth Press, Inc.) Vol. 9, No. 3/4, 2001, pp. 37-52; and: *Misinformation Concerning Child Sexual Abuse and Adult Survivors* (ed: Charles L. Whitfield, Joyanna Silberg, and Paul Jay Fink) The Haworth Maltreatment & Trauma Press, an imprint of The Haworth Press, Inc., 2001, pp. 37-52. Single or multiple copies of this article are available for a fee from The Haworth Document Delivery Service [1-800-HAWORTH, 9:00 a.m. - 5:00 p.m. (EST). E-mail address: getinfo@haworthpressinc.com].

37

structed and how it gained widespread acceptance. The Legend of Robert Halsey provides a cautionary tale about how easy it is to wrap even the guiltiest person in a cloak of righteous "witch hunt" claims. Cases identified as "false convictions" by defense lawyers and political activists deserve far greater scrutiny from the media and the public. *[Article copies available for a fee from The Haworth Document Delivery Service: 1-800-HAWORTH. E-mail address: <getinfo@haworthpressinc.com> Website: <http://www.HaworthPress.com> © 2001 by The Haworth Press, Inc. All rights reserved.]*

KEYWORDS. Child sexual abuse, backlash, politics, false accusation claims

Robert Halsey, convicted by a jury of sexually abusing two young boys on his school-van route near Pittsfield, Massachusetts, has become something of a folk hero in a political movement whose rallying cry is that there is a "witch hunt" in this country over child sexual abuse. Writing in the *The New York Review of Books,* Frederick Crews (1995) claimed that the criminal justice system "failed the Massachusetts school-bus driver Robert C. Halsey, who is serving *two consecutive life terms* for far-fetched misdeeds unwitnessed by any adults" (original emphasis; p. 45). Crews, a retired English professor from the University of California, Berkeley, argued the Halsey case is an example of "condemning the innocent to prison" on charges of child sexual abuse. The legend of Robert Halsey was entered into annals of Congress by Carol Hopkins of the San Diego-based "Justice Committee" who appealed for special relief for Halsey and others convicted of sexual abuse (Senate Committee, 1995). Robert Halsey's name also appears on the dedication page of *Satan's Silence: Ritual Abuse and the Making of an American Witch Hunt,* a foundational text in the "false-conviction" movement (Nathan & Snedeker, 1995).

That someone convicted of child sexual abuse could attain such prominent advocates in politics and academe is a testament to the organizational strength of the "false-conviction" movement. This movement draws together traditional advocates of civil liberties with a host of other interests. These groups are quick to question the exercise of authority by police, prosecutors, and others. They often rally under the banner of skepticism, claiming to bring this much-needed quality to places where it has been ignored. But none of these self-identified skeptics has expressed any skepticism of the Halsey "false conviction" story.

However, in spite of the strident claims to the contrary, the evidence against Halsey was overwhelming. Few child sexual abuse cases are as strong as this one. The credible testimony of five children was corroborated with physical evidence and with medical evidence that was diagnostic of sexual abuse. That a case with such powerful evidence of guilt could be taken as a "false conviction" by someone who carries the banner of "skeptic" is beyond ironic; it demonstrates a failure of authentic skepticism that comes only from the blindness of a political advocacy position.

How can this be? The broad answer is that the false-accusation movement thrives in a political culture that is apparently so inclined, maybe even anxious, to accept this story that apparently none of them has scrutinized the claims about Halsey. On closer examination, then, the legend of Robert Halsey is actually a story of how even the clearly guilty can hide under the claim of a "modern day witch hunt." The first part of this article lays out the evidence against Robert Halsey, evidence never mentioned in any of the sources where he has been canonized. In short, the first part of this article debunks the idea that Halsey's conviction is somehow "questionable." The second part of this article tracks down the source of this (false) legend and then, through close textual analysis, demonstrates the power of denial in action. The Halsey legend demonstrates how effective certain tactics can be, even when employed on behalf of someone who is guilty. In this regard, the legend of Robert Halsey is best seen as a cautionary tale about the false-conviction movement and its power to rally people around the guilty.

DEBUNKING THE LEGEND

Robert Halsey, 60, was a part-time bus driver in Western Massachusetts in 1990, when he was given a route that covered a remote part of Lanesboro, where he was a life-long resident. The "bus" was actually a Suburban van, and the route covered a handful of kindergartners who arrived at school shortly after noon each day, and leaving after 3:00 pm. Sometimes, Andrew and William W., 5 year-old twins, were the only passengers in Halsey's van. Halsey drove this route for the entire 1990-91 school year, and part of the following year. There were more children on the route in 1991-92: the twins and often five or six other children. In February of 1992, Halsey was transferred to a different route, one with much older kids. But the actual circumstances surrounding his transfer were kept quiet for almost a year.

In a formal sense, the "case" began 11 months later, shortly after Andrew and William W.'s father handed out cigars in celebration of a new birth in their family. With cigar smoke permeating the house, the twins suddenly began talking about their former bus-driver, Robert Halsey, also an avid cigar smoker. Halsey smoked cigars on the bus, sometimes with all of the windows closed. He used lit cigars to intimidate, and he also threatened the kids with matches, according to the records. The twins described various forms of physical abuse on the bus, including restraints with rope and duct tape, and abuse with a plastic baseball bat. They also described (using words of a child) being anally raped by Halsey in a wooded area next to a desolate road he often used as a shortcut. They reported that while one boy was restrained on the bus, the other would be taken into the woods. Mr. W. contacted the police immediately. That all happened over a weekend, and the boys each received a simple forensic interview on Monday morning.

The most common objections to child interviews (e.g., Ceci & Bruck, 1995) simply do not apply in this case. There were no repeat interviews, the boys disclosed significant details after the most open-ended questions, and they were interviewed almost immediately after disclosure. Using a one-way mirror, these interviews were conducted in the presence of the police, the district attorney, and the parents. A school counselor with training in child interviewing asked Andrew if he knew why he was there. "To talk about the stuff that Bob did," he responded. "Tell me what Bob did," she said (tr. 7: 1283). The session lasted 45 minutes, during which time the boy told a detailed story of physical and sexual abuse. He told of being tied with rope and having his mouth taped shut sometimes when he was on the bus. He told of being threatened with knives, guns, and matches. He described several weapons in detail. He described being hit with a bat, and, more reluctantly, of being taken off the bus near the pond on Nobody's Road and sexually abused and humiliated in the woods.

Interviewed separately, William told a similar story. He spoke for an hour and was generally more forthcoming with details. He demonstrated how the kids were tied up and taped on the bus. He described being tied to a tree in the woods, while Halsey shot at a target above his head. He also said that Halsey chased him with a shopping cart sometimes (this turns out to be an important detail in this initial disclosure, one borne out by the finding of an unlikely grocery cart in the place he described). William also said that Halsey "put his finger in my butt" many times. The boy described Halsey ejaculating on his back, while being forced to lie face down in the woods.

The police arrested Halsey that night at his home. More than one observer described his demeanor as "calm and detached," both before and after his arrest (see generally the testimony of Detective Lieutenant Robert G. Scott, tr. vol. 7). After waiving the right to an attorney, Halsey gave a bizarre statement filled with nonsequiturs, sexual innuendo, and lies. For example, Halsey denied owning any pornographic videotapes, until he was confronted with tapes the police seized after searching his property. When first asked about the twin boys, Halsey denied knowing them! When confronted with evidence of his obvious lie, Halsey told the officer: "They would never say anything. They are my friends" (tr. 7: 1371; 1572-3). Halsey also made strange, contradictory claims about his own sexuality.[1] These were his last public statements on the matter. Halsey did not take the stand in his own defense.

Robert Halsey was charged with multiple counts of rape, assault and battery, and assault and battery with a dangerous weapon (including a gun, a knife, and a baseball bat). Word of Halsey's arrest spread quickly. Curiously, nobody came forward to say what a great bus driver he had been. Instead, various comments and related revelations slowly painted a much darker picture. Consider the words of a fellow bus driver days after Mr. Halsey's arrest:

> I think I knew there were a few problems–they were small things. He would like to stand where the children brush up against him–things like that. (Elfbenbein, 1993b, B1)

Soon, parents learned that Halsey had been transferred in 1992 after a young girl's parents lodged a complaint. It was also revealed that the police knew about the "inappropriate behavior" and helped encourage the bus company owner to transfer Halsey without any formal investigation or charges. Rumors about Halsey were so rampant in some circles that he had been removed from the approved driver list in bordering Mt. Greylock School District. Still, the charges did not escalate or expand, even though the case was highly publicized in Pittsfield. Halsey was charged with sexual abuse of the twins and physical abuse of one girl.

The state's case was built largely on the testimony of five children. The main witnesses were the twins, who disclosed spontaneously at home and then elaborated without any questionable interviewing techniques shortly thereafter. The boys' testimony was corroborated by physical and medical evidence. Two other children provided direct evidence about the duct tape, the baseball bat, and various weapons and threatening behavior.

Andrew W. described a varied pattern of what adults would see as humiliation, intimidation, and physical and sexual abuse. He described being taken off the bus near a pond on Nobody's Road and watching Halsey kill frogs and turtles. "I'm going to kill you, too," he said to the boys. Sometimes he taped their eyes and mouth shut. Andrew also described being anally penetrated: "He told me that he was sticking his finger in my butt" (tr. 4: 626). He described Halsey ejaculating, and putting candy on his exposed penis and making the boys take it. He described knives and guns in detail, and where Halsey kept them on the bus. He also described going to Halsey's house on occasion and being forced to sit in a box of smelly kitty litter while Halsey played pornographic video-tapes (tr. 4: 675-6).

William, his brother, was more timid on the stand. He described some of the same weapons, and how he was hit and restrained by Halsey. He described telling his mother that "he didn't like the bus." Her response, understandably, was that it had been very difficult to get the district to provide the van, and that he should be grateful there was a van. William described Halsey putting candy "down his pants" and masturbating in front of them on the bus (tr. 5: 865-69). William also accurately explained the directions to Halsey's house (tr. 5: 892-900). Halsey told the police that the boys had never been to his house. He never provided an explanation of how the boys knew where his house was located, and how the rooms were arranged inside.

The third child to testify, Lauren C., had moved to Florida with her family *before* Mr. Halsey's sudden reassignment in February 1992. Interviewed in Florida, where the family had not maintained any contact with anyone near Pittsfield, Lauren quickly corroborated several aspects of the twins' story: how her mouth and hands had been taped with duct tape, and how her feet were tied with rope[2] (tr. 6:1014-18). Lauren also described how Halsey would take kids off the bus one at a time, near a pond (tr. 6:1022). She described guns, knives, and his ever-present cigars.

Michala K., the fourth child to testify, lived near the school and rarely took the bus in the morning. But she regularly took the bus in the afternoon, sometimes going to her grandmother's house. Michala also described various weapons on the bus and where Halsey kept them (tr. 6: 1058-61). She testified that Halsey called her a "bitch" and hit her with a foam bat. One day he "choked" her, and she told her grandmother and her parents (tr. 6: 1062). That complaint led to Halsey's sudden reassignment.

Lauren's older sister, Ivory C., was the final child to testify. Ivory, who was nine years old at trial, testified that she was rarely on the bus because she was in school all day (the other kids who testified attended school for half-days). But she had seen the ropes, the bats, and the knives. She recalled an incident when Halsey threatened her with the words: "If you won't be quiet, I'll put tape over your mouth until you stop breathing" (tr. 6: 1038, 1093-94).

The children's testimony was corroborated in numerous ways by physical evidence. For example, the twins described being chased by a grocery cart in the area off Nobody's Road in 1990-91. One of the two men who live on that road testified that he found a grocery cart in the same location in 1991. He also found pornography in the area, but that testimony was prohibited because the children didn't mention pornography in the woods, just at his house.[3] The twins also described an impressive constellation of items later found in Halsey's home: guns, knives, baseball bats, duct tape and rope. While those items might seem commonplace, the descriptions in some cases were quite specific. A small black pocketknife and a sword-like dagger with a hand in the handle, for example, were among the items matching descriptions provided by the boys. The twins also provided an accurate description of Halsey's house, a place that Halsey claims they had never been. Both boys gave accurate descriptions of the *inside* of the house. On cross-examination, the best the defense could do is stump one boy on the color of the front door.

Medical findings are rare in sexual abuse cases (Adams et al., 1994). Findings of the clarity found in this case are even more rare. In short, the medical evidence that the twins had been sexually abused was beyond dispute. A pediatric specialist testified that both boys had multiple lacerations inside their anuses (tr. 7: 1161-70). In both cases, the lesions were in a pattern considered by the American Academy of Pediatrics to be "diagnostic of penetration by a foreign object into the anus" (tr. 7: 1171-2). The defense suggested that the boys might have been raped by someone else, but these insinuations about the "real molesters" were never supported by actual evidence.

The boys' pediatrician testified to having made additional physical findings that were "supportive" but not diagnostic of sexual abuse (tr. 7: 1173-80). Evidence was introduced concerning two incidents in the boys' medical history while Halsey was their bus driver. Once, their mother was so worried that both twins had itchy and irritated anuses that she discussed the matter with the pediatrician. The doctor told her it was either pinworms or sexual abuse. The mother considered the possibility of sexual abuse and eliminated it because she could not imagine the possibility either at school or at home. Understandably, she did not even consider "en route" to be a possibility. As a result, the boys took medicine for pinworms.[4]

There were a few other witnesses for the prosecution, including the school counselor and a therapist. The defense did not put Halsey on the stand. The entire defense consisted largely of a few bus drivers who said they had never seen Halsey act inappropriately, and a few teachers who said they never saw the twins behave in a manner that suggested they had been sexually abused.

Nobody who followed the trial was surprised by the verdict. The evidence was so overwhelming that the main puzzle around the courthouse was why Halsey had not agreed to a plea deal. Halsey was sentenced to two *consecutive* life terms, a sentence undoubtedly stiffer because of insistence on putting the kids through a trial.[5]

Since the medical and physical evidence so powerfully corroborated the children's testimony, there was little left to raise on appeal. Mr. Halsey's lawyer decided to argue mostly about the pornography seized from his client's house. His first grounds for appeal was that that 16 pornographic items that were in plain sight when the search was executed on his house should not have been seized because they were not mentioned in the warrant. These items were not actually admitted into evidence at trial, but testimony concerning the items was allowed. Halsey's second argument on appeal was that the testimony regarding the pornography was "so inflammatory as to deny him a fair trial." Halsey's other arguments on appeal were, in the words of the appellate court, "susceptible of summary comment."[6] The appellate court dismissed the arguments about the pornography as well, concluding that there was "no substantial risk of a miscarriage of justice" (*Commonwealth v. Halsey*, 1996, p. 778).

DECONSTRUCTING THE DISTORTIONS

How did the legend of Robert Halsey's "false conviction" gain widespread acceptance, and why hasn't anyone apparently noticed that the evidence against Halsey was actually overwhelming? The answer begins with the power of the Internet and the uncritical acceptance of information, particularly when it originates from a prestigious educational institution. The answer is also social. The credulous acceptance of the Halsey legend provides a case study in techniques and tactics used to minimize and deny sexual abuse, while promoting a narrative about "ritual abuse" and "witch hunts."

The Prestige of MIT.EDU

The legend of Robert Halsey's "false conviction" can be traced to a most unlikely source: the esteemed Massachusetts Institute of Technology. Jonathan Harris, a visiting associate professor of chemical engineering at MIT in the mid-1990s, assured Robert Halsey's position in the false-conviction movement by including Halsey's case on the "Witch Hunt Information Page," a Web site launched in 1994 and housed on an MIT server until almost two years after Harris left MIT to work for a financial institution in Florida (see Harris, n.d.). According to then-professor Harris, the site contained information "about the modern version of the witch hunts: ritual (and pseudo ritual) sexual abuse trials and those who have been wrongfully imprisoned by them." The Halsey case was one of several cases described on the Harris Web Site[7].

As it turns out, Halsey's case gained notoriety by the coincidence of geography and the apparent need to "pad" the (short) list of cases offered as proof of an allegedly broad social trend. The geographic coincidence is that Halsey's case was described briefly in the *Boston Globe* a couple of times ("Bus driver," 1993; Roche, 1993). Neither of those stories intimated or otherwise supported the claim that Halsey was falsely accused, but that did not deter Harris from concluding that the case deserved a place on his Web site. This is the complete text of Harris's description:

> "Robert Halsey [sic], of Lanesboro (Western MA near Pittsfield): A busdriver serving two consecutive life terms. Mr. Halsey drove a small school bus for 5 and 6 year olds in the rural town of Lanesboro, Massachusetts. This case started after Mr. Halsey tickled a girl and she complained. According to his attorney, Halsey admitted to the incident and was transferred to another route. In the investigation which followed a bizarre story of sexual abuse emerged. The Globe had two stories on this, one alleging very bizarre and unlikely events as well as the usage of the bogus symptoms of sexual abuse (the ones which appear on normal children and often not in abuse ones). It turns out the same therapist of the Baran case was involved. Also the same insurance company handling the Baran case handled this one. The insurance company person seemed to feel that there was some medical evidence that supported the molestation charges (she said this was a "different" story but did not elaborate). I don't know enough about this one, but hopefully it will be critically examined eventually" (available at the Harris Web Site, http://www.geocities.com/jg harris7/baran.html).

Even though the "Witch Hunt Information Center" was a personal project, not one reflecting MIT research, the Site gained immediate credibility because of the address.[8] The cases described on this Site soon gained an inappropriately hallowed status. This was undoubtedly where Professor Crews and Carol Hopkins of the Justice Committee found out about the alleged injustice against Robert Halsey.[9] At the end of his adjective-laden account of the Halsey case, Harris adds this puzzling caveat: "I don't know enough about this one, but hopefully it will be critically examined eventually." The puzzle is *for what purpose* Harris did not "know enough about this one"? Obviously, he thought he knew enough about it to post an abstract on something he called the "Witch Hunt Information Page." This "Information Page" was described in banner headlines as providing: "Information about the Modern Version of the Witch Hunts: Ritual (and pseudo ritual) sexual abuse trials and those who have been wrongfully imprisoned by them." Since there is no caveat in the name or explanation of this Page, it remains puzzling why Mr. Harris, if he "did not know enough," associated the Halsey case with such strong adjectives and conclusions. It is also not clear why Harris (1994) made the sarcastic claim that "ritual abuse is alive and well in Western Massachusetts" when the case did not involve claims of ritual abuse.

Curiously, none of the self-described skeptics who favored this Site found reason to question any of the cases, even though Harris's abstract of the Halsey case pointed out the need for further inquiry. The failure of several famous skeptics to heed Harris's caveat speaks volumes about the difference in standards they employ. Apparently even the most remote *possibility* of a false conviction justifies posting (and embracing) cases on the "Witch Hunt Information Center." Imagine if things were the other way around, and sexual abuse was being claimed based on a slim possibility that had not actually been checked out.

The Power of Denial

Why was Harris's description taken at face value by so many self-proclaimed skeptics? Why was the false conviction claim so effective that it was adopted by scholars such as Frederick Crews? Mertz and Lonsway (1998) proposed a general framework for analysis of "effective denials" of sexual abuse in society. Several elements in that framework help explain how someone as guilty as Robert Halsey can effectively be made out to be a "witch hunt" victim.

"Language 'Games'"

Language games can "divert the audience's attention from the underlying problem" by drawing fine semantic distinctions that seek to evade responsibility (Mertz & Lonsway, 1998). Harris employed a similar tactic by turning a choke into a "tickle," thereby seriously misrepresenting the physical assault that resulted in Halsey losing his kindergarten route. According to Harris, "this case started after Mr. Hasley (sic) tickled a girl and she complained." It is true that a complaint was lodged; however, the complaint, which resulted in a cover-up, pre-dated Halsey's arrest by almost a year. In addition, the substance of the complaint was never as innocuous as a tickle. The complainant actually used the word *choke* (tr. 6: 1062). She described other abuse as well, prompting the police officer who (quietly) intervened to tell the owner of the bus company that Halsey "could get 10 years" for what he did.[10] When the story emerged in the newspaper a year later, the other person to call it "tickling" was the owner of the bus company, who was facing civil liability for not firing Halsey.

It is almost unbearable to tell this case in the kind of detail conveyed through the trial testimony. Some of the evidence is beyond revolting. Halsey dominated, restrained, threatened, over-powered, taunted, humiliated, and forcefully penetrated two young boys, according to the records. There is vivid testimony detailing the various ways in which Halsey did *each* of these things. The criminal trial focused on threats, physical assaults, and sexual assaults. The testimony concerning the ways he humiliated the boys, towering above them, taunting them, is perhaps the most sickening. Leaving out the details here runs the risk of omitting evidence that makes his other actions somehow more comprehensible, better fitting his "character." Including them, however, runs the risk of overkill and charges of sensationalism. There were certain things that Halsey said and did to the kids, for example, that are well documented in the trial transcript. They are graphic, repulsive and *probably* unnecessary for portraying the weight of the evidence. It is worth noting, however, that this sensibility helps make it possible for the most repugnant cases to be minimized and mischaracterized.

How the word "tickle" came to describe choking and other physical abuse is a classic example of how much easier it is for society to use words that minimize abuse than it is to use more accurate and descriptive words. The police officer who used the word "tickle," testified that he did so with a clear sense of euphemism when conveying his message to the owner of the bus company that "something should be done" about Halsey (tr. 9: 1745-56). This case demonstrates how easily such euphemisms will be accepted or later repeated as literal. It also points out how the social discomfort of describing sexual abuse works in favor of the perpetrator (see also, Whitfield, this volume, item 23). These forces are at work even in the detailed account of Halsey's case in this article.

Jonathan Harris also made the "witch hunt" narrative plausible through the repeated use of loaded adjectives. In his 173-word account of the Halsey case, Harris used the words "bogus," "bizarre," "very bizarre," and "unlikely." Professor Crews later dismissed the case with the word "far-fetched." The use of powerful adjectives instead of facts is reminiscent of Senator Joseph McCarthy.[11] Indeed, given the evidence presented at Halsey's trial, there is nothing "far-fetched" about the state's case. Both of the boys had clear medical signs of abuse, and their testimony was corroborated in various ways by other physical evidence. Presumably, the "unlikely" quality has something to do with the *opportunity* to commit the crime. The defense raised two questions concerning the *opportunity* for Halsey to commit these acts: First, they suggested that Nobody's Road was blocked off during part of the year and therefore would have been inaccessible to the bus; second, they suggested there was not sufficient *time* to commit these acts and get the boys to school on time. In the abstract, these arguments are likely to resonate with the common experience most people have had with school buses. On most buses, the driver could not possibly find the time or place to abuse the kids in the manner claimed in this case. But this was a van, not a bus, and there were many times the twins were the only ones on board. Moreover, the route was in a "very remote" area of the county, and the schedule was "padded" by at least 25 minutes, possibly as much as 45 on most days.[12]

There was also detailed testimony to contradict the claim that Nobody's Road was inaccessible at times. Nobody's Road has two houses. Mory

Brenner, one of two residents of the road, testified that the cement blocks that were intended to block the road during the winter of 1990-91 were rolled on their side a little while after the city put them up, rendering it possible for vehicles to pass through. Even before they were moved, he testified, they "could always be gotten through" with a vehicle the size of a van (tr. 7: 1224-1225). In sum, the allegations might seem "far-fetched" if all you know is that a bus driver was accused of sexually abusing kids on his route. But every *detail* in this case makes the scenario more likely, not less. Nevertheless, the language contained on the "Witch Hunt Information Center" was effective in convincing others that Halsey, not the children, is somehow the victim (see also, Whitfield, this volume, false memory defense number 2).

Re-Frame the Issue, Attack the Source

Mertz and Lonsway (1998) describe two other basic strategies found in effective denials: "attack the source" and "re-frame the issue." Both play a prominent role in the false-conviction narrative that Jonathan Harris constructed for his Web page. Basically, Harris impugned the investigation by the sheriff's office and criticized the woman who interviewed the children. This approach simultaneously directed attention away from Halsey while undermining official sources in the case. Of course, these would be legitimate arguments if supported by facts. Harris's narrative, however, did not rely on facts; rather, it relied on innuendo, language games, and guilt-by-association.

The first step in this process was to impugn the investigation through insinuating words. According to Harris, the investigation did not "uncover" or "document" anything; rather, the "bizarre story of sexual abuse emerged" from the investigation. The bitter irony in Harris's attempt to reframe history is that officials in the Halsey matter should be faulted for covering up Halsey's case for almost a year, not for rushing to judgment and somehow charging an innocent man. Left entirely out of Harris's version of the investigation is what happened after the little girl complained that Halsey had "choked" her. Halsey was quietly reassigned to a route with high school students. No charges were filed, no children were interviewed, and no parents were told about the matter. In short, it would be much more accurate to say that the charges were originally covered up.

The investigation that resulted in Halsey's arrest was entirely separate from the complaint that was covered up 11 months earlier. The fact that the February 1992 complaint was never properly investigated (let alone prosecuted) is the reason why 200 angry parents attended a meeting shortly after Halsey's arrest (Elfbenbein, 1993a). While the reader of Harris's account would assume that the "tickle" charges triggered an investigation that ran amok, actually the complaint (which was far more serious than tickling) resulted in a cover-up that was eventually addressed a year later when the boys also disclosed abuse by Halsey.

Harris further impugned the investigation by distracting attention and blaming someone else: the school counselor who interviewed the twins for the police, shortly after they disclosed to their parents. As Harris put it: "It turns out the same therapist of the Baran case was involved" (1996, p. 8). This single sentence packs several more McCarthy-like tactics. First and most obviously, it employs guilt by association. The sins of the Baran case[13] are apparently visited upon the Halsey case by virtue of one overlapping person whose presence might signify nothing more than that both cases, almost seven years apart, happened in the same small county. Second, combining an incorrect word ("therapist") with a vague one ("involved"), Harris creates the phony specter of the bad therapist who somehow conjured up the allegations. That is the foundational narrative structure of a popular advocacy group for accused parents and others, the so-called False Memory Syndrome Foundation. Ms. Satullo was a counselor, not a therapist, at the kids' school. Moreover, she was trained in interviewing children, and her involvement in the Halsey case began with the initial forensic interview. She conducted these interviews while others watched through one-way glass. There were no objections about those interviews before, during, or after they were conducted.

A related version of "attack the source" is Harris' assertion that Halsey's case involved "the usage of the bogus symptoms of sexual abuse (the ones which appear on normal children and often not in abuse ones)"(1996, p. 8). *Who* used these alleged "bogus symptoms" and *how* are left out of the "witch hunt" narrative? There *was* testimony about the behavioral symptoms that can accompany sexual abuse, and about the dynamics that explain delayed disclosure. However, the testimony of Dr. Jeffrey Fishman was limited to general characteristics, nothing specific to the children in the case. Obviously, this kind of general evidence is relevant to the case, particularly since the defense insinuated that the delay required explanation. The testimony is also useful in deciding whether the unusual behavior the mother observed in the twins during 1991 is the kind of behavior that might be explained by sexual abuse. The testimony about the twins' "unusual behavior" is apparently what Harris dismisses as "bogus," although he provides no specific reason for impugning the evidence in this case. However, the "unusual behavior" was not nearly as normal and innocuous as Harris asserts. The kind of behavior the mother observed (and wondered about, going so far as to discuss the matter with the boys' doctor) included obscene outbursts (e.g., the boys started yelling "freaking asshole bait" that year) and anal compulsive behavior in the bathtub (e.g., they also spread their cheeks and said things like "see my butt hole") (tr. 6: 1112-1120).

However questionable this kind of evidence might sound in the abstract, it looks entirely different in the total context of the harsh reality of specific facts.

CONCLUSION

The legend of Robert Halsey demonstrates how easy it is to wrap even the guiltiest person in a cloak of righteous "witch hunt" claims. The implications of the legend, then, extend far beyond the fact that a man guilty of horrendous sex crimes against two five-year old boys has been embraced unskeptically by academics linked with two of the world's most distinguished universities, M.I.T. and the University of California, Berkeley. The success of Jonathan Harris's "witch hunt" narrative demonstrates the power of the "basic 'moves' " that Mertz and Bowman identified in their analysis of "effective denials." That these techniques can be effective for someone as guilty as Robert Halsey suggests just how simultaneously appealing and dangerous these moves can be. The need for skepticism of the "witch hunt" claim is clear. It is made all the more pressing by the untempered credulity with which self-identified skeptics have accepted the Halsey legend.

The Halsey case has also been explicitly associated with "ritual abuse" by Harris (1994) and Nathan and Snedeker (1995), each of whom employ the label to discredit the case. Just as the Halsey case was not a "witch hunt," it also had nothing to do with "ritual abuse" or Satan. That Harris (1994) and Crews (1995) could describe this case as "bizarre" and "far-fetched" suggests, most charitably, that they do not understand that some child molesters really do employ threats in conjunction with sexual abuse. The ability to dismiss as implausible behaviors that are well documented and all too common carries implications far beyond the Halsey case. What do the glaring inaccuracies in the legend of Robert Halsey say about the other cases embraced by the "witch hunt" movement? The answer will apparently remain unclear until a much-needed dose of skepticism is applied to the rest of the "witch hunt" claims.

NOTES

1. At one point, Halsey claimed that he could not have committed these acts because "I'm dead down there." He later contradicted himself with unsolicited assertions about recent sexual activities with his wife, claims also designed somehow to "prove" that he did not assault these boys.

2. Questions were raised at the trial about whether the detective mentioned rope before Lauren did, but all parties agreed that Lauren mentioned duct tape without prompting, and without any knowledge that the twins had told of duct tape in their interviews (not yet public in any sense), taken thousands of miles away.

3. Because the boys did not mention pornography in the woods, there was no legal foundation for introducing this evidence. The boys did mention the pornography in Halsey's house. But they didn't mention it in their very first interview, the one that formed the basis for the search and arrest warrants. Therefore the jury never heard the evidence concerning the pornography in Halsey's house. Ownership of pornography does not prove anything, of course; but what Halsey had in plain view did include depictions of anal sex, actions closely related to the allegations by the twins.

4. There was also a time that year that one of the boys came home badly bruised on the legs. He said he had been bruised on the playground. In the investigation of Halsey that took place more than a year later, the boy told police that Halsey had hit him with the plastic baseball bat. His medical chart documents the bruises.

5. The trial transcript indicates that the prosecution raised the issue of a plea bargain at side bars throughout the initial presentation of their case (see, particularly, proceedings after completion of opening statements, August 30, 1993; tr. vol. 3). They were hoping to spare the children the ordeal of cross-examination. Halsey declined.

6. The claim that Jane Satullo improperly "vouched" for the children mischaracterizes her testimony. Jane Weinstein, her name at the time, described the interview she had with each boy two days after disclosing to their parents. The interview came so soon after their disclosure that Ms. Weinstein was permitted to testify as a "fresh complaint witness."

The other claim was that evidence concerning Halseys demeanor at the time of his arrest and after being given his Miranda rights (to wit, that he was "calm, lucid") violated his right against self-incrimination. The court ruled, however, that the evidence was relevant to assessing the voluntariness of his statements to the police, an issue that Halsey raised at trial.

7. For about five years, Harris's description of the Halsey case was located at: <http://web.mit.edu/harris/www/baran.html>. The Site has since been resurrected and can currently be found at: <http://www.geocities.com/jgharris7/baran.html>.

8. Perhaps the best evidence is the (incorrect) entry in NetFirst, a directory of Web resources, which said the following about Harris's Web site and electronic list: "The organization responsible for running this group is the Massachusetts Institute of Technology, Cambridge, MA, based in the USA." In fact, it was Harris's personal page and in no sense was "run" (or approved) by MIT.

9. Harris's site contains a list prepared by Ms. Nathan. A subscription list requested from the list-server in January 1995 indicates that Professor Crews was then subscribed to WITCHHNT.

10. That testimony was also kept from the jury. But it was the topic of intense conversation at side bar. (See, e.g., tr. 9: 1745-65.)

11. Senator Joseph McCarthy did much the same thing, employing "shrill and exaggerated" language. McCarthy's indiscriminate attacks gave rise to the term "McCarthyism." One tactic of McCarthy's that is mirrored by Jonathan Harris in the context of Robert Halsey is the labeling of events as 'fantastic,' 'unbelievable,' 'incredible' and 'phenomenal.' (Oshinsky, 1983: 78).

12. The twins were picked up between 11:15 and 11:30 am for a 12:10 pm class. The prosecution provided evidence that the route to the school could be covered in less than 10 minutes on most days. The defense witnesses claimed it would take, at most, 27 minutes. Since there was evidence that Halsey routinely arrived for the twins at 11:15

am, even allowing the *defense* estimate of total driving time, Halsey could stop on Nobody's Road for 20 to 30 minutes a day.

13. The Baran case also turns out to be more complicated than the one-sided version
written by Harris (see, generally, Mehegan, 2000).

REFERENCES

Adams, J., Harper, K., Knudson, S., & Revilla, J. (1994). Examination findings in le-
gally confirmed child sexual abuse: It's normal to be normal. *Pediatrics. 94*(3):
310-317.
Bus driver faces more charges. (1993, Jan. 30). *Boston Globe*, p. 26.
Ceci, S., & Bruck, M. (1995). *Jeopardy in the courtroom: A scientific analysis of chil-
dren's testimony.* Washington, DC: American Psychological Association.
Commonwealth v. Halsey. (Berkshire County Superior Court, 1993) (10 volumes).
Commonwealth v. Halsey. (No. 94-P-477)(41 Mass. App. Ct. 200; 669 N.E. 2d 774)
(Appeals Court of Massachusetts. 1996).
Crews, F. (1995, Jan. 12). Response to letters to the editor. *New York Review of Books*, 42-48.
Elfbenbein, G. (1993a, Jan. 21). Lanesboro parents voice anger. *Berkshire Eagle*, B1.
Elfbenbein, G. (1993b, Jan. 22). Lanesboro school: At the eye of a storm. *Berkshire
Eagle*, B1.
Harris, J.(1994). "Ritual abuse is alive and well in Western Massachusetts." Posting on
WITCHHNT electronic list. (June 10).
Harris, J. (n.d.). *Bernie Baran, of Pittsfield, MA (serving three concurrent life terms).*
Retrieved August 21, 1996 from the World Wide Web: <http://web.mit.edu/harris/
www/baran.html>. This website has been moved to: <http://www.geocities.com/
jgharris7/baran.html>.
Mehegan, D. (2000, Oct. 1) "Firm Convictions," *Boston Globe Magazine*, pp. 12, 17-23.
Mertz, E., & Lonsway, K. (1998). The power of denial: Individual and cultural construc-
tions of child sexual abuse. *Northwestern University Law Review 92*(4): 1415-58.
Nathan, D., & Snedeker, M. (1995). *Satan's silence: The making of an American witch
hunt.* New York: Basic Books.
Oshinsky, D.M. (1983). *A conspiracy so immense: The world of Joe McCarthy.* New
York: Free Press.
Roche, B. J. (1993, Jan. 21). Small-town school bus driver charged with rape of chil-
dren. *Boston Globe*, p. 76.
Senate Committee on Labor and Human Resources; Subcommittee on Children and
Families. (1995, May 25). Testimony of Carol Lamb Hopkins. S. HRG. 104-77. pp.
70-76.

FORENSIC ISSUES

The "False Memory" Defense: Using Disinformation and Junk Science In and Out of Court

Charles L. Whitfield

SUMMARY. This article describes a seemingly sophisticated, but mostly contrived and often erroneous "false memory" defense, and compares it in a brief review to what the science says about the effect of trauma on memory. Child sexual abuse is widespread and dissociative/traumatic amnesia for it is common. Accused, convicted and self-confessed child molesters and their advocates have crafted a strategy that tries to negate their abusive, criminal behavior, which we can call a "false memory" defense. Each of 22 of the more commonly used components of this defense is described and discussed with respect to what the science says about them. Armed with this knowledge, survivors, their clinicians,

Charles L. Whitfield, MD, FASAM, is in private practice in Atlanta, Georgia. He is a member of the Leadership Council on Mental Health, Justice and the Media, and on the faculty of Rutgers Institute on Alcohol Studies, Rutgers University, New Brunswick, NJ.

Address correspondence to: Charles L. Whitfield, Box 420487, Atlanta, GA 30342.

[Haworth co-indexing entry note]: "The 'False Memory' Defense: Using Disinformation and Junk Science In and Out of Court." Whitfield, Charles L. Co-published simultaneously in *Journal of Child Sexual Abuse* (The Haworth Maltreatment & Trauma Press, an imprint of The Haworth Press, Inc.) Vol. 9, No. 3/4, 2001, pp. 53-78; and: *Misinformation Concerning Child Sexual Abuse and Adult Survivors* (ed: Charles L. Whitfield, Joyanna Silberg, and Paul Jay Fink) The Haworth Maltreatment & Trauma Press, an imprint of The Haworth Press, Inc., 2001, pp. 53-78. Single or multiple copies of this article are available for a fee from The Haworth Document Delivery Service [1-800-HAWORTH 9:00 a.m. - 5:00 p.m. (EST). E-mail address: getinfo@haworthpressinc.com].

and their attorneys will be better able to refute this defense of disinformation. *[Article copies available for a fee from The Haworth Document Delivery Service: 1-800-HAWORTH. E-mail address: <getinfo@haworthpressinc.com> Website: <http://www.HaworthPress.com> © 2001 by The Haworth Press, Inc. All rights reserved.]*

KEYWORDS. Dissociative amnesia, traumatic amnesia, child sexual abuse, child molesters, pedophiles, enablers, "false memory," "false memory" defense, disinformation

In a civil lawsuit brought by an adult daughter against her father for sexually abusing her when she was a child, the following is an example of a closing argument for the defense:

> Ladies and gentlemen of the jury, I ask you to finally lift this burden off his back, to let him stand tall and proud again. And when you do, realize that you will be helping Roberta, too, because she cannot get better if she keeps pursuing a dream based on a false memory. She needs to know you have seen the truth; she needs to face the truth herself. For it is only the truth that can reunite this family and allow love to return to it. [The lawyer for the defense now pauses for effect.] . . . All you need to do to help this family is to reach a verdict for the defendant. When you do, realize that good can come out of this lawsuit. The defendant himself holds no hard feelings toward Roberta for these terrible accusations. He realizes that Roberta has been misguided [by her therapist]. He still loves her. He and Gertrude want their daughter back. So bring in a verdict that can accomplish that–a verdict for the defendant. Help to free Roberta from her terrible confusion that has misled her. Help to show her the truth. [With those final words, the defense attorney looks at the face of each juror and then returns to his seat.] (Roseman, Craig & Scott, 1997, p. 454).

This is a typical and perhaps convincing ending of a closing argument in many of these cases. We can see how at least one of the two sides plays upon the other in presenting their evidence for their client. The problem is that even those who have indeed committed child sexual abuse almost universally claim innocence, and they use the same defense as above (Levy, 2000).

Attorneys for accused, convicted or found-responsible child molesters tend to use a superficially sophisticated argument, which can be described as the "false memory defense." This defense is fraught with disinformation, smoke screens, and other untruths that are a distortion of what the available science of the psychology of trauma and memory shows. In this article, this seemingly sophisticated, but actually mostly contrived and often erroneous defense, is described and it is compared in a brief review to what the science says about the effect of trauma on memory.

INTRODUCTION

Many who are accused and some who are convicted of child molestation, an especially harmful kind of criminal behavior, have made a number of claims. A principal claim is that dissociative (also called traumatic) amnesia and other detrimental effects resulting from child sexual abuse (CSA) do not exist (Brown, Scheflin, & Hammond, 1997; Brown, Scheflin, & Whitfield, 1999; Whitfield, 1995b, 1997b). Assisted by their attorneys, some family members, and other advocates in order to defend themselves, these "false memory" advocates have made many erroneous statements to discount the experience of survivors of child sexual assault and to attack helping professionals. They have blitzed the media and tried to influence the clinical, academic, and legal professions with what is mostly disinformation (J. Freyd, 1993; Freid, 1994; Brown, Scheflin & Whitfield, 1999; Hovdestad & Kristiansen, 1996; Loftus, 1993; Pope, Hudson, Bodkin, & Oliva, 1998; Pope, 1995, 1998; Pope & Brown, 1996; Whitfield, 1995a, 1995b, 1998a).

They have claimed that their accusers' experience as a survivor of CSA was invalid, and that *they,* the accused, were the "real" victim (Roys, 1995; D. T. Roys, personal communication, November 1997). While there have been many factors to account for this defense (see Whitfield, Silberg, & Fink, this volume), since early 1992 perhaps the organized hub of this group has been the False Memory Syndrome Foundation (FMSF). The FMSF has claimed that persons accusing parents or other parent figures of having molested them as children had a "false memory syndrome" ("fms"). The FMSF further claims that the alleged "false" memories were "implanted" by outside sources, such as therapists, self-help groups or even books and other "suggestive" influences. They tried to make "fms" appear scientific in order to help it gain entrance into the courtroom and academia.

They have taken a criminal act and major betrayal of children, families and society and cleverly framed it as a "memory problem." Prior to and since the FMSF was founded in March 1992, there has not been a single case report documenting the existence of any clinical condition known as "false memory syndrome" published in any of the peer-reviewed clinical or scientific literature (Brown, Scheflin & Whitfield, 1999; Dallam, this volume; Whitfield, 1995b, 1997b). This lack remains to this day, a full nine years later, in spite of the FMSF's pledge in 1993 to promote and support research on their made-up "syndrome" (FMSF flyer, August 1993). A condition known as "false memory syndrome" is not included in any of the diagnostic codebooks and is not recognized as a bona fide clinical disorder by any of the mental health professional associations or societies. It is not included or even mentioned in any edition of the *Diagnostic and Statistical Manual of Mental Disorders* (DSM) (American Psychiatric Association, 1994; Pope, 1998; Pope & Brown, 1996; Whitfield, 1995a, 1995b). There is also no convincing evidence in the clinical and scientific literature that anyone can "suggest" or "implant" enduring false memories of childhood sexual abuse, or induce the long-term effects of child sexual abuse in individuals or groups of people without actually abusing them (Brown, Scheflin & Whitfield, 1999; Whitfield, 1995b). Some forensic psychologists and sociologists affiliated with the FMSF have coined another term as part of the false memory defense: "recovered memory therapy." Like "fms," "recovered memory therapy" ("rmt") is not recognized by the DSM-IV or any other authoritative source (Briere, 1996; Brown, Scheflin & Whitfield, 1999; Pope, 1998), yet some "fms" advocates, defense attorneys and their expert witnesses continue to use the term.

COMPONENTS OF THE "FALSE MEMORY" DEFENSE

A problem with the "false memory" defense was that these theories were not based on careful clinical observation or solid research. Rather, they were based mostly on speculation, usually made by non-clinicians, some of whom were themselves accused of unethical behavior or had a personal or financial interest in the accused being innocent (Brown, Scheflin, & Hammond, 1997; Crook & Dean, 1999a, 1999b; Freid, 1994; Pope, 1995; Stanton, 1997; Whitfield, 1995b).

The "false memory" defense is one of the most sophisticated ones to appear in the history of the denial and minimization of the existence and effects of child abuse, especially CSA, and it manifests as a peculiar but not surprising socio-cultural-political-legal phenomenon of the 1990s. It may present itself as any of a number of kinds of disinformation which the accused, the convicted, and their advocates used regularly (Brown et al., 1999; Dallam, this volume; Cheit, this volume; Emrick, 1994, 1996; Roys, 1995; Scheflin & Brown, 1996; Stanton, 1997; Whitfield, 1995b). These defense strategies are listed in Table 1, and each is briefly described below.

"The Looking Good" Defense

The "false memory" defense commonly starts with a "Looking Good" defense, which claims that the accused or defendant is innocent, an upstanding

TABLE 1. Components of the False Memory Defense

1. The "Looking Good" Defense
2. The Accused/Defendant is the Real Victim
3. Choose Someone Else to Blame
4. Try to Blame the Plaintiff
5. Plaintiff Has Not Shown External Evidence of CSA
6. Hire and Use a "False Memory"/ "FMS"–Advocating Expert Witness
7. Inappropriately Introduce Satanic Ritual Abuse, Alien Abduction, and "Past Life" Experience
8. Regularly Take Quotes and Citations Out of Context
9. Try to Use Biased Articles and/or Opinions
10. Misinterpret the Effects of Trauma
11. Negate Dissociative Amnesia
12. Claim "Childhood Amnesia" When Accuser Has Early Memories
13. Claim Other Reasons Why They Were Accused
14. Propose Other Explanations for Accuser's Symptoms
15. Try to Combine "Common Sense" with a "Law of Probability"
16. Use Contrived Terms and Other Pseudoscientific Jargon
17. Make Up Other Special Categories with No Scientific Support
18. Try to Discredit Every Corroborating Witness
19. Erroneously Try to Equate Retraction with "Proof" of "False" Memory
20. Try to Impeach Other Witnesses or Those Who Have Filed Reports
21. Try to Intimidate and Impeach Plaintiff's Expert Witness
22. Play on Our Individual and Collective Wishes and Doubts

member of the community, a family man/woman, churchgoing, hard working, and respected (Emrick, 1994; Pope & Brown, 1996; Whitfield, 1995b). This is one of the oldest strategies in courtroom history; that is, simply make your external appearance look better so that those who may be judging your alleged criminal behavior will thereby think better of you. For example, in the murder trial of George Franklin, whose daughter had also accused him of sexually abusing her (Terr, 1994), his attorney had him clean himself up appreciably before appearing in court. Previously disheveled, he now looked neat and clean (A.W. Scheflin, personal communication, October 1999). Nonetheless, he was convicted of murder, although a few years later he was released from prison on a procedural technicality. In another instance, Pamela Freyd, co-founder and director of the FMSF, explained that her accused members were not pedophiles or child molesters because "We are a good-looking bunch of people, graying hair, well-dressed, healthy, smiling. . . . Just about every person who has attended [our meetings] is someone you would want to count as a friend" (P. Freyd, 1992, p. 1).

Just as most of the other defensive components described below, the science shows the opposite of what the "false memory" advocates claim. Looking good or bad is not a factor. The disorder of pedophilia and its usually resulting crime of CSA have no socio-economic restrictions or boundaries. There is no such stereotypic abuser. People from all socio-economic strata are equally represented among the pedophile/child molesting population (Salter, 1995; Whitfield, 1995b). Interviews of convicted and self-confessed child molesters reveal that one cannot rely on self-report when assessing whether someone is a sex offender. Despite their initial and enduring complete and convincing denial, when they are finally in appropriate treatment or prison, many offenders ultimately relate their crimes in horrific detail. In these special and safe circumstances, molesters commonly describe how they fooled people in their communities for years by "looking good," by being so kind and responsible that no one would believe an accusation of sexual abuse or assault (Roys, 1995; Salter, 1998; Whitfield, 1998b). This "looking good" appearance is part of the "grooming" behavior that the molester commonly uses with the child and the family or others to make them all feel a false sense of safety when the child is in his or her care (Emrick, 1994; also cited in Whitfield, 1995b). In this regard, if appropriate, the victim's attorney can offer evidence of "grooming" behavior and expert testimony that "looking good" is consistent with the superficial persona of a child abuser (W. Murphy, personal communication, October, 1997; Salter, 1998; Whitfield, 1995b).

The Accused/Defendant Is the Real Victim

In a strange but common way of thinking, the molester and their knowing or unknowing accomplices try to turn the tables on the accuser by saying that the accuser simply made a mistake. This strategy claims that, in a strange kind of sleight-of-hand, the *defendant* is actually the victim here, just as the plaintiff and family are too, since the *real* offender(s) is/are the inducers or "implanters" of "false memories" or "false memory syndrome." This strategy is commonly used now to help defend child molesters (Emrick, 1994; Roys, 1995; Salter, 1995).

In spite of recent attempts to claim that CSA is not harmful (Rind, Tromovitch, & Bauserman, 1998; see critiques of this in the present volume), the science shows that the detrimental effects of CSA do harm the child (Briere, 1996; Courtois, 1999; Dallam, Gleaves, Cepeda-Benito, Kraemer, & Spiegel, in press; Felitti et al., 1998; Herman, 1992; Kendler et al., 2000; McCauley et al., 1997; Whitfield, 1998c), and not the abuser. The victim's attorney can argue that such a position is a "red herring" designed to distract attention from the gruesome facts of the case (W. Murphy, personal communication, October 1997).

Choose Someone Else to Blame

"False memory" advocates try to divert the blame to others. They claim that the actual causes of the "false memories"–which they say are the "real perpetrators," that "victimize" the innocent accused defendant–may include any one or more of the following:

1. The *therapist*–The "fms" advocate may offer varying kinds of "evidence," often in the form of opinion articles that appear in journals, but written by authors who are frequently one or more of their own FMSF advisory board members. Examples include the opinions of Loftus (1993), who, in spite of having no clinical training or expertise and basing her ideas and reports mostly on her experiments on normal memory, she tries to negate the existence of dissociative amnesia and other effects of CSA. Another example is the report of a controversial and methodologically weak survey of therapists' experience. The author claimed that therapists commonly suggested "false" memories of CSA to their patient/clients (Yapko, 1994a, 1994b). But there are no other data to support this contention. In fact, Whitfield and Stock (1996) and others (e.g., Brown, Scheflin & Whitfield, 1999) have found that individual and group therapy were among the lowest associations as triggers of recovered memories of CSA.
2. The *therapy group*–In looking at comments about group therapy, we usually find claims and speculation only and no peer reviewed or data based studies.
3. The *books*–Any self-help or recovery oriented book. As with most of these ideas, they are simply claims and speculation, with no documentation by peer reviewed or data-based studies.
4. The *media*–Movies, talk shows, other venues. Likewise, claims and speculation only, since there are no peer reviewed or data-based studies.
5. The *plaintiff*–they claim, was too "suggestible" to the above items 1 through 4 and was looking for a "complex" answer (molested by the accused) to a "simple" explanation ("false memory syndrome"). The truth is that "fms" is itself a complex, controversial, elusive, and unproven hypothesis that remains neither properly researched nor peer-reviewed. Using the law of parsimony, what they call a "complex" answer is in fact the simplest explanation for the plaintiff's symptoms (Cheit, 1998, 1999, 2000; Roseman et al., 1997; Whitfield, 1995b).

Try to Blame the Plaintiff

They use this strategy often, especially if the allegations are unusual, and then focus on the plaintiffs to try to make them and their behavior look bizarre or crazy. Usually the plaintiffs are still doing active work in their recovery process, with all of the emotional swings that occur, and consequently these may make them appear as though they are "crazy" on the surface. Often when the effects of recovery from trauma are considered, it is actually clinically *appropriate* for the people to manifest a broad range of symptoms, such as intrusive posttraumatic stress symptoms, dissociative symptoms, and painful psycho-physiological reactivity (Brown, Scheflin & Whitfield, 1999; Herman, 1992; Whitfield, 1995b). Reliable recovered memories are typically accompanied by significant emotional distress and the occurrence of psychiatric symptoms concurrent with recovery of the memory (Brown, Scheflin & Whitfield, 1999; Courtois, 1999; Whitfield, 1994, 1998c).

Recent research has addressed the natural history and phenomenology of recovered memories (Brown, Scheflin & Whitfield, 1999). Memory of the trauma persists both as an explicit, narrative memory and an implicit, behavioral and somatic memory. While these clinical findings often evolve in the order shown in Figure 1, they may also evolve in a different sequence. Working through these phases over time in the process of recovering the narrative memory strengthens recovery by decreasing dissociation and leading to a sense of mastery over the traumatic experience (Brown, Scheflin & Whitfield, 1999).

Plaintiff Has Not Shown External Evidence of CSA

The "false memory" defense usually includes strong statements that the plaintiff has not shown direct (external or "hard") evidence that the abuse actually happened. The plaintiffs are usually criticized for not having eyewitness testimony, physical findings (such as scars), or other evidence that may appear in a medical record, photos, and confessions. However, all of these are actually rare in CSA cases (Briere, 1996; Brown et al., 1997; Whitfield, 1995b, 1998c).

Circumstantial evidence may be present though. This may include, for example, the presence of post-traumatic stress disorder (PTSD) without another obvious traumatic cause (Rowan & Foy, 1993) or other common effects of child sexual abuse, which the legal system may not understand (Whitfield, 1997b, 1998c). If the belief system of the judge or jury leans in the "false memory" direction, it may be difficult to convince them that the abuse happened without overwhelming evidence.

FIGURE 1. The Effects of the Evolution of Memory Recovery in Childhood Sexual Abuse*

Clinical Findings**	Example References
1. Transference re-enactments (in &/or out of therapy)*** ↓	Burgess et al., 1995; Terr, 1994; Laplanche & Pontalis, 1973
2. Somatic & psychological symptoms ↓	Cameron, 1996; van der Kolk & Fisler, 1995; Pomerantz, 1999
3. Flashbacks, abreactions & age regressions ↓	above plus: Roe & Schwartz, 1996; Kristiansen et al., 1995; Whitfield, 1995b,1997c,1998c
4. Dreams & nightmares ↓	Whitfield, 1995b,1997c, 1998c; Kristiansen et al. 1995
5. Fragmented narrative memory (triggered by reminder events) ↓	Cameron, 1996; Kristiansen et al., 1995; Van der Kolk & Fisler, 1995
6. Obsessive thoughts of trauma ↓	Terr, 1994
7. Organized narrative memory ↓	van der Kolk & Fisler, 1995 (none showed initial return of memory as narrative memory, which tended to occur last)

(Brown, Scheflin, & Whitfield, 1999)
*Working through these stages as they occurred decreased dissociation and led to a sense of mastery over the trauma.
**Clinical findings are from Davies & Frawley, 1994, Whitfield, 1995b, 1997c, 1998c, and other cited references, and all may be manifestations of PTSD. *Triggering events* commonly initiate these kinds of memory (Whitfield, 1995b). These clinical findings tend to progress from being vague to clearer.
***These clinical findings may occur in different sequences, e.g., #2 may be the initial experience, then skip to #5, and then continue as #6 and #7.

Some courts, such as in the case of *Crook v. Murphy* (1994; Yule, 1994), have allowed circumstantial or indirect evidence that, taken as a whole, helps to show that the plaintiff was sexually abused as a child. This may be a different kind of circumstantial evidence than some courts are used to considering and admitting. It includes clinical findings that a therapist may have observed, recorded, and accumulated during evaluation and therapy that may also include information concerning internal corroboration of traumatic memory and consistency (for a discussion of internal corroboration, see Terr, 1994; Whitfield, 1997c, 1998c).

This kind of circumstantial evidence may end up suggesting that the accused person(s) committed the offense. Nonetheless, it is circumstantial evidence, which is accepted in most states as being equal to or as strong as direct evidence for indicating that a crime such as child abuse happened. Most courts may instruct the jury regarding this: "The law makes no distinction between direct and circumstantial evidence as to the degree of proof. Each is respected for such convincing force as it may carry." (See details of circumstantial or internal corroboration in Whitfield 1997c; 1998c.)

Hire and Use a "False Memory"/"FMS" Advocating Expert Witness

The defendant hires an "expert" witness who is often on the FMSF board, a fact frequently not mentioned on their resume. In their testimony they tend to make vague claims as to the effects of CSA. They are often not clinicians and have frequently published commentary or opinions on trauma and memory that are not consistent with the research. They tend to claim that they know the "true science" of CSA and memory, when instead they are actually presenting their own pseudoscientific version or interpretation of the published evidence (or a version from the FMSF). Some have been questioned as to their ethics (see Crook & Dean, 1999a, 1999b), or the obvious bias in their writings (e.g., see Wakefield & Underwager, 1993; Whitfield, 1995b; Dallam, 1999). At times some of these advocates for "fms" have sued those who publically disagree with them or with whom they are otherwise in conflict (Legg, 1997; *Singer & Ofshe v. American Psychological Association et al.,* 1992, 1993, 1994a, 1994b; *Underwager & Wakefield v. Salter,* 1994). Still others have been disqualified from testifying as expert witnesses for the defense because of their inadequate qualifications (see examples in Whitfield, 1995b) or admonished for their inappropriate behavior (see examples in Peterson, 1990).

Screening the Expert Witness. How can a judge determine who is acceptable as an expert witness in these kinds of cases? An important question to consider asking before accepting such an expert witness might be, "Does the proposed witness understand the clinical evolution of dissociative/traumatic amnesia, PTSD, and dissociative disorders as presented in the *DSM-IV* and elsewhere?" An affirmative answer and demonstration of such an understanding would speak in favor of accepting the person as an expert witness (Whitfield, 1997b).

Another useful screening question may be, "What data-based research or writing have you published on traumatic memory, as contrasted with ordinary or normal memory?" If proposed experts have published only their opinions and comments on what they imagine or think traumatic memory is, and their statements lack clinical or scientific merit, this may argue against accepting them as expert witnesses. The judge may ask to examine a copy of their articles on traumatic memory and, if in doubt, have an expert on trauma psychology provide an opinion as well. By contrast, having published scholarly articles on traumatic memory in the clinical or scientific literature that have been widely accepted by trauma psychologists would speak in favor of accepting a person as an expert witness. A final question is, "What clinical experience do you have in providing treatment to survivors of child sexual abuse or sex offenders concerning their long term recovery?" If they have little or no clinical experience, it is unlikely that they will have the full knowledge and experience required to provide reliable or valid testimony with respect to these issues.

In summary, if a proposed expert witness answers yes to the first question and demonstrates a clear understanding of traumatic amnesia, PTSD, and dissociative disorders; has demonstrated an accurate understanding of traumatic memory by publishing scholarly articles or books, and has specialized clinical experience in helping these special populations, he or she is more likely to provide accurate and helpful information to the trier-of-fact. One way to save court time and expenses for both sides and to avoid this kind of bias is to have the court hire a neutral clinical evaluator who has expertise and extensive experience in treating traumatized populations (Lazo, 1995). Defense attorneys in these cases can be expected to protest, but if appropriate, under the federal rules of evidence, the decision of whether to appoint an expert witness for the court is within the judge's discretion.

Inappropriately Introduce Extreme Situations of Satanic Ritual Abuse, Alien Abduction, and "Past Life" Experience

False memory advocates often introduce the notion of extreme situations, such as satanic ritual abuse, alien abduction, and "past lives" and then say that, "If you believe these, I guess you will believe 'repressed memories' or the like, too." This intrusion into the deposition or court record is nearly always of their own making and is, therefore, inappropriate when this is not part of their history. In fact, in and out of court, this smokescreen notion is usually another of their diversionary tactics.

Regularly Take Quotes and Citations Out of Context

False memory advocates regularly juxtapose quotes and citations out of context in their media packets, quotes, legal briefs and other writings with irrelevant, contrived, propagandistic, and/or generalized pro-"false memory" information in a hoped-for convincing effect. They can often be challenged on this inappropriate and unscientific pattern. A case example of this occurred in the 1996 lawsuit of Pamela and Peter Freyd v. Charles Whitfield for alleged "defamation," which judged in favor of Whitfield (Legg, 1997). During the Freyds' deposition of Whitfield, they handed him a page of brief quotes or "snippets" that they had selected from the position papers on memory of several professional organizations, such as the American Psychiatric and Psychological Associations, and asked for his opinion about them. He responded by saying that these were all statements taken *out of context* from these much longer position papers. So that he could comment, he asked to see the full paper for each one, which they were unable to provide. He objected on the record to their inappropriate and inaccurate use of these documents. They did not pursue this line of questioning.

Try to Use Biased Articles and/or Opinions

In a similar way, in an attempt to discredit and invalidate the plaintiff and witnesses and anyone who may disagree with them (in or outside of court), false memory advocates try to use biased articles and/or opinions. They often use their own published writing wherein they distort the science of the effects of CSA (Brown, Scheflin & Whitfield, 1999; Pope, 1995; Pope & Brown, 1996). For example, in trying to show that all traumas induce only remembering but not forgetting, Pope et al. (1998) reported their own selection of 63 research studies on trauma with a pool of over 10,000 victims of various types of trauma, including accidents, natural disasters, wars, etc., none of which described any clear cases of dissociative amnesia. However, this report contained several scientific errors, such as: (1) in 39 of their 63 analyzed studies, amnesia was not addressed, (2) in two studies amnesia is not reported in the results, (3) 19 studies actually support the reality of dissociative (traumatic) amnesia, (4) two studies report injury-specific amnesia only, and (5) one study is on flashbulb memory (i.e., memory of a sudden traumatic, often public event) of the Challenger explosion (Brown, Scheflin & Whitfield, 1999).

Furthermore, besides featuring mostly public events only, their selected 63 studies did not involve the hidden abuse of a child or adolescent by a primary caregiver. There is now substantial evidence that this type of betrayal trauma is more threatening because the victim is simultaneously abused by, and dependent upon, the perpetrator (J. Freyd, 1996). Oftentimes, the non-offending spouse or other parent figure does not protect the child. Because the 63 studies do not involve private childhood sexual abuse, Pope and Hudson (1995) did not include them in their review of the relevant literature on repression. Had Pope et al. (1998) been more discerning, appropriate or complete in their selection from the available literature, they would have found 68 more data-based reports which showed that dissociative amnesia is a finding in every one of these studies of the effects of CSA (Brown, Scheflin & Whitfield, 1999). In their conclusions about this article Brown, Scheflin and Whitfield (1999) said, "In our opinion, based upon the prevailing scientific data, the fact that the majority of people remember certain traumas does not negate the fact that a significant minority do not remember, and that dissociated amnesia, or repressed memory, for sexual abuse is a commonly observed phenomenon in some individuals across virtually all of the research that has addressed the issue" (p. 32).

Misinterpret the Effects of Trauma

The "false memory" advocates usually manifest a poor understanding and interpretation of the effects of trauma, especially of child sexual abuse, which they regularly introduce as a strategy into their defense. They can be challenged on these as well from the vast published reports and knowledge about the effects of CSA (e.g., Briere, 1992, 1996; Brown, Scheflin & Whitfield, 1999; Brown, Scheflin, & Hammond, 1997; Chu, 1998; Courtois, 1989, 1999; Felitti et al., 1998; Herman, 1992; McCauley et al., 1997; Whitfield, 1995b, 1997c; Berliner & Elliott, 2001; Brown, this volume).

Negate Dissociative Amnesia

False memory advocates regularly use another defense strategy wherein they try to confuse dissociative (i.e., traumatic) amnesia with their own version of it, which they commonly call "repression." They then claim that repression does not exist. They try to invalidate or exclude research and data on the existence of dissociative/traumatic amnesia and other documented findings in the effects of trauma. The reality of dissociative amnesia has been the primary target of the "false memory" movement since its existence, although its spokespeople have shrewdly tried to shift their focus over time (Brown, Scheflin & Whitfield, 1999). However, the science shows that the evidence for its existence is strong, is peer reviewed, and meets *Daubert v. Merrell Dow Pharmaceuticals* (1993) standards, depending on the individual court's interpretation. The science shows that traumatic amnesia is an authentic and common part of denied and unprocessed trauma (see American Psychiatric Association, 1994; Brown et al. 1997; Brown, Scheflin & Whitfield, 1999; Scheflin & Brown, 1996; Whitfield, 1997a, 1997b).

Claim "Childhood Amnesia" When Accuser Has Early Memories

Some defense lawyers will also hire "false memory" advocating expert witnesses to try to support a "childhood amnesia" defense (also called "infantile amnesia"). Here, "fms" advocates claim that a person cannot remember *any* event before three or four years of age, much less remember one or more traumas. The reason, they claim, is that the very young child's brain is too immature or insufficiently developed to be able to have memories of such events. Once again, they cite experiments and studies on normal memory and try to generalize them, often inappropriately, to traumatic memory. The available data from published case reports based on careful clinical observation, as well as data from numerous survey studies, indicate that this defense is not hard and fast; indeed, it is clearly untrue in many cases, as indicated below.

For example, in a prospective study, Burgess, Hartman, and Baker (1995) evaluated and monitored 19 children who had been sexually abused (corroborated in court) by day-care staff. Their ages at the time of the abuse ranged from 3 months to 4.5 years (M = 2.5 years). Three independent clinicians evaluated each child just after the abuse became evident and then every five years thereafter. At each evaluation, they checked for four kinds of memory: cognitive (or verbal), behavioral, visual, and somatic. The most common kind of nonverbal memory manifested was somatic (100%), followed by behavioral (82%) and visual (59%). Eleven (58%) of the children always verbally (cognitively) remembered the abuse, five (26%) partially remembered, and three (16%) totally forgot experiencing any abuse. In a separate prospective study of 12 children of similar ages, Burgess and Hartman (1996) reported similar results.

In Williams' (1994) follow-up study of 129 women who had childhood sexual abuse documented in emergency room medical records, 5 of 11 women (45%), who were under 4 years old at the time of being sexually abused, remembered the abuse. If Williams' data are combined with those from Burgess et al. described above, they result in a total of 42 very young children (i.e., less than 4 to 4.5 years of age) studied prospectively, of whom 23 (55%) later remembered and 19 (45%) were amnestic for sexual abuse that was also shown by direct evidence (Burgess et al., 1995; Williams, 1994).

Other studies have found similar results (Bauer, 1996; Bruhn, 1990; Hewitt, 1994; Terr, 1991, 1994). In fact, after extensive research, Bauer concludes that many very young children (i.e., 2 years old and younger) remember certain events for long durations (Bauer, 1996). Because language skills are not fully developed at these very young ages, abused children are not usually able to talk about their traumatic experiences in the way that an older person would. For example, in the Oklahoma City bombing, most of the traumatized survivors were supported by their family and peers when they reported what happened to them and how the experience affected them. They were able to more effectively consolidate their traumatic memories into memory storage through a process that memory researchers call *rehearsal*. Trauma clinicians explain that talking about (or rehearsing) a traumatic event or experience is the best way to help anyone remember the event. This sequence is shown in Figure 2 (Brown, Scheflin & Whitfield, 1999; Whitfield, 1997b, 1997c).

Young children who are traumatized at a preverbal stage of development are at a significant disadvantage because they are not able to process the expe-

FIGURE 2. The Process of Memory Retrieval

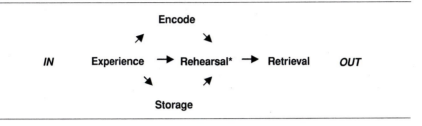

Threats, dissociation and *lack of language skills* block rehearsal.

rience by talking about or rehearsing it (Terr, 1991, 1994; Whitfield, 1995b). This disadvantage is compounded by the fact that, in most cases of child sexual abuse, the offender threatened the child with serious harm if he or she were to disclose the abuse, as shown in Figure 2 (Emrick, 1994, 1996; D. T. Roys, personal communication, November 1997; Whitfield, 1998b).

Claim Other Reasons Why They Were Accused

Using this strategy, the defendant claims or proposes other reasons why they were accused, exposed, or why they believe that the plaintiff brought suit (e.g., that the accuser was angry at the defendant for another reason) (Roseman et al., 1997). It is also common for the defense to argue that the victim has a motive to lie. This claim can sometimes be rebutted simply by arguing that it makes no logical sense. W. Murphy (personal communication, October 1997) said, "I can sometimes stretch that argument by saying, 'If this victim wanted to be vengeful and falsely accuse this person of a crime, why would she choose rape since it is the most painful, stigmatizing and revictimizing process to endure. She could have made it a lot easier on herself if she claimed that he hit her, stole from her, etc.' "

Propose Other Explanations for Accuser's Symptoms

The accused often proposes other explanations for the accuser's symptoms, such as having an unhappy marriage, job problems, or that they are "mentally ill." When the alleged abuser's defense claims there are other explanations for the victim's symptoms, the plaintiffs can argue to the jury that they, the jury, have also been divorced, had a loved one die, etc., and that it is painful, but it doesn't look like this victim's situation, and thus the argument does not make sense (W. Murphy, personal communication, October 1997).

Try to Combine "Common Sense" with a "Law of Probability"

The accused often also tries to combine what they may call "common sense" with a "law of probability" that the defendant could not have abused the plaintiff (Roseman et al., 1997). Drawing from the first and last defense items (# 1 above and # 22 below), the first "common sense" ploy is to say that for such a "fine family" here and the "upstanding" person that the accused is, child abuse of any kind, much less molestation, just "makes no sense."

A second "common sense" strategy is to take each bit of evidence presented by the victim, examine it in isolation, and then show how it (alone) is "improbable." This maneuver takes each piece of evidence and tries to negate it individually, instead of weighing the total evidence. For example, a man accused of sexually abusing his daughter as a child argued that since his wife "slept very lightly," which she agreed to in her testimony, she would have known it if he had done it, and he argued several other such details similarly. However, the totality of the evidence showed that he had likely sexually abused his daughter. Criminal and civil justice is about sorting out and ruling on the totality of the weight of evidence, not on isolated details of common sense or odds-making (Brown, Scheflin & Whitfield, 1999; Roseman et al., 1997). W. Murphy (personal communication, October 1997) suggests: "Compare the 'pieces' argument to a puzzle and argue that one puzzle piece does not make a picture; the jury has a responsibility to view the pieces together, and they took an oath to do that. In the same way that puzzle pieces, when put together, form only one picture, the victim's evidence points to only one conclusion."

Use Contrived Terms and Other Pseudoscientific Jargon

Accused molesters tend to use contrived terms and other pseudoscientific jargon, such as "false memory syndrome," "recovered memory therapy" or "parental alienation syndrome." These have never been established through empirical or data-based studies (Brown et al., 1997; Brown, Scheflin & Whitfield, 1999; Whitfield, 1995b, 1997b). As mentioned above, these terms are not found in the DSM-IV or the ICD-10, and while their advocates have maneuvered and at times even promoted them in some sectors of the popular media, they are not accepted by mainstream mental health (Brown, Scheflin & Hammond, 1997; Brown, Scheflin & Whitfield, 1999; Dallam, 1999; Whitfield, 1995b).

Make Up Other Special Categories with No Scientific Support

To further their argument, exposed or accused molesters may contrive other terms or categories with no scientific support. Examples include "robust repression" vs. "partial repression" to try to confuse and negate cases involving dissociative amnesia. These kinds of terms were used to try to invalidate the sexual abuse of Ross Cheit and Frank Fitzpatrick when they were children. Both had dissociative amnesia and then recovered memories of the abuse decades later, and in both cases their offender eventually confessed (Cheit, 1998, 1999, 2000; Whitfield, 1995b).

Try to Discredit Every Corroborating Witness

The accused or convicted molester often tries to discredit and impeach every corroborating witness, including other family members who have been abused. This and the other defenses are commonly used by sex offenders when they are molesting and also by supporters in and out of court (R. Emrick, cited in Whitfield, 1995b; D. T. Roys, personal communication, November 1997; Salter, 1998).

Erroneously Try to Equate Retraction with "Proof" of "False" Memory

Retractors are those who recall memories of child abuse, disclose them, and later say that they were not real, commonly claiming that a therapist or another source "implanted" the memories. Their retraction is often triggered by family pressure and/or "false memory" advocates (Brown, Scheflin & Whitfield, 1998; Scheflin & Brown, 1999; Summit, 1983; Whitfield, 1995b). They also may file malpractice lawsuits (Scheflin & Brown, 1999).

Without knowing the facts, "false memory" advocates have accepted that these retractors' "secondary" claims (the primary claim is of the trauma memory) are true. They base their assumption on their tenuous theory that the retractor was originally wrong, but is now remembering accurately. In fact, like one leg of a three-legged stool, retractor stories make up a substantial base of the conception of "fms" (the other two legs include denial by the accused or convicted molester, and a few studies on normal memory, along with a few controversial anecdotal reports) (Whitfield, 1995b, 1997b). This new reversed claim then may raise a "plausible alternative explanation" for such cases.

For at least the last decade, accused and convicted child molesters have erroneously tried to equate the common phenomenon of retraction with "proof" of "false" memory. Since 1984, Summit has clearly described his vast experience with this frequent part of the process of CSA (Summit, 1983; Whitfield, 1995b). Armstrong (1999) recently asked, "What kind of person would first accuse her parents of abuse and then declare this belief to be false and accuse her therapist of abuse? We know little of the psychology of a 'recanter,' someone whose beliefs about her own nature and that of the people she loves appear to transform so totally and then abruptly transform again" (p. 520).

The science shows some helpful findings. For example, in a study of 30 malpractice law suits by retractors against their former therapists for "implanting false memories" or "implanting DID," Scheflin and Brown (1999) found that most of the 30 had recovered their memories and/or had the diagnosis of DID made *before* the sued therapist had seen them. There were many other kinds of direct and circumstantial evidence in these cases. Nearly all 30 retractors had been previously given multiple co-morbid psychiatric diagnoses that are extensively reported in the clinical scientific literature to be associated with or caused by childhood trauma, especially child sexual abuse (e.g., Herman, 1992; Whitfield, 1997c, 1998c). These included: major depression (e.g., Kendler et al., 2000), anxiety disorders (e.g., McCauley et al., 1997), PTSD (e.g,, Rowan, Foy, Rodriguez, & Ryan, 1994), major dissociative disorders (e.g., Whitfield, 1997c), personality disorders such as borderline personality disorder (e.g., Herman, 1992), and major addictions such as chemical dependence and eating disorders (e.g., Felitti et al., 1998; Herman, 1992; McCauley et al., 1997). Ninety percent (27 of the 30) had a diagnosis of either DID (11 retractors) or Dissociative Disorder, Not Otherwise Stated (DD-NOS) (17 retractors) (Scheflin & Brown, 1999).

Nearly all of the therapists sued had given the retractors appropriate stage-oriented trauma treatment. In *none* of the 30 cases was there any mention or evidence of "recovered memory therapy" or a single-minded focus on recovering memories of abuse. Scheflin and Brown (1999) said, " . . . later, after encounters with pro-false memory (mis)information, the patient came to misattribute the source of his/her abuse memory to the defendant therapist and forgot that it had been self-reported, sometimes being recovered outside the context of therapy" (p. 685). In fact Scheflin and Brown (1999) found that if any false information was implanted, it likely occurred by exposure to *pro-false memory* sources close to or after the time of the identified therapy sessions. They said, " . . . in all 30 cases the plaintiff failed to report his or her vulnerability to post-therapeutic suggestive influences that might have been operative in the shaping of the retraction belief itself . . . the most striking finding from our analysis was [that] the significant post-therapeutic suggestive influences associated with the development of the retraction belief could be identified in every one of the 30 cases" (p. 687).

They conclude, "In our analysis of these 30 cases, significant exposure to false memory (mis)information occurred in the great majority of the cases and had a significant impact on the progressive shaping of retraction beliefs. . . . What do these data tell us? That sometimes litigious patients, plaintiff attorneys, and other individuals intentionally solicit other former patients in order to influence them" (Scheflin & Brown, 1999, p. 688).

Both in and out of court, the potentially erroneous claims of retractors and their advocates had not previously been tested. While rare, at best some scientific data suggest that false memories for the gist of complex traumatic events can occur. However, these usually appear only under a specific set of conditions (i.e., from extreme interviewing wherein most of the content about abuse themes is being supplied by the interviewer and does not originate from the interviewee) (Brown, Scheflin & Whitfield, 1999). While this can happen in excessive police interrogations or in political brainwashing interrogations (Marks, 1979; Sargent, 1957; Scheflin, 1995; Scheflin & Opton, 1978), most psychotherapy is not conducted in this way (see several citations in Brown, Scheflin & Whitfield, 1999). For such an "implantation" to happen, there must be at least two conditions about the retracting person: (1) they must have a personality trait of sufficient memory suggestibility; and (2) they must be subjected to a documented extensive and rigorous pattern of systematically suggested misinformation within and across interviews. In other words, it must be demonstrated that the interviewer actually is supplying most of the content about abuse-related themes within and across sessions, and that these themes are not originating from the patient (Brown, Scheflin & Whitfield, 1999).

Evidence Criteria. In their extensive monograph Brown, Scheflin & Whitfield, (1999) stated: "In our opinion the false memory suggestion argument represents a gross overgeneralization from rather complex sources of data and has seriously misled judges in the courts. Based on a careful review of a large body of research on human suggestion effects, several reasonable conclusions can be drawn. We recommend that these conclusions be used by the courts as a set of criteria by which to evaluate the evidence in cases where allegations have been made that a false abuse-related memory has been implanted" (p. 83). In order to demonstrate this claim, they concluded that the evidence must show the criteria listed in Table 2.

In other words, the record must reflect that the great proportion of abuse-related themes are unequivocally supplied by the interviewer, and does *not* originate with the patient. Brown and Scheflin (1999) have seen numerous malpractice cases where a plaintiff has sued a former therapist for "implanting" abuse memories that were subsequently retracted, where the medical record consistently showed that the abuse-related content originally came from the patient, now plaintiff, either inside or outside the context of therapy. The patient subsequently as plaintiff, over and against the medical record, made the misattribution error of attributing the source of the suggestion to the therapist. Since this distinction often gets obscured, the trier-of-fact must carefully eval-

TABLE 2. Evidence Criteria that a False Abuse-Related Memory May Have Been Suggested or Implanted by an Authority Figure: A Recommended Standard of Evidence for the Court

---

1. **Patient:** Shows a specific trait of high memory suggestibility.
2. **Clinical record:** Contains a pattern of systemic misinformation within and across interview sessions.
3. **Interaction:** Reflects uncritical acceptance by patient of the specific abuse-related suggestions.
4. **Ruled out:** reflects no extra-therapeutic sources of the alleged false abuse memory, i.e., therapy alone is proximate cause.
5. **Ruled out:** A pattern of post-therapeutic suggestive influences *

*This pattern may include, but is not limited to, such influences as:
a. Strong family pressures to retract,
b. Exposure to "false memory" media, literature, or personal influences,
c. Other retractors who may have sued a therapist,
d. Coaching or consultation by "false memory" experts, attorneys or advocacy groups, and
e. Retraction occurs in context of heated custody dispute.
(from Brown, Scheflin & Whitfield, 1999)

---

uate the medical record to distinguish between patient-reported abuse and therapist-suggested abuse themes.

The vulnerability to suggestive influences does not stop once the therapy has terminated. In many of these malpractice cases the plaintiff has made the logical error of alleging therapist-implanted memories of abuse that never occurred, while failing to consider the likelihood that the retraction belief is actually the product of *post*-therapeutic suggestive influences. Retraction beliefs are likely to be the product of post-therapeutic suggestive influences when the plaintiff has been subjected to any one or more of those influences (a-b) at the bottom of Table 2. Under such circumstances, the plaintiffs' complaints and recollections about alleged therapeutic malpractice may be significantly distorted, unreliable and unduly contaminated by post-therapeutic false memory influences. "Canned" plaintiff malpractice complaints, wherein the language mirrors the arguments found in popular pro false memory books, is evidence of uncritical acceptance of the suggested false memory information on the part of plaintiff.

Try to Impeach Other Witnesses or Those Who Have Filed Reports

Besides trying to discredit corroborating witnesses, the accused try to impeach other witnesses or those who have filed reports, such as therapists, child protective services, the police, and others who intervene. In depositions and during cross-examinations the defendant uses every possible strategy to make the witness or reporter look wrong.

Try to Intimidate and Impeach Plaintiff's Expert Witness

The accused molester tries to intimidate and impeach the plaintiff's expert witness with minutiae or irrelevant details that are often not within their appropriate working clinical knowledge. For example, "fms" advocate lawyer C. Barden so deposed a trauma expert by asking him many inappropriate, irrelevant or distracting questions, apparently in an effort to intimidate the witness (see Barden's deposition of Dr. van der Kolk of 12/27/96 on website www.tjcesq.com/html/van_der_Kolk_12_27.html).

Play on Our Individual and Collective Wishes and Doubts

Of all the defenses, this may be the most effective one that actual abusers use to manipulate us to believe them. We all so much want the abuse *not* to have happened, and so when an accused person, whether they are guilty, says that they did not do it and uses any one or a combination of the above excuses or defenses, it may activate several parts of our own inner life, including our personal wants, emotions and beliefs. The accused and/or exposed molester plays on our individual and collective wishes and doubts that an adult would sexually assault a child. It is as though we don't want to believe it, and so every bit of evidence that is presented to us, no matter how convincing, is then filtered out through the fine mesh of our beliefs and doubts. With this kind of internal pressure to disbelieve any and all evidence, our objectivity and reasoning capacities are then not open to allow us to carefully listen, consider and weigh what we hear from both sides.

Salter (1998) interviewed convicted child molesters in prison, who, with nothing else to lose, told her that their chief enablers in their enacting their crime are the "good" people who do not want to believe that crimes of child sexual abuse occur. They describe how people easily hand over their children to them. They explain that this is because most people are not suspicious, they trust others, and do not believe their children will be harmed by other adults who look attractive and act polite. A way to handle this major potential block to justice is to focus on the science, both clinical and basic, of trauma psychology and offender psychology.

CONCLUSION

Child sexual abuse is widespread, and traumatic amnesia for it is common. Accused, convicted and self-confessed child molesters and their advocates have crafted a strategy that tries to negate these facts, which we can call a "false memory" defense. In this article each of the more commonly used parts of the defense have been described, and what the science indicates about them has been presented. Armed with this knowledge, survivors, their clinicians, and their attorneys will be better able to refute this defense of mostly disinformation.

REFERENCES

American Psychiatric Association. (1994). *Diagnostic and statistical manual of mental disorders*. (4th ed.). Washington, DC: American Psychiatric Association Press.

Armstrong J. G. (1999). False memories and true lies: The psychology of a recanter. *The Journal of Psychiatry & Law*, *27*, 519-547.

Barden, C. (1996). Deposition of Dr. van der Kolk of 12/27/96 on website www.tjcesq.com/html/van_der_Kolk_12_27.html.

Bauer, P. J. (1996). What do infants recall of their lives? *American Psychologist*, *51*, 29-41.

Berliner, L. & Elliott, D. M. (2001). Sexual abuse of children. In: *The APSAC Handbook on Child Maltreatment*. Thousand Oaks, CA: Sage.

Briere, J. N. (1992). Methodological issues in the study of sexual abuse effects. *Journal of Consulting and Clinical Psychology*, *60*, 196-203.

Briere, J. N. (1996). *Treatment of adults sexually molested as children: Beyond survival* (Rev. 2nd ed.). New York: Springer.

Brown, D. & Scheflin, A.W. (1999). Factitious disorders and trauma-related diagnoses. *The Journal of Psychiatry & Law*, *27*, 373-422.

Brown, D., Scheflin, A.W., & Hammond C. (1997). *Trauma, memory, treatment & law*. New York: W.W. Norton.

Brown, D., Scheflin, A., & Whitfield, C. L. (1999). Recovered memories: The current weight of the evidence in science and in the courts. *The Journal of Psychiatry and Law*, *26*, 5-156.

Bruhn, A. R. (1990). *Earliest childhood memories*. New York: Praeger.

Burgess, A. W., & Hartman, C. R. (1996, July). Sadistic child abuse and traumatic memories. Paper presented at Trauma and Memory: An International Research Conference, Durham, NH.

Burgess, A., Hartman, C. R. & Baker, T. (1995). Memory presentations of childhood sexual abuse. *Journal of Psychosocial Nursing*, *33*(9), 9-16.

Cameron, C. (1996). Comparing amnesiac and nonamnesiac survivors of childhood sexual abuse: A longitudinal study. In K. Pezdek & W. P. Banks (eds.). *The Recovered Memory/False Memory Debate* (pp. 41-68). New York: Academic Press.

Cheit, R.E. (1998). Consider this, skeptics of recovered memory. *Ethics and Behavior*, *8*(2), 141-160.

Cheit, R. E. (1999). Junk skepticism and recovered memory: A reply to Piper. *Ethics & Behavior*, *9*, 295-318.

Cheit, R. (2000). <http://www.brown.edu/Departments/Taubman_Center/Recovmem/Archive.html>.

Chu, J. A. (1998). *Rebuilding shattered lives: The responsible treatment of complex post-traumatic and dissociative disorders*. New York: Basic Books.

Courtois, C. A. (1989). *Healing the incest wound: Adult survivors in therapy*. New York: Norton.

Courtois, C. A. (1999). *Recollections of sexual abuse: Treatment principles & guidelines*. New York: W.W. Norton.

Crook v. Murphy. Super. Ct. Benton County, WA (1994) 91-2-01102-5; D.D.

Crook, L. & Dean, M. (1999b). Lost in the shopping mall: A breach of professional ethics. *Ethics & Behavior, 9*(1), 39-50 (available on the internet at http://users. owt.com/crook/memory/).

Crook, L. S., & Dean, M. (1999a). Logical fallacies and ethical breaches. *Ethics & Behavior, 9*(1), 61-68.

Dallam, S. J. (1999). Parental alienation syndrome: Is it scientific? In E. St. Charles & L. Crook (Eds.), *Expose: The failure of family courts to protect children from abuse in custody disputes* (pp. 67-94). Los Gatos, CA: Our Children Charitable Foundation.

Dallam, S. J., Gleaves, D. H., Cepeda-Benito, A., Kraemer, H. C., & Spiegel, D. (In press). The effects of childhood sexual abuse: A critique of Rind, Tromovitch and Bauserman. *Psychological Bulletin*.

Daubert v. Merrell Dow Pharmaceuticals. (1993). 113 S. Ct. 2786 (1993).

Davies, J. M. & Frawley, M. G. (1994). *Treating the adult survivor of childhood sexual abuse: A psychoanalytic perspective*. New York: Basic Books.

Emrick, R. L. (1994, October). Child sexual abuse: A closer look at offenders, offense cycle, process of abuse and victim trauma. Presented at a Workshop on Treating Child Molesters, Baltimore, MD.

Emrick, R. L. (1996). *Sexual offenders: A provider's handbook*. Thousand Oaks, CA: Sage.

False Memory Syndrome Foundation Newsletter. (1993, August). Philadelphia: False Memory Syndrome Foundation.

Felitti, V. J., Anda, R. F., Nordenberg, D., Williamson, D. F., Spitz, A. M., Edwards, V., Koss, M. P., et al. (1998). The relationship of adult health status to childhood abuse and household dysfunction. *American Journal of Preventative Medicine, 4*, 245-258.

Freid, S. (1994, January). War of remembrance: How the problems of one Philadelphia family created the False Memory Syndrome Foundation and triggered the most controversial debate in modern mental health. *Philadelphia*, pp. 66-71, 149-157.

Freyd, J. J. (1993). Dr. Jennifer Freyd goes public: Parents are FMSF founders (her personal account of being sexually abused as a child). *Moving Forward, 2*(S), 6-11.

Freyd, J. J. (1996). *Betrayal trauma*. Cambridge, MA: Harvard University Press.

Freyd, P. (1992, Feb 29). FMS Newsletter, p. 1.

Herman, J. (1992). *Trauma and recovery*. New York: Basic Books.

Hewitt, S. K. (1994). Preverbal sexual abuse. *Child Abuse and Neglect, 18*, 819-824.

Hovdestad, W.E. & Kristiansen, C.M. (1996). A field study of "False Memory Syndrome": Construct validity and incidence. *The Journal of Psychiatry and Law, 24*, 299-338.

Kendler, K.S., Bulik, C.M., Silberg, J., Hettema, J.M., Myers, J., & Prescott, C.A. (2000). Childhood sexual abuse and adult psychiatric and substance use disorders in women: An epidemiological and co-twin control analysis. *Archives of General Psychiatry, 57*, 953-959.

Kristiansen, C. M., Felton, K. A., Hovdestad, W. E., & Allard, C. B. (1995). The Ottawa study: A summary of the findings. Unpublished manuscript. Carleton University, Ottawa, Ontario, Canada.

Laplanche, J. & Pontalis, J. B. (1973). *The language of psycho-analysis.* New York: W.W. Norton.

Lazo, J. (1995). True or false: Expert testimony on repressed memory, *Loyola of Los Angeles Law Review, 28*, 1345-1414.

Legg, B. E. (1997). Grant of summary judgment in: *Freyd & Freyd v. Whitfield*: Civil No. L-96-627 U.S. District Court, Baltimore, Maryland.

Levy, B. J. (2000). Plaintiff and defense expert witnesses in the sexual abuse case. *Journal of Aggression, Maltreatment & Trauma, 3*(2), 113-132.

Loftus, E. F. (1993). The reality of repressed memories. *American Psychologist, 48*, 518-537.

Marks, J. (1979). *The search for the Manchurian candidate: The CIA and mind control.* New York: Times Books.

McCauley, J., Kern, D.E., Kolodner, K., Dill, L., Schroeder, A.F., DeChant, H.K., Ryden, J., Derogatis, L., & Bass, E.B. (1997). Clinical characteristics of women with a history of childhood abuse: Unhealed wounds. *Journal of the American Medical Association, 277*, 1362-1368.

Peterson, R. H. (1990). Closing remarks in *State of Washington v. Paul R. Ingrahm.* Superior Court of Washington in & for Thurston County. Report of proceedings, vol VII, no 88-1-752-1.

Pomerantz, J. (1999). Memories of abuse: Women sexually traumatized in childhood. Unpublished manuscript; cited in Brown, Scheflin, & Whitfield, 1999 (above).

Pope, H. G., Hudson, J. I., Bodkin, J. A., & Oliva, P. (1998). Questionable validity of 'dissociative amnesia' in trauma victims. *British Journal of Psychiatry, 172*, 210-215.

Pope, H.G., Jr. & Hudson, J.I. (1995). Can memories of childhood sexual abuse be repressed? *Psychological Medicine, 25*, 121-126.

Pope, K. S. (1995). What psychologists better know about recovered memories, research, lawsuits, and the pivotal experiment. *Clinical Psychology: Science and Practice, 2*(3), 304-315.

Pope, K. S. (1998). Pseudoscience, cross-examination, and scientific evidence in the recovered memory controversy. *Psychology, Public Policy, & Law, 4*(4), 1160-1181.

Pope, K. & Brown, L. (1996). *Recovered memories of abuse.* Washington, DC: American Psychological Association.

Rind, B., Tromovitch, P., & Bauserman, R. (1998). A meta-analytic examination of assumed properties of child sexual abuse using college samples. *Psychological Bulletin, 124*(1), 22-53.

Roe, C. M. & Schwartz, M. (1996). Characteristics of previously forgotten memories of sexual abuse: A descriptive study. *Journal of Psychiatry and Law, 24*, 189-206.

Roseman, M. E., Craig, W.B. & Scott, G. G. (1997). *You the jury: A recovered memory case-allegations of sexual abuse.* Santa Ana, CA: Seven Locks Press.

Rowan, A. B., & Foy, D. W. (1993). PTSD in child sexual abuse. *Journal of Traumatic Stress*, *6*, 3-20.

Rowan, A. B., Foy, D.W., Rodriguez, N., & Ryan, S. (1994). Post-traumatic stress disorder in a clinical sample of adults sexually abused as children. *Child Abuse Neglect*, *18*, 51-61.

Roys, D. T. (1995). Exit examination for sexual offenders. *Sexual Abuse: A Journal of Research and Trauma*, *7*, 85-106.

Salter, A. (1998). Truth, lies and sex offenders. Thousand Oaks, CA: PAL Video, Sage.

Salter, A. C. (1995). *Transforming trauma: A guide to understanding and treating adult survivors of child sexual abuse*. Thousand Oaks, CA: Sage.

Sargant, W. (1957). *Battle for the mind*. Westport, CT: Greenwood Press.

Scheflin, A. W. (1995). The history of mind control: What we can prove and what we can't. CKLN FM, Toronto, Mind Control Series, Part 6, Toronto the International Connection, Producer/interviewer Wayne Morris.

Scheflin, A. W. & Brown, D. (1996). Repressed memory or dissociative amnesia: what the science says. *Journal of Psychiatry & Law*, *24*, 143-188.

Scheflin, A. W. & Brown, D. (1999). The false litigant syndrome: "Nobody would say that unless it was the truth." *The Journal of Psychiatry & Law*, *27*, 649-705.

Scheflin, A. W. & Opton, Jr., E. M. (1978). *The mind manipulators*. New York, NY: Paddington Press.

Singer v. American Psychological Association et al. (1992, September 30). Amended Complaint. United States District Court, Southern District of New York, 92 Civ. 6082.

Singer v. American Psychological Association et al. (1993, August 9). Memorandum and Order. United States District Court, Southern District of New York, *92* Civ. *6082*, WL 307782.

Singer v. American Psychological Association et al. (1994a, January 31). Complaint for civil conspiracy, etc. Superior Court of the State of California in and for the County of Alameda, Case No. 730012-7.

Singer v. American Psychological Association et al. (1994b, June 17). Order. Superior Court of the State of California in and for the County of Alameda, Case No. 730012-8.

Stanton, M. (1997). U-turn on memory lane. *Columbia Journalism Review*, July/August, 44-49.

Summit, R. (1983). The child sexual abuse accommodation syndrome. *Child Abuse and Neglect*, *7*, 177-193.

Terr, L. (1991). Childhood traumas: An outline and overview. *American Journal of Psychiatry*, *148*, 10-20.

Terr, L. (1994). *Unchained memories*. New York: Basic Books.

Underwager & Wakefield v. Salter. (1994, April 25). U.S. Court of Appeals, Seventh Circuit.

Van der Kolk, B. & Fisler, R. (1995). Dissociation and the fragmentary nature of traumatic memories: Overview and exploratory study. *Journal of Traumatic Stress*, *8*, 505-525.

Wakefield, H. & Underwager, R. (1993). Interview on pedophilia. *Paidika: The Journal of Pedophilia, 3*(1), 2-12.

Whitfield, C. L. (1994). The forgotten difference: Ordinary memory vs. traumatic memory. *Consciousness and Cognition, 4*, 88-94.

Whitfield, C. L. (1995a). How common is traumatic forgetting? *Journal of Psychohistory, 23*(2), 119-130.

Whitfield, C. L. (1995b). *Memory and abuse: Remembering and healing the effects of trauma.* Deerfield Beach, FL: Health Communications.

Whitfield, C. L. (1997c). Internal verification and corroboration of traumatic memories. *Journal of Child Sexual Abuse, 6*(3), 99-122.

Whitfield, C. L. (1997a). Memory and trauma. In Burgess, A.W. (ed.): *Advanced practice in psychiatric mental health nursing* (pp. 171-186). Stanford, CT: Appleton & Lange.

Whitfield, C. L. (1997b). Traumatic amnesia: The evolution of our understanding from a clinical and legal prospective. *Sexual Addiction & Compulsivity, 4*(2), 3-34.

Whitfield, C. L. (1998a). Adverse childhood experience and trauma (editorial). *American Journal of Preventive Medicine, 14*(4), 361-364.

Whitfield, C. L. (1998c). Internal evidence and corroboration of traumatic memories of child sexual abuse with addictive disorders. *Sexual Addiction & Compulsivity, 5*, 269-292.

Whitfield, C. L. (1998b, August). Traumatic amnesia from child sexual abuse: Observations on 40 child molesters in group therapy weekly over nine months. Workshop presentation at the Georgia Council on Child Abuse annual conference, Atlanta, GA.

Whitfield, C. L. & Stock, W. E. (1996, July). Traumatic amnesia in 100 survivors of childhood sexual abuse. Presented at the national conference on trauma & memory, Univ. of New Hampshire.

Williams, L. M. (1994). Recall of childhood trauma: A prospective study of women's memories of child sexual abuse. *Journal of Consulting and Clinical Psychology, 62*(6), 1167-1176.

Yapko, M. (1994b). *Suggestions of abuse.* New York: Simon & Schuster.

Yapko, M. (1994a). Suggestibility & repressed memories of abuse: A survey of psychotherapists' beliefs. *American Journal of Clinical Hypnosis, 36*(3), 163-7.

Yule, R: Final statements and ruling in *Crook v. Murphy* (supra) (1994, March 4).

(Mis) Representations
of the Long-Term Effects
of Childhood Sexual Abuse in the Courts

Daniel Brown

SUMMARY. This study addresses the (mis) representations made by pro-false memory attorneys and expert witnesses in court regarding the long-term effects of childhood sexual abuse (CSA). Five pro-false memory positions were identified: (1) there is no causal connection between CSA and adult psychopathology; (2) the evidence is insufficient; (3) CSA does not cause specific trauma-related outcomes like borderline and dissociative identity disorder; (4) other variables than CSA explain the variance of adult psychopathology; and (5) the long-term effects of CSA are general and non-specific. Examining the testimony revealed that such pro-false memory testimony was based solely on a partial understanding of retrospective data and that pro-false memory experts do not cite the more recent prospective data. Reviewing the totality of the scientific evidence demonstrates that such pro-false memory testimony is inaccurate and has the potential of misleading the jury. Prospective

Daniel Brown, PhD, is Assistant Clinical Professor in Psychology, Harvard Medical School, Adjunct Professor, Simmons School of Social Work, Boston MA, and trauma clinician and forensic expert witness regarding trauma and memory issues for the courts.

Address correspondence to: Daniel Brown, PhD & Associates, 997 Chestnut Street, Newton Upper Falls, MA 02464 (E-mail: danbrown1@rcn.com).

[Haworth co-indexing entry note]: "(Mis) Representations of the Long-Term Effects of Childhood Sexual Abuse in the Courts." Brown, Daniel. Co-published simultaneously in *Journal of Child Sexual Abuse* (The Haworth Maltreatment & Trauma Press, an imprint of The Haworth Press, Inc.) Vol. 9, No. 3/4, 2001, pp. 79-107; and: *Misinformation Concerning Child Sexual Abuse and Adult Survivors* (ed: Charles L. Whitfield, Joyanna Silberg, and Paul Jay Fink) The Haworth Maltreatment & Trauma Press, an imprint of The Haworth Press, Inc., 2001, pp. 79-107. Single or multiple copies of this article are available for a fee from The Haworth Document Delivery Service [1-800-HAWORTH 9:00 a.m. - 5:00 p.m. (EST). E-mail address: getinfo@haworthpressinc.com].

79

studies provide sufficient evidence to causally link CSA to a number of areas of adult psychopathology including multiple, co-morbid psychiatric conditions, and possibly to link early parent-infant attachment pathology to the development of borderline and dissociative identity disorder. *[Article copies available for a fee from the haworth document delivery service: 1-800-HAWORTH. E-mail address: <getinfo@haworthpressinc.com> Website: <http://www.HaworthPress.com> © 2001 by The Haworth Press, Inc. All rights reserved.]*

KEYWORDS. Abuse, sexual abuse, psychopathology, law and psychiatry, expert testimony

INTRODUCTION

Over the past decade the interface between childhood sexual abuse (CSA) and the law has expanded dramatically in two areas: (1) adult plaintiff civil actions against alleged perpetrators of CSA; and (2) plaintiff civil actions against former therapists for alleged malpractice (Brown, Scheflin & Hammond, 1998). In the former situations, plaintiff expert witness, arguing in favor of traumatization effects, have represented to the courts that CSA causes long-term damage in the form of some sort of psychological problems. Defense expert witnesses, arguing a pro-false memory position, typically say that CSA does not cause the damage that the plaintiff alleges, or that recovered memories of CSA are unreliable and should not be admitted as court testimony are (Brown, Scheflin & Whitfield, 1999). In the latter situations, the plaintiff is generally an adult patient who had recovered memories of CSA (and sometimes other forms of abuse) in therapy, later retracted the memories, and subsequently sued the therapist(s) for allegedly implanting false abuse memories. In these such cases, plaintiff pro-false memory expert witnesses typically argue that CSA does not cause the forms of psychopathology that plaintiff manifested in therapy. They charge that the defendant therapists were negligent to have assumed a causal connection between CSA and adult psychopathology and to have used this assumption as the justification to "search" for recovered memories (Ofshe & Watters, 1994).

The critical issue in each of these scenarios is whether there is a causal connection between CSA and specific forms of adult psychopathology. The purpose of this article is to critically examine the way a pro-false memory argument in each of these respective areas has been represented (or misrepresented) to the courts, and to evaluate these representations against the current scientific evidence. As Ceci (1994) once said, nobody is neutral in the recovered/false memory controversy; the real issue is how "off-center" a given position is in one direction or another. I have been an expert witness largely for the adult plaintiff in suits against alleged perpetrators of CSA, and as an expert mainly for the defense in malpractice suits against clinicians allegedly for negligently implanting false memories of childhood abuse and/or negligently implanting a 'false' diagnosis of dissociative identity disorder. Therefore, my own position is "off-center" in the direction of the pro-trauma, rather than the false-memory position. Nevertheless, I have served as an expert witness in well over 50 such cases, and, therefore, I have had considerable experience observing the patterns of how pro-false memory arguments are represented to the courts. In other areas, it has been shown that pro-false memory testimony often has misrepresented the available scientific evidence. For example, some of these include allegedly implanting false abuse memories (Scheflin & Brown, 1999), allegedly suggesting a false dissociative identity disorder diagnosis (Brown, Frischholtz, & Scheflin, 1999), and the status of repressed/dissociated memories (Brown, Scheflin, & Whitfield, 1999).

Pro-False Memory (Mis) Representations of the Long-Term Effects of CSA in the Courts

From a review of over 50 deposition and/or trial testimonies of pro-false memory expert witnesses, I have been able to identify five basic pro-false memory arguments made to the courts in testimony given under oath: (1) there is no causal connection between CSA and adult psychopathology; (2) the evidence for such a connection is insufficient; (3) CSA does not cause specific trauma-related outcomes like borderline and dissociative identity disorder; (4) other variables than CSA explain most of the variance of adult psychopathology; and (5) the long-term effects of CSA are general and non-specific. Each is described below.

1. There is *no causal connection* between adult psychopathology and CSA.
   a. *No causal connection.* One pro-false memory expert witness in a number of malpractice cases, Paul McHugh, has testified that there is no causal connection between CSA and adult psychopathology:

   I do not believe that necessarily finding abuse in a person's childhood in and of itself explains disorders that turn up in adulthood . . . because we know many people are sexually abused in childhood and have no mental illness later on, and people with mental illness don't . . . necessarily have child abuse. So the connection there would not be done

(*Daly et al. v. Wisconsin Patient's Fund et al.* 1999, Vol. 1, p. 161) . . . Many people are sexually abused as children, and except for the disruption in the relationship that they remember and suffer from, they seem to emerge well. Many do not, though. And . . . psychiatrists cannot attribute any particular psychiatric state directly to any particular childhood event. So what could be relatively serious outcomes usually relate to the sexual abuse being embedded in other serious problems in childhood . . . There is no clear link between that event [CSA] . . . and later psychiatric disorders that reach clinical significance. (1999, Vol. 2, pp. 457-459)

b. *Low or unknown frequency of damage.* A related argument illustrated by the above testimony is that even where CSA might cause long-term harm, the prevalence of long-term damage is quite low and "many" abuse survivors do well. Pro-false memory attorney/psychologist R. Christopher Barden has made a related argument, namely that establishing a causal relationship between CSA and adult psychopathology is meaningless unless the respective "base rates" for CSA and adult psychiatric sequelae have been established:

[How do you compare the base rates (of psychopathology) in the normal psychiatric population . . . with sequelae known from child sexual abuse, how do you compare that if you don't know what they are, . . . ?] (*Burgess v. Rush-Presbyterian-St.Luke's Medical Center et al.* 1996. Questions by attorney Barden in the deposition of Dr. Bennett G. Braun, pp. 464-465.)

c. *It is negligent to assume a causal connection between CSA and adult psychopathology.* This argument essentially has been made by pro-false memory expert August Piper:

The [defendant] doctor is thinking that her depression is a direct result of sexual abuse . . . the literature just does not support this kind of thinking on his part. Any one of probably a dozen articles and scholarly journals talked about the fact that sexual abuse alone is not a sufficient cause for people's psychological problems, and the doctor should have known that. (*Greene vs. Megellan Health Services et al.* 1997. Deposition of August Piper, pp. 54-5)

2. CSA does not cause specific trauma-related outcomes like dissociative identity disorder, eating disorders, or personality disorders like borderline personality disorder. Paul McHugh has testified in several cases that trauma-related conditions do not arise from CSA. For example, he says: "As I said to you, there is no evidence that multiple personality disorder and CSA have any connection." (*Daly et al. v. Wisconsin Patient's Fund et al.* Vol. 1, pp. 108-109)

3a. *CSA may or may not cause specific psychiatric conditions in adulthood but the evidence is insufficient.* The main advocate for the "insufficient evidence" position has been pro-false memory expert, James I. Hudson:

> [What problems, if any, are documented to be caused in an adult's life by sexual abuse during childhood?] Certainly individuals would have distress after the event and may well have unpleasant feelings and distress surrounding certain issues as an adult on the basis of that. . . . [Are there any scientific studies that either confirm or refute that?] Well, there is really a lack of good literature on the adult effects of CSA, specifically, whether specific psychiatric disorders can be caused by them . . . [. . . there is inadequate information . . . to either confirm or refute ongoing adult problems as a result of childhood abuse?] Problems. I would say there seems to be adequate evidence that there would be problems . . . exactly the nature of them and whether specific disorders are caused by it is . . . unknown (*Tyo v. Ash et al.* 1999, pp. 110-112) . . . It is possible that CSA can be a cause of major depressive disorder. It's just not been established, no . . . as to having CSA as a child and then years or decades later developing a psychiatric disorder, we don't have evidence for that, but certainly causing distress and problems, we don't have strong evidence for that. (*Hess et al. v. Wausau,* 1999, pp. 163-164)

3b. *On the basis of insufficient evidence, defendant therapists in malpractice suits negligently have promoted a "false belief" that CSA causes adult psychopathology.* This more extreme position has been put forth by pro-false memory expert, Richard Ofshe:

> And then from the mid-1980's, the idea of sexual abuse being the cause of adult symptoms, as in, for example, the presumption that bulimia was caused by sexual abuse, was an idea that some people were promoting. As it turns out, there is no evidence for it. [It was being promoted because] the talk therapies were on the decline. And one could look at the interest in trauma therapies as an attempt to revitalize this talk therapy industry . . . [that had] develop[ed] from a psychodynamic paradigm, all of which traced back on speculations and . . . misreports about the efficacy of . . . treatment. (*Greene v. Magellan Health Services et al.* 1998, pp. 78-80)

4. *CSA may or may not cause specific psychiatric conditions in adulthood but other variables explain most of the variance.* This more tempered argument does not preclude a causal connection between CSA and adult psychopathology,

but hypothesizes that it would explain only a small part of the variance of the overall adult psychopathology. Not surprisingly, those favorable to a pro-false memory position who devote more time to research than clinical practice take this position:

> [Are there some patients . . . who suffered abuse as children who do not go on to develop psychopathology as adults?] Many. . . . The issue is the causal connection between the abuse and later psychopathology. That has been less more firmly established . . . [Well, in those patients who do actually suffer abuse and go on . . . to develop causally connected psychopathology as adults, that group of patients, you're acknowledging that happens, right?] . . . You know, let me try to be fair to your question. As a clinician, I know that people are influenced by many, many things; they're influenced not only by traumatic experience . . . and are affected by many things in their lives that actually moderate whether or not psychopathology will be expressed later on, things like social support, how the family reacts, things like genetic vulnerability . . . So I think it's very difficult to talk about these causal connections because there are so many potential mediators or moderators . . . (*Daly et al. v. Wisconsin Patient's Fund et al.*, 1999, pp. 78-81. Deposition of Steven Jay Lynn)

> There appears to have been a pattern of conveying information of the kind I've already mentioned, the notion that sexual abuse is a very important determinant of adult psychopathology, when in fact the evidence suggests that it's not an especially important one. It's one among many possible influences and not by any means always the strongest. (*Carlson v. St. Paul Fire and Marine Insurance et al.*, 1999, p. 101. Deposition of William M. Grove)

5. If CSA causes anything at all, its long-term effects are general and non-specific:

> [Much has been made in this case of assuming causality. With a current diagnosis of an eating disorder or a borderline personality disorder or perhaps of what we now call dissociative identity disorder, working backwards from that and then assuming abuse as the causal factor. What is the current state of the research and learning on that?] . . . my reading of the eating disorder literature in relationship to childhood sexual abuse . . . is that the eating disorder risk might be increased if you are abused, but no more so than lots of other disorders . . . that there is some kind of unique link between eating disorders and sexual abuse is not supported. However, all sorts of bad things about your childhood, including physical or sexual traumatization *are thought to increase your risk in general*

(emphasis added) for various kinds of psychiatric disorders. That might be one of them. Secondly, the studies done on eating disorders patients which purport to show this do not, in fact, validate that they were ever abused . . . the attempt to go backwards and reason from the clinical picture or diagnosis to the supported historical event of abuse would not be possible to do that in a reasonably certain way in the individual case. (*Greene v. Megellan Health Services et al.* 1998, pp.144-148. Deposition of William M. Grove)

The critical question is whether these pro-false memory arguments accurately portray or essentially misrepresent the scientific evidence on the long-term effects of CSA. My position will be that these arguments mislead the courts because they are based on a biased interpretation of a highly select body of evidence, namely the retrospective studies on CSA that appeared in the professional literature in the 1980s and early 1990s. More important, *none* of the pro-false memory experts in any of the over 50 court cases reviewed ever cited in their testimony the rapidly accumulating body of prospective studies on the long-term effects of CSA. In essence, such pro-false memory testimony, from a scientific point of view, is both premature and inaccurate.

The Evidence from the Retrospective Studies

A good deal of the above mentioned testimony by pro-false memory expert witnesses takes as its source of data a few, select critical reviews of the retrospective studies on the long-term effects of CSA. While almost 500 citations appeared in the professional literature from the mid-1970s to the early 1990s on the effects of CSA (Neumann, Houskamp, Pollock, & Briere, 1996), pro-false memory expert witnesses rarely cite individual articles in their court testimony, and, instead, they rely on several strategic critical reviews (Beitchman et al., 1992; Kendall-Tackett, Williams, & Finkelhor, 1993; Rind & Tromovitch, 1997; Rind, Tromovitch, & Bauserman, 1998; cf. attorney Barden's citation of these studies in *State of Rhode Island v. Quattrocchi, 1996*). The gist of the pro-false memory interpretation of these data is that a causal connection between CSA and adult psychopathology has not been scientifically established in these retrospective studies, and that even where long-term effects are suggested, the prevalence rate is low and the effects are so variable that no clear-cut pattern of damage can be reliably and validly identified as causally connected to CSA. Piper's interpretation of these data is perhaps representative:

Many if not most abused children go on to function normally as adults and, at least as assessed by currently available tools, show no significant

harm from the experience. (*Greene vs. Magellan Health Services et al.,*
1997, p. 617)

Since this representation of the retrospective studies is not entirely accurate, a
brief review of their actual claims might be useful.

Kendall-Tackett et al. (1993) wrote an important review of the effects of
CSA in later childhood. They review 45 retrospective studies presenting quan-
tified, longitudinal data appearing in the literature from 1984-1991. Comparing abuse and non-abused children across these studies, they found that a
"wide range of symptoms" were reported in sexually abused children. The
most commonly studied symptom was sexualized behavior but that "other
symptoms . . . included anxiety, depression, withdrawn behavior, somatic
complaints, aggression, and school problems" (p. 165). Differences in reported symptoms between the abused and non-abused children included:
"fears, nightmares, general posttraumatic stress disorder (PTSD), withdrawn
behavior, neurotic mental illness, cruelty, delinquency, sexually inappropriate
behavior, regressive behavior . . . running away, general behavior problems,
self-injurious behavior, internalizing, and externalizing" (p. 165). However,
they add that in comparison to non-abused children seen in a clinical context,
the abused children were "less symptomatic . . . except in regard to sexualized
behavior and PTSD" (p. 165). When looking at specific symptoms, such as
anxiety, depression, somatic complaints, etc., the authors found that "sexual
abuse status alone accounted for a very large percentage of the variance"
(p. 166) with high effect sizes specifically for acting out, internalized (depression and withdrawal), sexualized and aggressive behaviors, but that "no one
symptom characterized a majority of sexually abused children" (p. 164). Approximately one-third of the abused children did not show symptoms. They
add that these data "hint at possible developmental patterns" (p. 167), in that
different patterns of effects, like sexualized behavior, appear, disappear, or re-
appear at different ages, while other symptoms, notably depression, appear
across different developmental periods. They note that "one half to two thirds
of all children became less symptomatic, whereas 10-24% became more so" in
the first year or two after the abuse (p. 173). According to the authors, a number of variables affect symptom patterns over time, such as duration and frequency of the abuse, penetration, use of force, and the relationship between the
victim and the perpetrator. They concluded:

> The present review confirms the general impression that the impact of
> sexual abuse is serious and can manifest itself in a wide variety of symp-
> tomatic and pathological behaviors. There is virtually no domain of
> symptomatology that has not been associated with a history of sexual

abuse . . . However, some sexually abused children may also appear to have no apparent symptoms. (p. 173)

Overall, sexualized behavior and PTSD were consistently seen in abused as compared to non-abused children in the clinic, but these were also sometimes seen in non-abused children as well. They added that there is no "specific syndrome" resulting from CSA.

Beitchman et al. (1992) wrote an important review of the long-term effects of CSA in adults. They reviewed 32 retrospective studies appearing from 1977 to 1988 and found that women with a history of CSA as compared to women without such a history have: a greater evidence of sexual disturbance (especially in clinic patients and victims specifically of father-daughter incest); "a small but significant increased rate of homosexual activity" (p. 105); major depressive episodes and suicidality; and a weak but significant tendency toward more victimization experiences. They also found "insufficient evidence to confirm a relation between a history of CSA and a post-sexual abuse syndrome or multiple or borderline personality" (p. 101). They correctly add that with respect to such syndromes parent-child relational disturbance may contribute more to the variance of such specific syndromes than sexual abused acts per se. The predictors of long-term effects of sexual abuse were: duration of abuse, use of force, penetration, and relationship of victim and perpetrator. Beitchman et al. qualified their conclusions by adding that while there indeed are a variety of effects consistently found more in sexually abused relative to non-abused women, "To what extent the sequelae are due to sex abuse per se is still not known" (p. 115).

The third review study relied upon by pro-false memory experts is the Rind et al. meta-analytic review (Rind & Tromovitch, 1997; Rind, Tromovitch & Bauserman, 1998; see critiques by Dallam and by Wittenberg et al. in this volume, of the methodological flaws in this review study). Christopher Barden entered this study into the record in *State of Rhode Island v. Quattrocchi* (1996) with the following conclusions stated in the study:

> We found that, contrary to the implications and conclusions contained in previous literature reviews that were focused on biased samples, in the general population, CSA is not associated with pervasive harm and that harm, when it occurs, is not typically intense . . . conclusions about a causal link between CSA and later psychological maladjustment in the general population cannot safely be made because of the reliable presence of confounding variables. (Rind & Tromovitch, 1997, p. 237)

The essence of the Rind and Tromovitch approach has been to summarily dismiss the conclusions of previous critical reviews, like Kendall-Tackett et al. (1993) and Beitchman et al. (1992), along with previous meta-analytic reviews, like Jumper (1995) and Neumann et al. (1996), with the argument that these reviews were based largely on clinical and legal samples not representative of the general population. The Rind and Tromovitch conclusions are at odds with nearly all of the previous peer reviewed critical reviews and meta-analytic studies on the long-term effects of CSA, as noted.

What conclusions can safely be drawn from these reviews of the retrospective studies on the long-term effects of CSA that could appropriately serve as the basis of expert witness testimony in the courts? These studies, with the exception of Rind and Tromovitch (1997), clearly establish clinically significant long-term effects. They emphasize that there are a wide range of possible long-term effects and that no single symptom nor specific syndrome is the likely outcome. Rather, the specific pattern of symptoms for any given victim depends on a complex number of abuse-specific intervening variables (like duration and frequency of abuse, penetration and force, and relationship between victim and perpetrator). Some reviews, notably, Kendall-Tackett et al. (1993) raise the important question that different symptom patterns may occur at different developmental points in the same victim over time. These studies also qualify their conclusions, in that being based in retrospective data, they cannot firmly establish causality. In addition, the observed long effects associated with CSA may be associated with other variables such as family pathology or parent-child attachment disturbance.

Pro-false memory expert witnesses who have relied solely upon the above mentioned reviews as the source of their expert testimony are accurate when testifying about such things as "no causal connection," non-specific effects, or effects possibly accounted for by other variables. However, testimony about "insufficient evidence" runs contrary to the data in these reviews. Testimony about the non-specificity of effects misses the conclusions drawn by Kendall-Tackett et al. specifically about sexualized behavior and PTSD.

However, the main point is not the extent to which these pro-false memory expert witnesses have correctly or incorrectly represented these retrospective data. The far more important point is that the court cases reviewed did not have *any* pro-false memory expert witness cite the far more relevant prospective studies. The courts are best to consider the totality of the evidence relevant to the question of the long-term effects of CSA. Pro-false memory expert witnesses have been remiss in their duty to the courts by failing to include in their testimony prospective data that may answer and clarify many of the points, not the least of which includes establishing which areas of long-term effects are *causally* linked to CSA. Therefore, the important prospective studies that have appeared in the literature will briefly be reviewed here. Only genuine prospective studies that include both abused and matched normal, non-abused control subjects are reviewed because such studies can establish causal relationships between CSA and adult psychopathology. Other important longitudinal studies of CSA exist (e.g., Burgess, Hartman, & Baker, 1995) but lack the control conditions necessary to establish causality.

The Evidence from the Prospective Studies

Silverman, Reinherz and Giaconia (1996) conducted a 17-year longitudinal study on a community sample of all 519 children registered in kindergarten classes in a public school system. Detailed behavioral data were collected cross-sectionally in the children through self-report inventories and structured interviews at five data collection points (at ages 5, 9, 15, 18, and 21). In order to ascertain "the link between abuse and specific mental disorders" emerging over time, specifically in mid-adolescence and early adulthood, the data were used from ages 15 and 21. At age 21, nearly 11% [n = 40] of the 375 respondents reported physical or sexual abuse before age 18. These retrospective self-reports of abuse were significantly correlated with other, independent measures of abuse and violence. Thus, while this study is somewhat limited by the retrospective measure of abuse reports, nevertheless, the reports have some validity. The total sample was divided into two main groups, an abused group consisting of 22 physically abused (10 males and 12 females) and 25 (23 females and 2 males) sexually abused subjects, and a non-abused control group. These groups were matched on all demographic and academic variables.

At mid-adolescence the physically abused males differed significantly from the non-abused group only in reported suicidal ideation, while physically abused females differed significantly from the control group in a number of ways–degree of social withdrawal, suicidal ideation, manifestation of somatic complaints, anxious and depressive symptoms, problems with attention and thinking, and expression of aggressive behaviors. By early adulthood (age 21) the physically abused males and females, as compared to the normal control subjects, were significantly more likely to manifest one or more psychiatric conditions (major depressive disorder, posttraumatic stress disorder, antisocial personality disorder in both males and females, and drug abuse or dependence in males. The striking finding was the extent to which both physically abused males and females exhibited at least one (58.3%), two (41.7%) or more than two (16.7%) major psychiatric disorders in the physically abused group compared to the non-abused control group (30.9% one, 9.7% two, 1.7% three psychiatric conditions). The high rates of co-morbidity were striking as was the six-fold increase in suicidality in the abused young women.

At mid-adolescence the sexually abused females (there were not enough sexually abused males in the sample to evaluate) significantly differed from the non-abused girls in their somatic complaints, anxious and depressive symptoms, social problems, problems with attention and thinking, and expression of aggressive behaviors and suicidal ideation. By early adulthood (age 21), sexually abused females differed significantly in their manifestation of one (69.6%), two (43.5%) or more than two (13%) major psychiatric conditions as compared to the normal, control group (27.4%, 7.3%, and 1%, respectively). The psychiatric conditions included: major depressive disorder, posttraumatic stress disorder, antisocial personality, and alcohol abuse or dependence. The authors state, "These sexually abused females were nearly three times more likely than non-sexually abused females to have at least one active psychiatric disorder," and the prevalence of multiple, co-morbid psychiatric disorders was quite high. "Child and adolescent sexual abuse before the age of 18 posed a serious threat to nearly every aspect of psycho-social functioning for females during mid-adolescence and early adulthood" (p. 718).

Overall, the authors concluded that this longitudinal study "revealed distinct profiles of problematic functioning at ages 15 and 21 for subjects who were physically and/or sexually abused before the age of 18" (p. 719). They added:

> Alarming rates of psychopathology and co-occurring disorders were found among physically and sexually abused young adults at age 21 . . . an overwhelming proportion of abused subjects displayed co-morbidity of psychiatric disorders. (p. 720)

More than two-thirds of sexually abused girls met criteria for a major psychiatric condition in early adulthood. These data support the concept of *developmentally delayed effects,* with at least some of the effects being less obvious in later childhood, problematic behaviors emerging predominately in mid-adolescence, and significant psychiatric conditions appearing in early adulthood.

The generalization of these findings is limited by the fact that abuse was based on retrospective self-reports, so that it was never firmly established that the abuse occurred nor was the severity of the abuse ever determined. The study also lacked any way to segregate abuse effects from other important variables (e.g., family pathology) that might have contributed to the psychopathology emerging in early adulthood. Despite these limitations, these data suggest possible differences in the manifestation of the long-term effects of abuse at different developmental periods. For abused children relative to normal, non-abused children, mid-adolescence is much more likely to be characterized by the emergence of a variety of distinct behavioral problems (drug or alcohol abuse, suicidal and aggressive behavior, and antisocial behavior), cognitive problems, and/or the appearance of anxious, depressive, and somatic symptoms, all of which cause "significant impairments in functioning" (p. 709). By early adulthood the behavioral problems are somewhat less apparent, and the symptom patterns become organized into major psychiatric disorders.

The limitations of the Silverman et al. (1996) study are adequately addressed in a prospective study of the long-term effects of childhood neglect and physical and sexual abuse conducted by Cathy Spatz Widom and her associates (Widom & Shepard, 1996; Widom & Morris, 1997; Widom, 1999). This gold standard prospective study utilizes a large sample size. It originally consisted of 1,575 children followed over a 20-year period (1,196 respondents were interviewed at the 20-year follow-up point). The respondents included: 520 cases of neglect, 110 cases of physical abuse, 96 cases of CSA, and 543 normal control subjects demographically matched for age, sex, race, and socio-economic status.[1] The neglect and abuse cases were all selected from a review of juvenile and court records and the matched control subjects were selected from a review of hospital and elementary school records, all in the late 1960s. Neglect and abuse cases were selected when there was a high level of evidence establishing that neglect or abuse did indeed occur (the neglect or the physical or sexual abuse had been court substantiated, which included a review of court testimony and physical evidence). Neglect cases were selected for rather extreme neglect, where the evidence was unequivocal (e.g., "Failure to provide adequate food, clothing, shelter, and medical attention"; Widom, 1999, p. 1224). Selected physically abused children, for example, all had clear-cut physical injuries as a result of the physical abuse, such as bruises, welts, burns, lacerations, wounds, or broken bones. Selected sexually abused children "varied from relatively nonspecific charges of 'assault and battery with intent to gratify sexual desires' to more specific charges of 'fondling or touching in an obscene manner' " (Widom & Morris, 1997, p. 36), all of which cases had been court substantiated. Thus, in contrast to the Silverman et al. (1996) retrospective self-report study, the Widom prospective study was conducted with reasonable assurance that neglect or abuse had been factually established as having occurred. Furthermore, by comparing the findings after 20 years for both the neglect and abused children to the demographically matched control group of normal, non-abused children, it was possible to establish a *causal* relationship between childhood neglect/abuse and adult psychopathology. Both the neglect/abuse and demographically matched control children were then followed over a 20-year period and then re-interviewed.

The long-term effects of neglect have not yet been reported by Widom, but the analysis of abuse effects have been published. In the study on physical abuse (Widom & Shepard, 1996), one striking finding was that 40% of subjects with documented severe physically abused children interviewed after 20 years failed to report the abuse, and that 64% of those who reported the abuse never considered it to be physical abuse, even where lacerations and broken bones had been reported. These data suggest that strong forces (possibly by the perpetrator and/or the family environment) mediate the minimization and cognitive distortion of an accurate appraisal of the physical abuse as abuse for many physically abused children. With respect to the long-term effects of physical abuse, it was found to be causally related to subsequent arrests for violent behavior, suicidality, antisocial personality disorder, and alcoholism.

With respect to the long-term effects of CSA, Widom and Morris (1997) found that 37% of the subjects with documented histories of CSA interviewed after 20 years failed to report the sexual abuse and 36% of those who reported the abuse never considered it to be sexual abuse. As with physical abuse, forces operate over time that serve to minimize or distort an accurate understanding of documented sexual abuse as abuse. With respect to the long-term effects of CSA, officially documented CSA was significantly causally related to alcoholism and suicidality but not depression in women, whereas self reported CSA also predicted the development of depression over time. In essence, these findings suggest that suicidality and alcoholism are typical expected effects of CSA over time. Whether depression is associated with CSA may depend on the nature of the cognitive appraisal the survivor makes of the abuse. The long-term effects of sexual abuse for men were less clear-cut because of the small sample size of sexually abused men in the study.

In a subsequent article, Widom (1999) examined whether lifetime and current posttraumatic stress disorder (PTSD) was causally related to documented neglect and/or physical and sexual abuse in childhood. The total sample of 1,196 subjects were given the Diagnostic Interview Schedule (DIS) for PTSD at the 20-year mark. Over one-third (37.5%) of the group with a documented history of CSA, 32.7% of those with documented physical abuse, and 30.6% of those with documented severe neglect met the criteria for *lifetime* PTSD, in contrast to 20.4% for lifetime PTSD of the normal, non-abused control subjects. A total of 22.9%, 19.1%, and 17.3% of the respective groups met the criteria for *current* PTSD as compared to 10.4% in the control group. These findings all reached statistical significance and demonstrate that "Childhood victimization was associated with increased risk for lifetime and current PTSD" (p. 1223). However, Widom points out that childhood victimization is not a sufficient condition for the development of PTSD and that "family, individual, and lifestyle variables also place individuals at risk and contribute to the symptoms of PTSD" (p. 1223). The study showed that subjects with documented neglect or abuse were significantly more at risk for exposure to traumatic events in life than normal control subjects. Through analysis of co-variance the author attempted to ascertain relative contribution of the target neglect/abuse, later traumatic exposure, and other non-abuse variables to the subsequent development of PTSD. The target neglect, physical, and sexual abuse did not significantly predict a lifetime PTSD diagnosis but did predict lifetime PTSD symptoms when all other factors were partialled out, and accounted for a small percentage of the overall variance (9%). Thus, Widom concluded that "childhood experiences of abuse and neglect also contributed independently to a person's risk of PTSD, even when known risk factors were controlled" (p. 1227), but that even where lifetime PTSD symptoms are causally related to childhood neglect and physical and sexual abuse, that does not necessarily mean that the individual will meet sufficient diagnostic criteria for a diagnosis of PTSD. Widom also emphasizes that her findings show that neglected children, not just abused children, are at risk to develop PTSD over time.

Additional results from this Widom 20-year prospective study have also been reported using a similar method of analysis as in the PTSD study. The development of alcoholism (Widom, Ireland & Glynn, 1995) and antisocial personality (Luntz & Widom, 1994) were also found to be significantly causally related to documented childhood neglect and physical and sexual abuse.

The third longitudinal study on the long-term effects of CSA is currently still in progress. Putnam (1998) is conducting a 20-year prospective study of 77 sexually abused girls, 15 maltreated but not sexually abused girls, and 72 normal, non-abused girls. The two control groups (maltreated and normal girls) were demographically matched to the target group of abused girls. The abused girls were referred from Child Protective Services, and were not necessarily in treatment. Hence, the study represents essentially a non-clinical sample of abused girls. The average age of onset of the abuse was 11 years of age, and ranged from 8 to 14 years of age across subjects. Abuse occurred by a father in 23% and by a father figure in 58% of the girls, and multiple perpetrators were reported for 41% of the cases. The design called for data collection every two years. Data were collected in a number of ways, through self-report, administration of psychological inventories, and interviews of subjects, parents, and teachers. The real value of this study in comparison to the Silverman et al. and Widom studies is that it includes a much more comprehensive evaluation of possible effects of abuse over time, including behavioral, interpersonal, biological, and developmental effects.

Putnam (1998) reported some of the preliminary results, even though the last data-collection point had not been completed. At that time, the girls had reached late adolescence or early adulthood, so that some of the long-term effects were quite evident. The prospective design, using both sexually abused and matched non-abused girls was used to establish significant causal relationships between sexual abuse and the subsequent development of problems over time. With respect to symptom and behavioral effects, documented CSA in contrast to no abuse was significantly related to the development of attention deficit hyperactivity disorder (ADHD) in later childhood, and alcoholism, anxiety, depression, suicidality, self-mutilating behavior, and hyper-sexualized behaviors in adolescence and early adulthood. Interpersonally, sexually abused girls relative to the non-abused control girls showed a fundamental difference in the selection and patterning of their interpersonal behavior. Sexually abused girls were significantly less likely to have same-aged girls as friends, and were significantly more likely to select older boys and men for friendships and intimate relationships. They also were significantly more likely to have had intercourse at an earlier age, to have had a greater number of sexual partners, and to have been physically abused by their partners than the non-abused girls. Around male strangers the sexually abused girls relative to the non-abused girls were significantly more likely to exhibit hyper-sexualized behaviors, and they also showed a greater preoccupation with sexualized thought and fantasy than their non-abused counterparts. CSA relative to no abuse was also significantly associated with the development of multiple somatic complaints and somatization disorder in later childhood, adolescence and early adulthood. Multiple pain complaints were especially common among the sexually abused girls over time. Developmentally, CSA relative to no abuse was significantly related to developmental failures in the regulation of affect and impulses and in the consolidation of a cohesive self representational system. Thus, significant affect regulatory deficits and self pathology could be observed in sexually abused children over time, exactly the kind of effect and self deficits typically found in individuals with personality disorder and dissociative disorder diagnoses.

One very valuable result emerging from the Putnam study was the discovery that the long-term effects of CSA clearly change over time and manifest in different ways at different developmental periods. He calls these developmentally delayed or time-released effects "sleeper effects," in that the most important damage of sexual abuse may not be readily apparent in later childhood, but rather may emerge only in adolescence or adulthood, and not always in ways that are expected. For example, Putnam's data demonstrate that ADHD and depression were more likely to occur at younger ages. Then, the symptom picture clearly shifts to anxiety-related and PTSD symptoms in the same children at older ages. Likewise, the occurrence of dissociative symptoms is significantly more likely at younger than older ages. Dissociative symptoms decline with time and tend to decline concurrent with the emergence of anxiety and PTSD symptoms.

Putnam also found that of all the possible predictors of long-term effects, dissociation was the strongest predictor of suicidality, violent behavior, somatization, severity of psychopathology and the emergence of multiple, co-morbid psychiatric conditions over time. One possible interpretation of these data is that sexually abused girls who utilized a dissociative coping style may have appeared to be higher functioning in the short-run after the abuse, but by virtue of disrupting processing of the abuse via dissociation, in the long run more severe forms and varieties of symptom presentations and multiple, co-morbid psychiatric conditions emerge over time. The implication is clear: Sexually abused girls who appear well adjusted and high functioning after the abuse are not necessarily free of damage and may simply be manifesting "sleeper effects," which predict more severe forms of psychopathology emerging later in life. Thus, previous studies that have concluded that sexual abuse is not always damaging may have done so prematurely, in that they have failed to account for sleeper effects.

Taken together, these three studies clearly and consistently document the long-term damage occurring as a result of CSA. These studies cause us to re-think the conclusions of the earlier generation of retrospective studies as represented in the critical reviews by Beichtman et al. (1992) and Kendall-Tackett et al. (1993). The real value of the prospective studies is that they allow us to establish significant causal relationships between CSA and adult psychopathology

We can classify the effects as *causally related* or *possibly causally related* depending on whether the finding has been replicated across more than one of the three prospective studies. Behaviorally, physical abuse is causally related to later suicidality, violent behavior and antisocial behavior. Sexual abuse is causally related to the development of suicidality, possibly to self-mutilatory behavior and hyper-sexualized behavior; causally related to alcoholism and antisocial behavior in females and possibly drug dependence in males. With respect to symptom effects, CSA is causally related to anxiety, depression, and possibly causally related to PTSD, dissociative, and somatization symptoms. With respect to interpersonal effects CSA is possibly causally related to the selection and biased patterning of friendships and intimate relationships with older boys and men compared to same sex peer friendships, and also an earlier and greater degree of sexual activity within these relationships. Moreover, these longitudinal studies also clearly establish the fact that the long-term effects of CSA are quite severe, at least for a substantial portion of victims, in that the emergence of multiple, co-morbid psychiatric disorders in early adulthood is causally related to CSA. The firm establishment of these causal and possibly causal relationships does not preclude the contribution of family environment variables and other variables to the overall psychopathology observed at any given point in time, but these prospective studies unequivocally demonstrate that CSA *per se* makes a significant independent causal contribution to this psychopathology. The results are summarized in Table 1.

TABLE 1. Effects of Childhood Sexual and Physical Abuse as Shown by Prospective Studies

Effects	Silverman et al.	Widom et al.	Putnam
Problem Behaviors			
**Suicidal ideation	P, S	P, S	S
*Self-mutilation			S
**Aggressive behavior	P, S	P	
**Alcohol abuse/dependence		P, S	S
* Drug abuse/dependence	P, S		
Relational Behavior			
*Social withdrawal	P, S		
*Social problems	S		
*Hyper-sexualized behavior			S
*Older partners/lack of peer friendships			S
**Antisocial behavior	P, S	P, S	
Psychiatric Symptoms/Disorders			
**Anxiety	P, S		S
**Depression	P, S	?S	S
*Somatization			S
*Dissociation			S
*Attention/thinking problems	P, S		
*ADHD			S
**PTSD	P, S	P, S, N	
**Multiple, co-morbidities	P, S		S
Developmental Effects			
*Self pathology			S
*Affect dysregulation			S
**Developmentally-delayed effects	P, S		S

Key: P = physical abuse
   S = sexual abuse
   N = neglect
   ** shown as causal (replicated)
   * possibly causal (yet-to-be-replicated)

VARIABLES MODERATING THE LONG-TERM EFFECTS OF CSA

Early on, Gartner and Gartner (1988) and Brown (1990) emphasized that even where long term effects are associated with CSA, it is difficult to partial out the specific contribution of the sexually abusive act(s) *per se* and the contribution of other variables to the overall variance of long term damage, such as family pathology (Nash et al., 1993) or parent-child attachment pathology (Gauthier, Stollak, Messe, & Aronoff, 1996). The retrospective studies of the 1970s and 1980s tended to address abuse-specific variables (e.g., duration and frequency of abuse, penetration, force, and victim/perpetrator relationship) possibly mediating the range of potential long term effects, and these studies generally did not address other variables that might contribute to the overall long term effects. The prospective studies of the 1990s have also addressed abuse-specific mediating variables but with a different emphasis. More recently, two variables have emerged as possibly better predictors of long-term effects than duration, frequency, penetration or force. These are betrayal trauma (J. Freyd, 1996) and peritraumatic dissociation. Freyd, for example, has demonstrated that certain types of long term effects are more likely when the perpetrator is a close family member and wherein the child victim is dependent on that person for their ongoing development.

Peritraumatic dissociation pertains to the utilization of a dissociative coping style during a traumatic event or shortly thereafter as a way of adjusting to everyday life after the trauma. The use of peritraumatic dissociation around traumatization is a stronger predictor of the manifestation of chronic PTSD than other variables like duration and severity exposure from months to several decades after the abuse in war veterans (Bremner et al., 1992; Marmar et al., 1994; Shalev et al., 1996; Tichenor et al., 1996) and in civilians exposed to disasters (Cardena & Spiegel, 1993; Holon, 1993; Marmar et al., 1996; Shalev et al., 1996). The presence of dissociation also was a very strong predictor of both the range and severity of the long term effects of CSA (Putnam, 1998). There is some evidence that the use of a dissociative coping style predicts having no thoughts about (Grassian & Holtzen, 1996) or recovering memories about CSA years after the abuse (Sheiman, 1993). The consistent finding across these studies is that a specific personality characteristic, namely the use of a dissociative coping style, as compared to some other way of dealing with the abuse around the time of the abuse, may be the variable best predicting both the range and severity of long term effects. The Putnam (1998) data also suggest, echoing an earlier Kendall-Tackett et al. (1993) conclusion, that dissociation accounts for the "sleeper effects" (i.e., that victim who copes with CSA largely through dissociation are expected *not* to show significant effects at certain developmental periods and that the pattern of effects clearly varies over time within the same individual).

THE LONG TERM EFFECTS OF NEGLECT

For the past two decades, trauma experts have held the view that borderline and multiple personality disorder are *caused* by early physical and sexual abuse because there is a high incidence of abuse in the histories of borderline (e.g., Herman, Perry, & van der Kolk, 1989) and dissociative identity disorder patients (Putnam, 1985). However, research showing an association between childhood abuse and adult psychopathology merely establishes a correlation and does not establish *causality*. The conclusions of at least some of the retrospective reviews on the long-term effects of CSA (e.g., Beitchman et al., 1992) have not supported this conclusion.

Extensive research on parent-child attachment behavior has recently provided a viable alternative explanation for the etiology of borderline and dissociative identity disorder. Live observation of mother-child interactions in the first years of life using the Strange Situation Paradigm (Ainsworth, Blehar, Waters, & Wall, 1978) has led to the general classification of two main types of attachment behavior: secure and insecure attachment. Three main subtypes of insecure attachment behavior have been identified: preoccupied anxious attachment, avoidant attachment, and disorganized attachment. The disorganized, insecure attached child alternates between extreme dependent and avoidant behaviors. Somewhere between 55% and 82% of maltreated children manifest a disorganized attachment style in childhood (Lyons-Ruth & Jacobvitz, 1999), and the presence of a disorganized attachment style in early childhood has been implicated in the long-term development of borderline personality disorder (Solomon & George, 1999).

Liotti (1999) proposed that disorganized, insecure attachment behavior predicts the development of dissociative psychopathology later in life. Using Bowlby's concept of internal working models (i.e., the internal working representations guiding relational behavior), Liotti believes that a normal infant forms "multiple internal working models" for any given attachment relationship. Normally these multiple internal working models become integrated into a unified system over the course of child development in the context of a secure attachment relationship. However, in the context of an insecure, typically disorganized relationship to the primary care-giver, the infant fails to integrate the models and persists with "multiple" and "incoherent" models.

Putnam (1994), emphasizing behaviorally observable states rather than internal representations, makes almost the same point. He believes that multiple, discontinuous and discrete states of consciousness are "the fundamental unit of organization of consciousness and are detectable from the first moments following birth" (p. 278). It is a "normal developmental process that smoothes out the transitions across states of consciousness in normal individuals" (p. 288) so that such discrete states become more difficult to detect in later childhood. However, Liotti (1999) and Main and Morgan (1996) believe that significant parent-child attachment pathology may interfere with smoothing out these discontinuous states. As a result significant switching of states of consciousness may persist in such children over time and later develop into dissociative symptoms or a dissociative disorder.

Consistent with this hypothesis, Main and Morgan (1996) found that a frequent response to "frightened-frightening behavior" of the parent of the disorganized attached infant was "trance-like states." They also reported that certain behaviors enacted in a dissociated state were also commonly observed in disorganized infants. They emphasize, "One of the primary signs of infant disorganized attachment status is behavior resembling the dissociative trance" (p. 124). Hornstein (1996), studying older children with dissociative disorders, found:

> In children, these "switches" between alternate personality states are frequently observable as a rapid age regression, sudden shifts in demeanor or personality characteristics, or marked variations in ability and skill level. The younger the child, the less elaborated these alters are relative to the often extensive elaboration of separate "personality characteristics" seen in the alters of adult MPD patients. (p. 146)

However, apart from the prevalence of shifting and regressive states in childhood, and sometimes rudimentary alter behavior, it is quite clear that the long term effects of disorganized attachment do not appear until later developmental periods. Cole, Alexander and Anderson (1996) describe "a major developmental task . . . the integration of multiple aspects of self, including the integration of positive and negative qualities" beginning with the maturation of concrete operational thinking in the 8 or 9 year-old child (cf. also Harter, 1999). Disorganized attached children with their persistent multiple internal working models and shifting states are at a disadvantage. They may fail at this normal integrative task and are left with significant self pathology, manifested both as a failure to form an integrated self representational system and also as the persistence of discontinuous self states. During the developmental phase of normal adolescent identity consolidation internal conflict between different self states becomes greatly intensified, at least during mid-adolescence (Harter, 1983; 1999) Disorganized attached adolescents may find it especially difficult to master this normal developmental process, once again resulting in the failure to consolidate a unified identity, on the one hand, and the persistence of discontinuous self states, now experienced as intense internal conflict between "parts." Following the disorganized attached individual over these normal developmental periods, it becomes understandable why the full manifestations of dissociative identity disorder, in the form of alter personality behavior that takes executive control, would not be expected to emerge at least until late adolescence or early adulthood, although childhood DID also exists (Hornstein, 1996).

There is a growing body of experimental data that supports this model. Main and her associates have collected videotaped documentation of trance-like states and related dissociated behaviors in a large number of disorganized attached infants (Main & Morgan, 1996). Cole et al. (1996) found that in disorganized attached infants frequency of dissociative states progressively increased over the preschool years. Since documented observations of parent-child attachment behavior using the Strange Situation Paradigm began over 20 years ago, some researchers have used these data as part of a prospective study of the long term effects of infant attachment pathology. While these data are not yet complete, Carlson (1997) has reported some preliminary findings. She found that disorganized attachment in infancy significantly predicted the manifestation of dissociative states in preschool children and in adolescents. All the adolescents found to have significant dissociative experiences in her sample came from the disorganized attachment group (Main & Morgan, 1996).

Thus, the emerging view from these studies is that major dissociative disorders like DID and DDNOS are causally related to infancy disorganized attachment and not necessarily to childhood sexual or physical abuse per se, although abuse may certainly compound the subsequent clinical manifestations in the vulnerable child. Main and Morgan summarize the current view:

> With respect specifically to the dissociative disorders, it would seem reasonable to presume that looking backwards from an existing dissociative disorder in childhood or adulthood, we may find the expected relation to infant disorganized attachment status with mother or another primary care-giver. (p. 131)

Likewise, these data suggest that the etiology of borderline personality disorder is more likely to be found in infant disorganized attachment than in abuse per se (Alexander, 1992). Ross (1996) understands borderline and dissociative identity disorder as related forms of psychopathology along a continuum:

> To my way of thinking, borderline personality disorder is a simple form of DID in which the personality states are less crystalized, less personified, fewer in number, and not separated by the same degree of amnesia. Inversely, DID is a complex variant of borderline personality disorder . . . borderline personality disorder exists on a continuum of increasing severity, with DDNOS having a greater degree of complexity than pure borderline personality and DID the greatest degree of elaboration and crystallization . . . At the present time, the existing data unequivocally re-

fute the commonly advanced proposition that DID patients are "really just borderlines." (p. 13)

Thus, borderline and dissociative identity disorder may each arise from the same infant disorganized attachment pathology. They share a common feature, namely the persistence of contradictory internal representational models and related shifting states of consciousness. The only difference between splitting in the borderline and alter behavior in the DID patient, as Ross suggests, is the number and degree of complexity of internal representations and related shifting states.

THE LEGAL IMPLICATIONS OF DEVELOPMENTALLY-DELAYED AND "SLEEPER" EFFECTS

In false memory malpractice cases, the plaintiff typically argues that the defendant therapist negligently "implanted" false memories of abuse and/or a false dissociative identity disorder through suggestive influence. In order to emphasized that the defendant clinician(s) caused harm through his or her therapy, the plaintiff typically argues that the problems occurring in his or her life were proximately caused by the defendant's therapy. A common strategy used in such cases is to argue that the retractor plaintiff was generally high functioning and/or did not show a wide range of or severe symptoms prior to treatment by the defendants. They in turn imply that the treatment by the defendant clinician *caused* the emergence of symptoms and/or deterioration in functioning. Logically, this argument, of course, fails to consider that the symptoms may have emerged independent of the treatment, their occurrence concurrent with the treatment does not necessarily establish a causal connection to treatment. However, to suggest this causal connection to the jury, the plaintiff's attorney or expert witnesses typically will argue that there was no evidence of significant psychopathology in childhood, adolescence or early adulthood and/or no deterioration in functioning prior to the treatment by the defendant clinician(s).

The data reviewed above strongly suggest that the long-term effects of CSA and neglect show changing patterns at different developmental periods, with sleeper effects common in later childhood and early adolescence and with the full manifestations of psychopathology being developmentally-delayed and not developing until at least early adulthood or later, especially in victims who utilize a dissociative coping style around the time of the abuse. It is reasonably well established that anxiety-related and depressive symptoms and behavioral problems emerge at mid-adolescence and that multiple, co-morbid psychiatric disorders first appear in early adulthood. Clinical observations suggest that major dissociative disorders emerge progressively after that for many patients later diagnosed with DDNOS or DID, with clinical features like time loss and disremembered experiences first emerging and alter behavior sometime later. If these clinical features and then the alter behavior arise concurrent to therapy, it does not logically follow that the defendant's treatment *caused* the DID or DDNOS any more than it would logically follow that a clinician *caused* schizophrenia simply because auditory hallucinations first emerged in the treatment of a young schizophrenic. With schizophrenia it is well established that psychotic symptoms typically first emerge in late adolescence or early adulthood as a developmental observation (Bowers, 1974), irrespective or whether the patient is in treatment. There is no reason to expect that borderline or dissociative identity disorder follows anything other than the developmentally released effects commonly observed in other mental disorders like schizophrenia. Therefore, there is no scientific basis to the argument that a previous higher level of functioning or lack of severe psychopathology in a plaintiff prior to the defendant's treatment somehow establishes that the defendant *caused* harm. In fact, the data reviewed herein suggest the opposite, namely that a higher previous level of functioning and lack of manifestations of severe psychopathology at earlier stages of development is likely to be the consequence of a dissociative coping style, and related delayed or "sleeper" effects. Plaintiff attorneys and expert witnesses fail to include these data on sleeper and other developmentally released effects in their testimony.

CONCLUSION

From the scientific data reviewed here it is clear that pro-false memory expert witness' testimony that there is *no causal connection* between CSA and adult psychopathology is not accurate. It is certainly not "negligent" for a clinician to assume a such causal connection, as some pro-false memory experts have testified, nor is a clinician promoting a "false belief" if operating from the framework that a relationship exists between CSA and adult psychopathology. The evidence from prospective studies do not support the pro-false memory testimony. On the contrary, these data establish a causal relationship between CSA and specific areas of adult psychopathology such as suicidality, antisocial behavior, anxiety, PTSD, and alcoholism, and a possible (yet-to-be-replicated) causal relationship with respect to self-mutilation, depression, somatization, and dissociation. This is not to imply that all adult manifestations of these forms of psychopathology arise from CSA nor that clinicians are justified in reading back from adult symptoms to infer CSA. Yet, a clear causal relationship between

CSA and these forms of adult psychopathology has been established in general. Whether this causal connection applies to a specific case is another question. Nevertheless, pro-false memory testimony that the long term effects of CSA are "general and non-specific" is also not supported by the available scientific data.

Some pro-false memory experts have testified that "other variables" than CSA account for a good portion of the variance of adult problems. This appears accurate. The scientific data on disorganized attachment has helped to clarify that borderline and dissociative identity disorder are more likely to arise from infant-parent disorganized attachment pathology than from abusive acts per se, but since neglect/attachment pathology and subsequent abuse can occur in the same family, the long term effects of attachment-specific forms (like BPO and DID) and abuse-specific forms (like PTSD, depression, somatization, alcoholism) of psychopathology often co-vary in the same adult survivor.

Overall, the most remarkable finding from these prospective data is that severe, multiple, co-morbid psychiatric conditions arise in adulthood for a clinically significant sub-sample of victims of CSA, and that these conditions typically appear in individuals who previously were higher functioning. This finding is exactly the opposite to the impression that pro-false memory expert testimony give to the courts, namely that there is no evidence of specific areas of adult problems causally connected to CSA, and that even where problems may occur, the frequency and severity of damage is low. It appears that such pro-false memory testimony seriously distorts the available retrospective and prospective data and has the potential of misleading the judge and jury.

NOTE

1. Widom et al. failed to specify the prevalence of abuse and neglect in the control subjects. Thus, there is a possibility that some portion of the control subjects were also abused, and if so, the prevalence of causal relationships between childhood abuse/neglect and adult psychopathology reported in the study would be less than the expected rate.

REFERENCES

Ainsworth, M., Blehar, M.C., Waters, E., & Wall, S. (1978). *Patterns of attachment: A psychological study of the strange situation*. Hillsdale, NJ: Erlbaum.

Alexander, P.C. (1992). The application of attachment theory to the study of sexual abuse. *Journal of Consulting and Clinical Psychology, 60*, 185-195.

Beitchman, J.H., Zucker, K.J., Hood, J.E., DaCosta, G.A., Akman, D., & Cassavia, E. (1992). A review of the long-term effects of child sexual abuse. *Child Abuse and Neglect, 16*, 101-118.

Bowers, M.B. (1974). *Retreat from sanity: The structure of emerging psychosis*. New York: Human Sciences Press.

Bremner, J.D., Southwick, S., Brett, E., Fontana, A., Rosenheck, R., & Charney, D.S. (1992). Dissociation and posttraumatic stress disorder in Vietnam combat veterans. *American Journal of Psychiatry, 149*, 328-332.

Brown, D. (1990). The long-term variable effects of incest. In M. Fass & D. Brown (Eds.). *Creative mastery in hypnosis and hypnoanalysis: A Festschrift for Erika Fromm* (pp. 199-229). Hillsdale, NJ: Erlbaum.

Brown, D., Frischholz, E.J., & Scheflin, A.W. (1999). Iatrogenic dissociative identity disorder: An evaluation of the scientific evidence. *Journal of Psychiatry and Law, 27*, 549-637.

Brown, D., Scheflin, A.W., & Hammond, D.C. (1998). *Memory, trauma treatment, and the law*. New York: Norton.

Brown, D., Scheflin, A.W., & Whitfield, C.L. (1999). Recovered memories: The current weight of the evidence in science and in the courts. *Journal of Psychiatry and Law, 27*, 5-156.

Burgess, A.W., Hartman, C.R., & Baker, T. (1995). Memory presentations of childhood sexual abuse. *Journal of Psychosocial Nursing, 33*, 9-16.

Burgus et al. v. Rush-Presbyterian-St. Luke's Medical Center et al. 1996. State of Illinois, Cook County Circuit Court Case # 91-L-08493. Deposition of Bennett G. Braun 12/19/1996.

Cardena, E. & Spiegel, D. (1993). Dissociative reactions to the San Francisco Bay Area earthquake of 1989. *American Journal of Psychiatry, 150*, 474-478.

Carlson, E.A. (1997, April). A prospective longitudinal study of consequences of attachment disorganization/disorientation. Paper presented at the 62nd meeting of the Society for Research in Child Development, Minneapolis, MN.

Carlson v. St. Paul Fire and Marine Insurance Co. et al. State of Wisconsin, La Crosse County Circuit Court Case # 96-CV-321. Deposition of William M. Grove, 6/29/99.

Ceci, S.J. (August, 1994). Cognitive and social factors in children's testimony. Paper presented at the Annual Meeting of the American Psychological Association.

Cole, P.M., Alexander, P.C., & Anderson, C.L. (1996). Dissociation in typical and atypical development: Examples from father-daughter incest survivors. In L.K. Michelson & W.J. Ray (Eds.). *Handbook of dissociation: Theoretical, empirical, and clinical perspectives* (pp. 69-89). New York: Plenum.

Dallam, S.J., Gleaves, D.H., Cepeda-Benito, A., Spiegel, D., & Kraemer, H.C. (2000). The effects of childhood sexual abuse: A critique of Rind, Tromovitch and Bauserman (1998). Unpublished manuscript.

Daly et al. v. Wisconsin Patients Fund et al. State of Wisconsin, Green County Circuit Court Case # 98-CV-17. Deposition testimony of Paul McHugh. Vol. 1, 4/20/99; Vol. 2, 4/21/99. Deposition of Steven Jay Lynn, 3/22/99.

Freyd, J.J. (1996). *Betrayal trauma: The logic of forgetting childhood abuse*. Cambridge: Harvard University Press.

Gartner, A.F. & Gartner, J. (1988). Borderline pathology in post-incest adolescents: Diagnostic and theoretical considerations. *Bulletin of the Menninger Clinic, 52*, 101-113.

Gauthier, L., Stollak, G., Messe, L., & Aronoff, J. (1996). Recall of childhood neglect and physical abuse as differential predictors of current psychological functioning. *Child Abuse and Neglect, 20*, 549-559.

Grassian, S. & Holtzen D. (1996). Memory of sexual abuse by a parish priest. Paper presented at Trauma and Memory: An International Research Conference, University of New Hampshire, Durham, NH, July 26-28.

Greene v. Megellan Health Services et al. State of North Carolina, Mecklenburg County Superior Court, Case # 96-CVS-5235. Deposition of August Piper 10/24/97; Deposition of Richard Ofshe, 5/4/98; Deposition of William M. Grove, 5/4/98.

Harter, S. (1983). Developmental perspectives on the self system. In M.E. Hetherington (Ed.). *Handbook of child psychology: Socialization, personality, and social development* (4th ed., pp. 275-386). New York: Wiley.

Harter, S. (1999). *The construction of self: A developmental perspective.* New York: Guilford.

Herman, J.L., Perry, J.C., & van der Kolk, B.A. (1989). Childhood trauma in borderline personality disorder. *American Journal of Psychiatry, 146*, 490-495.

Hess et al. v. Wausau Insurance et al. State of Wisconsin, Marathon County Circuit Court, Case # 95-CV-138. Deposition testimony of James Irvin Hudson, 8/5/99.

Holon, A. (1993). The North Sea oil rig disaster. In J.P. Wilson & B. Raphael (Eds.). *International handbook of traumatic stress syndromes* (pp. 471-479). New York: Plenum.

Hornstein, N.L. (1996). Dissociative disorders in children and adolescents. In L.K. Michelson & W.J. Ray (Eds.). *Handbook of dissociation: Theoretical, empirical, and clinical perspectives* (pp. 139-159). New York: Plenum.

Jumper, S. (1995). A meta-analysis of the relationship of child sexual abuse to adult psychological adjustment. *Child Abuse and Neglect, 19*, 715-728.

Kendall-Tackett, K.A., Williams, L.M., & Finkelhor, D. (1993). Impact of sexual abuse on children: A review and synthesis of recent empirical studies. *Psychological Bulletin, 113*,164-180.

Liotti, G. (1999). Disorganization of attachment as a model for understanding dissociative psychopathology. In J. Solomon & C. George (Eds.). *Attachment disorganization* (pp. 291-317). New York: Guilford.

Luntz, B.K. & Widom, C.S. (1994). Antisocial personality disorder in abused and neglected children grown up. *American Journal of Psychiatry, 151*, 670-674.

Lyons-Ruth, K. & Jacobvitz, D. (1999). Attachment disorganization: Unresolved loss, relational violence, and lapses in behavioral and attentional strategies. In J. Cassidy & P.R. Shaver (Eds.). *Handbook of attachment: Theory, research, and clinical applications* (pp. 520-554). New York: Guilford.

Main, M. & Morgan, H. (1996). Disorganization and disorientation in infant strange situation behavior: Phenotypic resemblance to dissociative states. In L.K. Michelson & W.J. Ray (Eds.). *Handbook of dissociation: Theoretical, empirical, and clinical perspectives* (pp. 107-138). New York: Plenum.

Marmar, C.R., Weiss, D.S., Metzler, T.J., Ronfeldt, H.M., & Foreman, C. (1996). Stress responses of emergency services personnel to the Loma Prieta earthquake Interstate 880 freeway collapse and control traumatic incidents. *Journal of Traumatic Stress*, *9*, 63-85.

Marmar, C.R., Weiss, D.S., Schenger, W.E., Fairbank, J.A., Jordan, K., Kulka, R.A., & Hough, R.L. (1994). Peritraumatic dissociation and postraumatic stress in male Vietnam theater veterans. *American Journal of Psychiatry*, *151*, 902-907.

Nash, M.R., Hulsey, T.L., Sexton, M.C., Harralson, T.L., & Lambert, W. (1993). Long-term sequelae of childhood sexual abuse: Perceived family environment, psychopathology, and dissociation. *Journal of Consulting and Clinical Psychology*, *61*, 276-283.

Neumann, D.A., Houskamp, B.M., Pollock, V.E., & Briere, J. (1996). The long-term sequelae of childhood sexual abuse in women: A meta-analytic review. *Child Maltreatment*, *1*, 6-16.

Ofshe, R. & Watters, E. (1994). *Making monsters: False memories, psychotherapy, and sexual hysteria.* New York: Charles Scribner's Sons.

Putnam, F.W. (1985). Dissociation as an extreme response to trauma. In R.P. Kluft (ed.). *Childhood antecedents of multiple personality* (pp. 66-97). Washington, DC: American Psychiatric Press.

Putnam, F.W. (1994). The switch process in MPD. In R.M. Klein & B.K. Doane (Eds.) *Psychological concepts and dissociative disorders.* Hillsdale, NJ : Erlbaum.

Putnam, F.W. (1998). Developmental pathways in sexually abused girls. Presented at Psychological Trauma: Maturational Processes and Psychotherapeutic Interventions. Harvard Medical School, Boston, MA, March 20, 1998.

Rind, B. & Tromovitch, P. (1997). A meta-analytic review of findings from national samples on psychological correlates of child sexual abuse. *The Journal of Sex Research*, *34*, 237-255.

Rind, B., Tromovitch, P., & Bauserman, R. (1998). A meta-analytic examination of assumed properties of child sexual abuse using college samples. *Psychological Bulletin*, *124*, 22-53.

Ross, C.A. (1996). History, phenomenology, and epidemiology of dissociation. In L.K. Michelson & W.J. Ray (Eds.). *Handbook of dissociation: Theoretical, empirical, and clinical perspectives* (pp. 3-24). New York: Plenum.

Scheflin, A.W. & Brown, D. (1999). The false litigant syndrome: "Nobody would say that unless it was the truth." *Journal of Psychiatry and Law*, *27*, 649-705.

Shalev, A.Y., Peri, T., Cvaneti, L., & Schreiber, S. (1996). Predictors of PTSD in injured trauma survivors. *American Journal of Psychiatry*, *53*, 219-224.

Sheiman, J.A. (1993). "I've always wondered if something happened to me": Assessment of child sexual abuse survivors with amnesia. *Journal of Child Sexual Abuse*, *2*, 13-21.

Silverman, A.B., Reinherz, H.Z., & Giaconia, R.M. (1996). The long-term sequelae of child and adolescent abuse: A longitudinal community study. *Child Abuse and Neglect*, *20*, 709-723.

Solomon, J. & George, C. (Eds.). (1999). *Attachment disorganization.* New York: Guilford.

State of Rhode Island v. Quattrocchi, Superior Court. Case # P1/92-3759A, on appeal 681 A2d 879 (RI 1996).

Tichenor, V., Marmar, C.R., Weiss, D.S., Metler, T.J., & Ronfeldt, H.M. (1996). The relationship of peritraumatic dissociation and posttraumatic stress: Findings in female Vietnam theater veterans, *Journal of Consulting and Clinical Psychology, 64,* 1054-1059.

Tyo v. Ash et al. State of Texas, Dallas Country, 14th Judicial District Court. Case # DV-98-3843. Deposition of James Hudson, 7/20/99.

Widom, C.S. (1999). Posttraumatic stress disorder in abused and neglected children grown up. *American Journal of Psychiatry, 156,* 1223-1229.

Widom, C.S., Ireland, T.O., & Glynn, P.G. (1995). Alcohol abuse in abused and neglected children followed-up: Are they at increased risk? *Journal of the Study of Alcohol, 56,* 207-217.

Widom, C.S. & Morris, S. (1997). Accuracy of adult recollections of childhood victimization: Part 2. Childhood sexual abuse. *Psychological Assessment, 9,* 34-46.

Widom, C.S. & Shepard, R.L. (1996). Accuracy of adult recollections of childhood victimization: Part 1. Childhood physical abuse. *Psychological Assessment, 8,* 412-421.

Science or Propaganda?
An Examination of Rind,
Tromovitch and Bauserman (1998)

Stephanie J. Dallam

SUMMARY. An article, "A Meta-analytic Examination of Assumed Properties of Child Sexual Abuse Using College Samples," published in the July 1998 edition of the *Psychological Bulletin* resulted in an unprecedented amount of media attention and became the first scientific article to be formally denounced by the United States House of Representatives. The study's authors analyzed the findings of 59 earlier studies on child

Stephanie J. Dallam, RN, MSN, is Researcher for the Leadership Council. Prior to the Leadership Council, she worked in pediatric intensive care for 10 years at University of Missouri Hospital and Clinics, and is a former nursing instructor at the University of Missouri-Columbia. She has written numerous articles on issues related to the welfare of children.

Address correspondence to: Stephanie J. Dallam, 191 Presidential Boulevard, Suite C-132, Bala Cynwyd, PA 19004 (E-mail: sjd.scout@worldnet.att.net).

The author would like to thank David Gleaves, Joyanna Silberg, and Lynn Crook for useful comments and criticism. The author would also like to thank Els Grimminck for help with obtaining and translating Dutch newspaper articles.

[Haworth co-indexing entry note]: "Science or Propaganda? An Examination of Rind, Tromovitch and Bauserman (1998)." Dallam, Stephanie J. Co-published simultaneously in *Journal of Child Sexual Abuse* (The Haworth Maltreatment & Trauma Press, an imprint of The Haworth Press, Inc.) Vol. 9, No. 3/4, 2001, pp. 109-134; and: *Misinformation Concerning Child Sexual Abuse and Adult Survivors* (ed: Charles L. Whitfield, Joyanna Silberg, and Paul Jay Fink) The Haworth Maltreatment & Trauma Press, an imprint of The Haworth Press, Inc., 2001, pp. 109-134. Single or multiple copies of this article are available for a fee from The Haworth Document Delivery Service [1-800-HAWORTH, 9:00 a.m. - 5:00 p.m. (EST). E-mail address: getinfo@haworthpressinc.com].

sexual abuse (CSA) and concluded that mental health researchers have greatly overstated CSA's harmful potential. They recommended that a willing encounter with positive reactions would no longer be considered to be sexual abuse; instead, it would simply be labeled *adult-child sex.* The study's conclusions and recommendations spawned a debate in both the popular and scholarly press. A number of commentators suggested that the study is pedophile propaganda masquerading as science. Others claimed that the authors are victims of a moralistic witch-hunt and that scientific freedom is being threatened. After a careful examination of the evidence, it is concluded that Rind et al. can best be described as an advocacy article that inappropriately uses science in an attempt to legitimize its findings. *[Article copies available for a fee from The Haworth Document Delivery Service: 1-800-HAWORTH. E-mail address: <getinfo@haworthpressinc.com> Website: <http://www.HaworthPress.com> © 2001 by The Haworth Press, Inc. All rights reserved.]*

KEYWORDS. American Psychological Association, child sexual abuse, ethics, pedophilia, sexual politics, scientific freedom, United States Congress

THE CONTROVERSY

A study entitled "A Meta-analytic Examination of Assumed Properties of Child Sexual Abuse Using College Samples," published in the July 1998 edition of the prestigious *Psychological Bulletin,* resulted in enormous social controversy and debate. The study's authors, Rind, Tromovitch and Bauserman, analyzed 59 studies of college students and concluded that mental health researchers have greatly overstated the harmful potential of being abused. Despite finding that students who reported a history of child sexual abuse (CSA) were less well adjusted in 17 of the 18 types of psychological adjustment examined, Rind et al. (1998) suggested that the relationship may be spurious due to the confounding of CSA with family dysfunction. Rind et al. also reported that "men reacted much less negatively than women" (p. 22) and that "consent" was an important moderator of adjustment in males. They later summarized their findings, stating: "We showed that for boys in nonclinical populations, willing relations are generally experienced positively or neutrally and are not associated with maladjustment" (Rind, Bauserman, & Tromovitch, 1999, p. 2185). Rind et al. (1998) went on to suggest that when labeling events that have "heretofore been defined sociolegally as CSA," scientists should focus on the young person's perception of the experience: A willing encounter with positive reactions would no longer be considered to be sexual abuse; instead, it would "be labeled simply *adult-child sex*" (p. 46).

Not surprisingly, the study was immediately embraced by pedophile organizations. The North American Man/Boy Love Association (NAMBLA), a political and educational organization that advocates for the decriminalization of "consensual" pedophilic relationships, stated that the study confirmed that "the current war on boy-lovers has no basis in science." NAMBLA also publicly thanked the American Psychological Association (APA) for having the courage to publish the paper (Saunders, 1999).

The study did not come to the general public's attention until almost nine months after its publication. Alerted by a listener, popular radio talk-show host Dr. Laura Schlessinger discussed the study's findings on her show. On March 22, 1999, she told her 18 million listeners that she feared that the study "could be used to normalize pedophilia, to change the legal system" (Duin, 1999). Soon after Schlessinger aired her concerns, a number of other public commentators severely criticized the study and the APA's role in printing it. For example, in an article titled "Lolita Nation," newspaper columnist Debra Saunders (1999) stated that "the APA showed appalling judgment in printing this pedophilia propaganda."

Political leaders were also disturbed by the study's conclusions. Dr. Tom Coburn (R-Okla.) stated:

> As a practicing physician trained in science, I am shocked that the Psychological Association would publish a study that is clearly pedophilia propaganda masquerading as science. . . . The APA has brought itself and the entire psychological profession in disrepute by failing to filter junk science from a scientific journal. (Myers, 1999, p. 11)

In Alaska, Rep. Fred Dyson introduced a resolution (HJR 36)[1] calling on the APA to repudiate the study. The resolution was unanimously passed on April 30, 1999 and became a model for similar efforts in California, Delaware, Louisiana, Pennsylvania, Illinois, and the U.S. Congress.

Negative publicity resulted in a number of press releases and statements by APA leaders. On March 23, 1999, APA released a statement that reaffirmed its strong historical stand against CSA and stated that "publication of the findings of a research project within an APA journal is in no way an endorsement of a finding by the Association" (American Psychological Association, 1999). However, on May 14, 1999, APA Chief Executive Officer Raymond D. Fowler, PhD, defended the study on national television (MSNBC), stating: "It isn't a bad study, it's been peer-reviewed . . . it's a good study." On May 25, 1999, Fowler defended the study again in a letter emailed to APA division officers. Fowler said that the study passed a rigorous peer review process "and has, since the controversy, been reviewed again by an expert in statistical analysis who affirmed that it meets current standards and that the methodology, which is widely used by the National Institutes of Health (NIH) to develop guidelines, is sound." Suggesting that politicians and members of the media were misrepresenting the study's findings to further their political agenda, Fowler assured the officers that the APA was "working hard to try to correct the record with those politicians and members of the media who care about the facts."

The study was also criticized by several scientific organizations. On May 24, 1999, the Leadership Council on Mental Health, Justice and the Media, whose mission includes ensuring that the "the public receives accurate information about mental health issues" (Leadership Council, March 1999) issued a press release noting that Rind et al. improperly generalized from studies of predominantly noncontact experiences during adolescence in formulating some of their conclusions about the relative harmlessness of sex between adults and children. A few days later (May 27, 1999), Steven M. Mirin, MD, Medical Director of the American Psychiatric Association, expressed the Psychiatric Association's disagreement "with the implications of the authors' conclusions." Mirin stated, "From a psychological perspective, sex between adult and child is always abusive and exploitative because the adult always holds the power in the relationship. . . . Academic hair-splitting over whether the act should be considered adult-child sex or child sexual abuse . . . is not in the public interest and obfuscates the moral issues involved" ("Psychiatric Association Criticizes," 1999).

Apparently, the continued negative public reaction led Fowler to reconsider his support of the study. On June 9, 1999, Fowler hand-carried a letter to Majority Whip Tom DeLay (R-Tex) in which he admitted that the APA failed to "evaluate the article based on its potential for misinforming the public policy process." Fowler also acknowledged that "some of the language in the article when examined from a public policy perspective is inflammatory" and includes opinions "inconsistent" with APA's policy on child protection issues. Fowler pledged that in the future his organization would be more cognizant of the potential for publications to misinform the public on important issues. Fowler also announced that for the first time in its 107-year history of publishing it has sought independent expert evaluation of the scientific quality of an article. The next day, Fowler (June 10, 1999) announced that the American Association for the Advancement of Science (AAAS) had been asked to do the review, "because its credibility is unquestioned."

In July 1999, the meta-analysis by Rind et al. became the first scientific study to be formally denounced by the United States Congress. The House of Representatives and Senate both unanimously passed a resolution which rejected "the conclusions of a recent article published in the *Psychological Bulletin*, a journal of the American Psychological Association, that suggests that sexual relationships between adults and children might be positive for children." The resolution explained that "elected officials have a duty to inform and counter actions they consider damaging to children, parents, families, and society" (House Con. Res. 107).[2]

In response to criticism of their study, Rind, Tromovitch and Bauserman released a number of statements vigorously defending their results and conclusions. They claimed that their research "brought methodological rigor into an area that needed this" (Rind, Tromovitch, & Bauserman, November 6, 1999), and suggested that they had "an ethical duty" to report their findings (Rind, Tromovitch, & Bauserman, May 12, 1999). Claiming to be victims of political persecution, the authors characterized their critics as "religious and moralistic zealots" (e.g., Rind et al., November 6, 1999). A flyer for a continuing education workshop about the controversy offered by Rind and Carol Tavris stated:

> The enemies of Galileo and Darwin, the enemies of the natural science model are alive and well. . . . Not only are the "offending" data dismissed or trivialized, but the messengers can themselves be pressured into silence, recantation, or more simply be vilified by organs of academe and government alike. ("When Politics Clashes with Science," 2000)[3]

Concerned that the denouncement by Congress posed a threat to scientific freedom, a number of psychologists rushed to the study's defense (e.g., Berry, 2000; Tavris, 1999; Woll, 1999). For example, Stanley Woll (July 26, 1999), Professor of Psychology at California State-Fullerton, suggested that Rind et al. were victims of a "McCarthyesque witch hunt" which represented "a dangerous assault on the process of scientific research in general."

The AAAS's Committee of Scientific Freedom and Responsibility ultimately declined APA's request for a review of the study, saying they saw "no reason to second-guess the process of peer review used by the APA journal in its decision to publish the article in question" (McCarty, 1999, p. 2). AAAS also reported that they "saw no clear evidence of improper application of methodology or other questionable practices on the part of the article's authors" (p. 3). However, they added that, "if there were such problems, uncovering them would be the task of those reviewing it prior to publication or to readers of the published article" (p. 3). AAAS further noted, "The fact that the Committee has chosen not to proceed with an evaluation of the article in the *Psychological Bulletin* should not be seen either as endorsement or criticism of it" (p. 3). Despite the disclaimer, Rind and Tromovitch viewed the AAAS's decision as a vindication of their work. Tromovitch stated: "Their comments indicate to me that they consider our work to be up to par" (Burling, 1999).

The APA indicated that it had no plans to ask any other organization to review the study. In early December 1999, Ray Fowler went on a protracted sick leave citing stress. The debate over the study's merit remained unresolved. The purpose of the present article is to examine whether Rind et al. (1998) is best characterized as unpopular science or pedophile propaganda.

THE SCIENTIFIC EVIDENCE

When anybody makes a claim that is surprising or seems to be unlikely, science demands evidence. Thus, the first step in evaluating the conflicting views of the merit of Rind et al.'s (1998) work is to evaluate whether their findings are supported by appropriate data. Some have suggested that the results of the study by Rind et al. must be correct because the study passed peer review[4]; however, it is important to note that passing peer review is no guarantee that a study's results are correct. Without access to the original data, peer reviewers are often unable to determine the validity of a study's results (Whitely, Rennie & Hafner, 1994). There are really only two ways to determine whether the results of a study are valid: (1) replication of the study's findings using equal or higher quality methods, and (2) critical examination of the investigators' data and methodology.

Comparisons with Studies Using Equal or Superior Methodology

A review of the empirical literature examining the long-term consequences of CSA call into question the validity of many of Rind et al.'s (1998) key findings and conclusions. For example, Rind et al.'s conclusion about the relative harmlessness of CSA conflicts with the findings of three other meta-analyses of the relationship between CSA and maladjustment (e.g., Jumper, 1995; Neuman, Houskamp, Pollock, & Briere, 1996; Paolucci, Genuis, & Violato, 2001). In addition, little support can be found for their suggestion that the significant relationship found between CSA and maladjustment was likely spurious due to confounding between sexual abuse and family environment. Table 1 summarizes the results of large scale representative studies, prospective studies, and co-twin studies using nonclinical samples. These studies, which are considered the gold standard in terms of validity and reliability, reported significant associations between reporting CSA and a wide variety of mental, physical, and behavioral problems which persist even after controlling for family dysfunction.

TABLE 1. Results of Well-Designed Nonclinical Studies Which Controlled for Family Dysfunction

Study	Method	Results
Boney-McCoy & Finkelhor (1995)	Random, nationally representative probability sample of 2,000 youths aged 10-16 years	After controlling for family dysfunction, significant associations were found between CSA and increased levels of PTSD symptoms and school difficulties. Abused boys reported significantly more sadness than other children.
Boney-McCoy & Finkelhor (1996)	Longitudinal: Reinterviewed 1995 sample 15 months later	Sexual abuse during the 15-month interim was associated with PTSD-related symptoms and depression not present prior to the assault.
Dinwiddie et al. (2000)	Co-twin: Examined twins discordant for CSA drawn from 5,995 Australian male and female twins	The twin reporting CSA consistently displayed more psychopathology then their nonabused co-twin. However, only a single outcome reached statistical significance–the association between CSA and suicidal ideation in males.
Fergusson et al. (1996)	Prospective study of a birth cohort of 1,019 male and female youths	After controlling for family dysfunction, significant associations were found between CSA and higher rates of major depression, anxiety disorder, conduct disorder, substance use disorder, and suicidal behavior. Those whose abuse involved intercourse had the highest risk of disorder.
Fleming et al. (1999)	Subsample of 710 women selected from a larger study involving women randomly selected from electoral rolls in Australia	After controlling for family dysfunction, significant associations were found between CSA and higher reports of domestic violence, rape, sexual problems, mental health problems, low self-esteem, and problems with intimate relationships. CSA involving intercourse was associated with the highest risk of disorder.
Johnson et al. (1999)	Prospective study of a representative community sample of 639 youths	After controlling for family dysfunction, significant associations were found between CSA and increased rates of personality disorders during early adulthood.
Kendler et al. (2000)	Co-twin: Examined twins discordant for CSA drawn from a sample of 1,411 adult female twins	The twin reporting CSA was consistently at higher risk for lifetime psychiatric and substance use disorders compared to their nonabused co-twin with odds ratios generally increasing with the severity of the abuse.
Mullen et al. (1993)	Stratified, random community sample of 1,376 adult women in New Zealand	After controlling for family dysfunction, significant associations were found between CSA and higher levels of psychopathology, along with higher rates of substance abuse and suicidal behavior. A dose-response relationship was found with those suffering the most severe forms of abuse having the greatest level of psychopathology.
Stein et al. (1988)	Random community sample of 3,132 male and female adults	After controlling for family dysfunction, significant associations were found between CSA and meeting diagnostic criteria for at least one lifetime psychiatric disorder, especially substance abuse disorders, major depression, phobia, panic disorder, and antisocial personality.

Rind et al.'s (1998) finding that men react less negatively to CSA than women is another result that has not been supported by a large scale of nonclinical populations. In this instance, Rind et al.'s conclusions are limited by the fact that studies of college students have almost exclusively examined internalizing behaviors such as depression, anxiety, or eating disorders.

Studies which include measures of externalizing behaviors have demonstrated that the aftermath for abused boys may be worse or more complex for boys than for abused girls. For instance, Chandy, Blum and Resnick (1996) studied over 3,000 high school students. They found that sexually abused male adolescents were at higher risk for poor school performance, delinquent activities, and sexual risk taking. Sexually abused female adolescents, on the other hand, showed higher risk for suicidal ideation and behavior as well as disordered eating. Similar findings were reported by Garnefski and Arends (1998) who studied a large representative community sample of adolescents. They reported that the experience of sexual abuse carried far more negative consequences for boys than for girls regarding the use of alcohol, aggressive/criminal behavior, use of drugs, and the amount of truancy, as well as regarding suicidal thoughts and behavior. In fact, a burgeoning literature suggests that childhood abuse in males may precipitate a cycle of violence that is later manifested in various forms of adult aggression, including rape (e.g., Merrill, Thomsen, Gold, & Milner, 2001).

Critical Reviews of Rind et al. (1998)

Critical reviews of Rind et al. (1998) have raised serious concerns with the study's design, statistical analyses, and conclusions. Some of the major criticisms are summarized below (also see Whittenburg et al. in this volume).

Sample bias. A number of critics have noted that by restricting their analysis to convenience samples of college students, Rind et al. introduced a systematic bias in favor of their conclusion. Spiegel (2000) noted, "By design, Rind et al. ignored those so mired in drug abuse, criminal activity, prostitution, or financial and educational hardship, that they could not get it to college" (p. 64). Dallam et al. (in press) raised similar concerns and cited research showing a strong relationship between CSA and academic difficulties or dropping out of high school. Dallam et al. also demonstrated that Rind et al.'s contention that "the college data were completely consistent with data from national samples" (p. 22) was erroneous and was based on the misleading presentation of data from selected studies.

Duncan (2000) tested Rind et al.'s (1998) contention that studies of CSA in college populations should be considered generalizable to the population as a whole. She compared the semester-by-semester enrollment of college students with and without histories of abuse and found that students with a history of CSA were more likely than their nonabused peers to display symptoms of post-traumatic stress and to prematurely drop out of college, especially after only attending one semester. Duncan concluded that it was likely that investigators using college samples see "only the healthiest of survivors" (p. 987).

Measurement problems. Several critical reviews faulted Rind et al. for not standardizing their treatment of either their independent or dependent variables. For instance, Dallam et al. (in press) noted that Rind et al. uncritically combined data from studies of CSA with data from studies looking at other phenomena including consensual peer experiences, sexual experiences that occurred during adulthood, and homosexual approaches during adolescence.

Holmes and Slap (1999) noted that Rind et al. uncritically combined psychological outcomes measured by different instruments with varying validity, relevance, and different interval scaling and cut points. After reviewing the Rind et al study, Holmes and Slap concluded that "meta-analysis is not appropriate when methodological rigor, let alone the question asked, is so varied" (p. 2186).

Statistical analyses. Dallam et al. (in press) demonstrated numerous problems with Rind et al.'s statistical methods. For example, they noted that Rind et al. eliminated from analysis several studies of incest which showed the highest degree of harm, while including studies that did not even purport to examine CSA. Dallam et al. also documented numerous instances in which Rind et al. misreported or miscoded the original data from the studies they analyzed. Moreover, these errors were consistently in the direction of CSA being portrayed as less harmful than the findings of the original study suggested.

More importantly, Dallam et al. demonstrated that many of the findings that Rind et al. reported as being significant were actually statistical artifacts caused by their failure to correct for base rate differences in the rates of CSA in male and female samples. In this case, lower base rates of CSA in male samples caused effects sizes estimates for males to be attenuated and created the illusion that males were less harmed by CSA. After correcting for base-rate attenuation, Dallam et al. demonstrated that effect sizes for male and female samples were nearly identical.[5] In other words, contrary to Rind et al.'s claims, males were not less affected by their abuse.

Dallam et al. also found serious problems with Rind et al.'s moderator analysis of "consent" by gender. Based on their analysis, Rind, Bauserman and Tromovitch (1999) reported that with abused boys "willing relations . . . are not associated with maladjustment" (p. 2185). Dallam et al. reviewed the analysis and found that Rind et al. claimed to have measured a variable (i.e., willingness) that was not examined in the original studies. To get around this fact, Rind et al. *assumed* that detectable amounts of "willing" sexual experiences were included in any study that did not explicitly state that the student should report *only* unwanted experiences. Dallam et al. examined the original studies and replicated the moderator analysis. They found no evidence to support Rind et al.'s assumption that the studies in the "consent" group contained significant amounts of willing CSA. Moreover, after correcting for miscalculated effect sizes and base rate attenuation, Dallam et al. found no significant effects for male gender and "level of consent."

EVIDENCE FOR ADVOCACY

Rind, Tromovitch and Bauserman's attitudes toward sexual relationships between adults and children are important to evaluate for several reasons. First, the authors have claimed to be objective scientists who have suffered political persecution for publishing unpopular findings (e.g., Rind et al., November 6, 1999). Also, supporters of the study have claimed that critics are trying to suppress their article's important findings by unfairly tying the authors to pedophile groups (e.g., Tavris, 1999). To evaluate the validity of these claims, it is necessary to determine whether there is substance to the concerns raised by those who believe that Rind et al.'s paper is better characterized as propaganda than science.

Second, as Rind et al. themselves noted, research findings can be skewed by an investigator's personal biases. Rind et al. (1998) stated, "Reviewers who are convinced that CSA is a major cause of adult psychopathology may fall prey to confirmation bias by noting and describing study findings indicating harmful effects but ignoring or paying less attention to findings indicating nonnegative outcomes" (p. 24). The fact that Rind et al.'s results differed from those of most other researchers who have studied CSA raises the possibility that Rind et al. may have exhibited a confirmatory bias in the opposite direction (i.e., they ignored or downplayed findings indicating harmful effects).

Finally, critical reviews of Rind et al.'s paper have invariably found evidence suggestive of bias. For example, after reviewing the meta-analysis, Ondersma, Chaffin and Berliner (1999) stated:

> We believe that the primary flaw in the Rind et al. manuscript is not the science that it used, but its use of science. Through emphasis on certain key points and the omission of others, this article could be interpreted as using science to inappropriately question key moral and legal assumptions about CSA. (p. 3)

Erikson (2000) found evidence of bias in the fact that when the meta-analysis indicated evidence of harm, Rind et al. immediately looked for an alternative explanation. Conversely, as Dallam et al. reported, when the findings went in the direction of the authors' personal beliefs (e.g., as in their analysis of "consent"), Rind et al. ignored confounding variables and measurement problems. Moreover, as previously noted, Dallam et al. (in press) found most errors in Rind et al.'s paper to be in the direction of portraying CSA being less harmful than the original study's findings suggested.

By itself, however, evidence for bias does not support the inferential leap that Rind et al.'s paper should be considered pedophile advocacy. To make this determination, one must first clarify what it is that people supportive of pedophilia are advocating.

THE GOALS OF PEDOPHILE ADVOCATES

Brief History of the Modern Pedophile Movement

The origins of the modern pedophilia movement can be traced to the social changes that occurred during the 1960s and '70s. Encouraged by the increased tolerance for minorities and alternative lifestyles, underground pedophile groups began to go public in an effort to garner greater social acceptance (Schuijer, 1990). Just as pedophiles began to make political headway, the rise of feminism led to greater public awareness about the negative consequences of sexual abuse. Recognizing the futility of seeking decriminalization of pedophilia at a time when abuse victims were speaking out, pedophile groups changed their focus. By the early 1970s, pedophile groups began to portray themselves as champions of children's sexual emancipation (see Schuijer, 1990, p. 219). They conceded that sexual abuse was wrong but questioned whether all sexual contact between adults and children should be regarded as abusive. Claiming that children often initiated and benefited from sexual relationships with adults, pedophile groups advocated for the decriminalization of "consensual" relationships.

Although no formal "agenda" has been published by organizations supporting pedophilia, the overall goals of pedophiles can be gleaned from a number of sources. Sociologist Mary DeYoung (1989), for example, reviewed the literature that pedophile organizations such as NAMBLA published for public dissemination. She found that pedophiles sought to make their unpopular philosophy more palatable to the public by using four main techniques to justify and normalize their philosophy and practices (see Table 2).

Strategies for normalizing pedophilia have also been discussed in articles and books written by pedophile advocates and apologists. These strategies are summarized in Table 3 and briefly reviewed below. Because psychology is one of the primary sites for determining "normalcy" in our culture, changing the views of mental health professionals has been recognized as an important predecessor of the lifting of legal restrictions on deviant sexual behaviors (e.g., Mirkin, 1999, p. 10).

TABLE 2. How Pedophile Groups Justify Having Sex with Children

Techniques of Justification	Description
1. Denial of injury	The use of anecdotal accounts of children who appear to enjoy sex with adults to demonstrate the benefits and advantages of such relationships to children. Culpability for any harm that occurs to an abused child is displaced onto the reactions of others, such as the child's parents, and the criminal justice and mental health systems.
2. Condemnation of the condemners	Those who condemn sex between adults and child are portrayed as engaging in even more victimizing or exploitative acts than those for which pedophiles are accused.
3. Appeal to higher loyalties	The assertion that they serve the interests of a higher principle: the liberation of children from the repressive bonds of society. Also, the attempt to align with other, less stigmatized, organizations such as the woman's movement or the gay rights movement.
4. Denial of the victim	The conceptual transformation of children from victims of adult sexual behavior into willing partners.

Adapted from: De Young, M. (1989). The world according to NAMBLA: Accounting for deviance. *Journal of Sociology & Social Welfare, 16,* 111-126.

Strategies of Normalization

1. The adoption of value-neutral terminology. One of the fundamental steps that has been identified as necessary to change how society views pedophilia is to change the language used to describe pedophilic relationships. Harris Mirkin (1999), Associate Professor of Political Science at the University of Missouri-Kansas City, suggested that before pedophiles can advance socially, "neutral labels" must replace "words like 'child molestation,' and 'child abuse' " (p. 12). A similar point was made by Gilbert Herdt, an anthropologist who has studied sex between adults and children in other cultures. Joseph Geraci, chief editor of *Paidika: The Journal of Paedophila,* asked Herdt, "Is there a social acceptance process that paedophiles can engage in and nurture to improve their situation? A normalization process?" Herdt responded, "One of the steps would be the deconstruction of the language and categories being used. Buried in them are very, very old prejudices, fears and moral approbations" (Geraci, 1994, p. 17). According to Herdt, pedophile advocates need to replace "dull and reductionistic" terms like *pedophilia* and *abuse* when discussing sex between "a person who has not achieved adulthood and one who has" (p. 15). Moreover, words like "child" or "childhood" should be "resisted at all costs":

> . . . as soon as the category "child" is invoked, everything is completely slanted and biased. It is suddenly no longer possible to have a rational

discourse. Indeed, you could say that the category "child" is a rhetorical device for inflaming what is really an irrational set of attitudes. We would certainly have to use some other term. As I have said what we are discussing is desire, and the desire is for a person who is not yet an adult. (p. 14)

The importance of terminology was also discussed in a special double issue of the *Journal of Homosexuality* devoted to "Male Intergenerational Intimacy."[6] The special issue was guest edited by three members of the editorial board of *Paidika: The Journal of Paedophila*. In their introduction, they noted that "the choice of labels is never without political grounds or consequences" (Sandfort, Brongersma, & van Naerssen, 1990, p. 8). Because of its negative connotations, they avoided the term *pedophilia,* preferring to use words such as *man/boy love* and *intergenerational intimacy*. They explained that they chose the term *man/boy love* as it stresses the "unproblematic affectional side of the phenomenon," and the term *intergenerational intimacy* was used because "it gives man-boy contacts a less dangerous outlook" (pp. 7-8).

2. *Redefining the term "child sexual abuse."* Another recurring theme among those seeking to normalize pedophilia is the need to redefine or restrict the usage of the term *child sexual abuse*. For example, Gerald Jones (1990), an Affiliated Scholar in the Institute for the Study of Women and Men in Society at the University of Southern California, suggested that "intergenerational intimacy" should not be considered synonymous with child sexual abuse: "The crucial difference has to do with mutuality and control" (p. 278). Jones suggested, "Intergenerational attraction on the part of some adults could constitute a lifestyle 'orientation,' rather than a pathological maladjustment" (p. 288). However, before society could come to recognize the potential benefits of

TABLE 3. Strategies for Normalizing Pedophilia

---

1. The use of value-neutral terminology when describing "intergenerational" sexual relationships. Also, avoiding terms that have negative connotations (including terms such as "pedophile" or "pedophilia"), and avoiding terms which call attention to the fact that the sexual "partner" is a child.

2. Doing away with the term *child sexual abuse* or restricting its use to behavior that is demonstrably harmful.

3. Promoting the idea that children can consent to sex with adults.

4. Questioning the assumption that sex with adults is harmful to children.

   a. Blaming harm on those who intervene after CSA is discovered or disclosed.

   b. Publishing work showing positive or neutral effects.

   c. Proponents of man-boy love: Promoting the idea that studies showing harmful results are not applicable to boys; suggesting that boys are able to handle sex with adults at an earlier age than girls.

5. Promoting the "objective" study of sex between adults and children free of moral and ethical considerations.

---

intergenerational intimacy (p. 283), the use of the term *child sexual abuse* must first be limited to behavior meeting a strict definition of abuse (i.e., behavior that is demonstrably harmful).

3. *Promoting the idea that children can consent to sex with adults.* The reconceptualization of children as willing sexual "partners" along with the de-criminalization of "consensual" sexual relations is perhaps the key change sought by pedophile advocates. For example, on their website NAMBLA advocates for the decriminalization of "consensual, loving" pedophilic relationships, but "condemns sexual abuse and all forms of coercion" (http://www.nambla.de/welcome.htm).

To counter arguments that children cannot give informed consent, some have suggested that with children, consent should be understood as the simple willingness that an event should take place (e.g., Graupner, 1999, p. 31). Others have suggested that a young child's ability to vocalize preferences for toys or articles of clothing is sufficient evidence that they are capable of providing informed consent. For example, in his book *Understanding Loved Boys and Boylovers,* David L. Riegel (2000) stated, "Anyone who holds to the idea that a young boy cannot give or withhold informed consent has never taken such a boy shopping for new sneakers" (p. 38).

4. *Questioning the assumption of harm.* One of the greatest barriers to the decriminalization of sex between adults and children are the hundreds of studies demonstrating a consistent association between CSA and negative outcomes. Advocates of pedophilia have attempted to deal with this problem in a variety of ways. For example, they often blame any negative outcomes on parents or professionals who seek to prevent or intervene in the abuse.

Riegel (2000), for instance, asserted: "The acts themselves harm no one, the emotional and psychological harm comes from the 'after the fact' interference, counseling, therapy, etc., that attempt to artificially create a 'victim' and a 'perpetrator' where neither exists" (p. 21). Similar arguments are made by SafeHaven Foundation, an organization for "responsible boylovers." On their website, they wrote, "The child abuse industry . . . takes a boy who has enjoyed pleasurable and completely consensual sexual experiences with another boy or man, and traumatizes him in an attempt to convince him that what he did was 'wrong.' " They also suggested that "many of the supposed traumas elicited by psychotherapy turn out to be nothing more than the result of the False Memory Syndrome" (SafeHaven Foundation, 2001).[7]

Another way that pedophile advocates seek to counter negative research findings is through the publication of positive ones. For example, *Paidika* advisor Theo Sandfort (1987) joined with members of the Dutch National Pedophile Workshops and studied sexual "partners" referred by the organization's members. The pedophiles helped fund the study and boys provided glowing reports of the benefits they received from the relationships. More recently, a brief article titled "A New Approach to the Societal Emancipation of Affectionate Relationships between Minors and Adults," was published in the October 1997 IPCE online newsletter. The author, Titus Rivas (1997), stated, "It is necessary to find adults who as a child or adolescent experienced a positive relationship with an adult, and who after having grown up, still maintain that they have not suffered because of that relationship on a long term basis, but rather keep cherishing the memory of it." He solicits positive stories and cautions that it would be best if the referred adults were not now pedophiles. Rivas says that upon its publication, the report can be used as "a tool of emancipation."

One of the ways that advocates of "man-boy love" deal with negative research findings is by claiming that they are not applicable to boys. *Paidika* board member Dr. Edward Brongersma[8] (1990), for example, has suggested that research showing CSA to be harmful is unreliable because results involving female samples have been improperly generalized to males. According to Brongersma, "Conclusions based on studying sex between men and girls should never be applied to sex between man and boys" (p. 152). Contending that boys are better equipped to handle sex at an earlier age, in his book *Loving Boys: A Multidisciplinary Study of Sexual Relations Between Adult and Minor Males* (Vol. 1), Brongersma (1986) asserted, "A boy is mature for lust, for hedonistic sex, from his birth on; sex as an expression of love becomes a possibility from about five years of age" (p. 40).

5. *Promoting "objective" research.* Those who advocate normalizing pedophilia often argue that investigations of CSA have been distorted by researchers' biases against sex between adults and children (e.g., Brongersma, 1990). As such, they frequently call for a less emotional and more "objective" and scientific approach to the subject (e.g., Geraci, 1994, p. 17; Jones, 1990). A study that is frequently cited as embodying the type of "objective" research needed is Sandfort's (1987) study of boys' relationships with pedophiles. Although the study is considered the epitome of objectivity by advocates of intergenerational sexual relationships (e.g., Brongersma, 1990, p. 168; Jones, 1990, p. 286), critics have pointed to strong evidence which suggests that the study was "politically motivated to 'reform' legislation" (Mrazek, 1990, p. 318). Ethical concerns have also been expressed over the apparent lack of human subject safeguards and the fact that the boys were studied without the permission of their parents, many of whom were unaware of their child's (often illegal) relationship with the pedophile (Mrazek, 1990, pp. 317-18).

THE WORK OF RIND, TROMOVITCH AND BAUSERMAN

A review of Rind, Tromovitch and Bauserman's work reveals numerous intersections with pedophile publications or organizations, along with frequent instances in which they have promoted the same changes advocated by those seeking to normalize pedophilia.

Intersections with Advocacy Groups

Both Bauserman and Rind have published in *Paidika: The Journal of Paedophilia,* a scholarly journal published by pedophiles in the Netherlands. The journal's purpose was made explicit in its first issue: "Through publication of scholarly studies, thoroughly documented and carefully reasoned, we intend to demonstrate that paedophilia has been, and remains, a legitimate and productive part of the totality of human experience." ("*Paidika*: Statement of Purpose," pp. 2-3).[9]

Bauserman's (1989) article in *Paidika* reviewed the historical and cross cultural literature on sex between men and boys, and reported that "man-boy" relationships have traditionally provided boys with positive male role models and teachers. Bauserman also contributed an article to the *Journal of Homosexuality's* special double issue on "Male Intergenerational Intimacy" that was edited by members of *Paidika's* editorial board. Bauserman's (1990) article consisted of a spirited defense of Sandfort's research on boys' relationships with pedophiles. Rind's (1995a) contribution to *Paidika* was a favorable book review of *First Do No Harm: The Sexual Abuse Industry,* a book which promotes the notion of "false memories" being a major problem while at the same time arguing that sexual abuse is not necessarily harmful to children and that the age of sexual consent should be removed from the statute books (Goodyear-Smith, 1993). Rind (1995a) described Goodyear-Smith's book as "excellent" and argued that CSA is "a social problem much less serious in size and scope than an unwitting public has been led to believe" (p. 83).

After the publication of their meta-analysis in *Psychological Bulletin,* Rind, Tromovitch and Bauserman were the keynote speakers for an advocacy conference in the Netherlands. According to an announcement in the *International Pedophile and Child Emancipation (IPCE) Newsletter,*[10] the conference was being convened "expressly to throw light on the more positive side" of "adult-nonadult sexual contacts" ("The Other Side of the Coin," September 1998). The conference was hosted by the Foundation for Church Social Work in Paulus Kerk, Rotterdam, an organization headed by outspoken pedophile advocate Rev. Hans Visser.[11] An overview of the conference appeared in an article in the local Rotterdam newspaper titled "Dominee Visser Pleit voor het

Aanvaarden van Pedofilie" [Reverend Visser Pleads for the Acceptance of Pedophilia] ("Dominee Visser," December 18, 1998). The conference also featured talks by two members of *Paidika's* editorial board, Drs. Gert Hekma and Alex van Naerssen.

In their keynote address, Rind, Bauserman and Tromovitch (December 18, 1998) claimed that their research demonstrated that little if any harm can be attributed to CSA and blamed the erroneous assumption that CSA causes intense and pervasive harm on child abuse "hysteria."[12] After suggesting that the term "child sexual abuse" should be reserved for instances when "early sexual episodes are unwanted and experienced negatively," the authors concluded their presentation with the following disclaimer: "We want to emphasize that our presentation should not be taken to advocate behaviors *labeled* [italics added] as CSA." The full text of Rind et al.'s keynote address was reprinted in the *International Pedophile and Child Emancipation Newsletter* (Number E 4, January 1999) and is available online.[13]

The Author's Views and Positions

A review of Rind, Tromovitch and Bauserman's professional work shows that, at some time or another, one or more of the authors have followed and/or recommended almost every action outlined in Table 3. For example, Rind et al. (1998) recommended that professionals use value neutral terminology when discussing "willing" sex between adults and children. Rind and Bauserman expressed even stronger views in prior writings. In 1993, they conducted research to determine how terminology used to describe the relationships between and adult male and a boy affected college students' perceptions of sex between adults and children. They concluded that the indiscriminate use of terms suggesting victimization and harm when describing "adult-nonadult sexual relationships" can create a biased perception; "researchers can give their readers the impression that . . . these relationships are abusive even when the evidence . . . points to neutral or even positive outcomes" (Rind & Bauserman, 1993, p. 266). In another paper, Rind (1995b) reviewed human sexuality textbooks' coverage of the "psychological correlates of adult-nonadult sex" (i.e., CSA). Rind objected to the use of terms such as *victims, survivors, offenders,* and *perpetrators,* as these terms confuse "harm done to children or adolescents with violations of social norms" (p. 219).

In their 1998 paper, Rind et al. recommended restricting the usage of the term *child sexual abuse* to sexual episodes that are unwanted or experienced negatively. Such a recommendation appears to imply that Rind et al. believe that sex between adults and children can be noncoercive and that children can consent to sexual contact with adults.[14] It should also be remembered that this reconceptualization was first proposed by Jones (1990), who suggested the change would help professionals recognize the "possible benefits of intergenerational intimacy" (p. 276).[15]

Bauserman and Rind (1997) argued that negative feelings are not inherent in sexual contacts between boys and adults, "but depend on cultural views of these behaviors."

> In the absence of social taboos and moral condemnation, negative feelings such as guilt and shame and doubts and conflicts about masculinity should not arise for children and adolescents who experience such contacts. The cross-cultural and historical literature provides examples of societies where sexual contacts between boys and adults, rather than being condemned and pathologized, instead were approved of, encouraged, or even regarded as necessary for healthy development. (Bauserman & Rind, 1997, p. 135)

Rind (1998) suggested that "willing man-boy sex accompanied by positive reactions may be better informed by the ancient Greek model [i.e., sexual relationship in which the older male also acts as a teacher and guardian] than by models based on the female experience (e.g., rape and incest models)" (p. 399).

In addition to suggesting that sexual abuse is rarely harmful, Rind et al. have also blamed negative outcomes on those seeking to protect or treat abused children. For example, Rind et al. (December 18, 1998) blamed exaggerated beliefs about the harmfulness of CSA for child abuse hysteria, implantation of false memories, and iatrogenic creation of symptoms, which they claim "researchers in the child abuse industry" have seized upon "as further evidence for the pathogenicity of CSA." Rind (1995a) asserted that the consequence of CSA "is debatable because the traumatic behaviors attributed to the actual or fabricated sexual contact may instead have been induced by the interview tactics of the therapists and child abuse workers" (p. 82).

Rind et al. (1998) suggested that the current prohibition of sex between adults and children is based primarily on a cultural taboo, and advocated using empirical criteria in conceptualizing "early sexual relations," rather than legal or moral criteria (p. 46). In his defense of Sandfort's research on boys' relationships with pedophiles, Bauserman (1990) criticized those who believe that sexual relationships between men and boys "are by their very nature abusive and exploitive," or "that the younger partner is automatically incapable of consent" (p. 310). Bauserman stated, "It remains to be seen whether scientific objectivity can prevail against the need to defend the current dogma on man-boy sexual contacts" (p. 311).

CONCLUSION

In response to criticism, Rind, Tromovitch and Bauserman have cloaked themselves in the authority of science, implying that the controversy over their ideas is purely political and that their data are unimpeachable. This review suggests that this is a serious misrepresentation. A number of researchers have demonstrated that the Rind et al.'s (1998) data either fails to support their case, was presented in a misleading or biased way, or equally supports alternative explanations. A review of the authors' previous writings reveals that Rind and Bauserman formed many of their opinions about the relative harmlessness of sexual relationships between adults and children years prior to performing any meaningful research into the issue. In addition, the authors' views on sex between adults and children have more in common with the ideology of advocates of "intergenerational" sexual relationships, than those of other scientists who have studied this issue. After reviewing the available evidence, Rind et al. is perhaps best described as an advocacy paper that inappropriately uses science in an attempt to legitimize its findings.

As the public and political reaction to Rind et al.'s paper demonstrated, there are prices to be paid for faulty science. Poorly constructed or morally repugnant studies may shake public confidence in science and lessen the public's willingness to base public policy on legitimate scientific research. In addition, unless it is challenged and corrected, erroneous social science research has a way of infiltrating into legal and social structures where it may adversely affect all of our lives. To safeguard both scientific integrity and the public's welfare, professional bodies should be more strident in their insistence that research articles adhere to the ethical and scientific standards set forth by their profession and do not take "extra-scientific" leaps to promote personal agendas. As Ondersma et al. (in press) noted, "Both credibility and progress are jeopardized when scientific efforts are revealed as advocacy rather than a process for refining knowledge."

NOTES

1. The bill's history can be found at <http://www.legis.state.ak.us/ s/basp1000.dll? Get&S=21&Root=hjr36>.

2. The resolution's full title is: "Expressing the sense of Congress rejecting the conclusions of a recent article published by the American Psychological Association that suggests that sexual relationships between adults and children might be positive for children." The resolution can be found at <http://thomas.loc.gov/cgi-bin/query/ z?c106:H.+Con.+Res.+107>.

3. The original sponsors listed on the flyer were the following: University of Tennessee Psychology Department, UT Research Office, UT Science Forum, UT Chapter

of the Golden Key National Honor Society, and the Tennessee Psychological Association (TPA). Later, a letter was sent out by James Lawler, PhD, head of the Department of Psychology at the University of Tennessee-Knoxville, saying that the inclusion of TPA was in error and that it was not a co-sponsor. No explanation was offered.

4. Although APA CEO Dr. Raymond Fowler has suggested that the study by Rind et al. is sound because it passed peer-review, in a personal communication with this author (June 22, 1999), Fowler admitted that he never actually investigated how the study passed peer review, or if it even did. It was later revealed that Rind et al. was thoroughly rejected by its first set of peer-reviewers for the *Psychological Bulletin;* the authors were asked not to resubmit the paper (personal communication with original reviewer who wishes to remain anonymous). Apparently, Rind et al. resubmitted their paper after a change in editors, and the paper was given to a new set of reviewers. At least one of these reviewers also rejected the article. It remains unclear what portion (if any) of the second set of reviewers recommended the paper for publication.

5. Although Rind et al. (1998) acknowledged the problem, they chose not to correct for it, saying "the attenuation is small in absolute magnitude for small effect sizes," and that "effect sizes would increase *at most by .03*" [italics added]. (p. 41). It is important to note that .03 was the exact difference in magnitude that Rind et al. reported between male and female effect sizes ($r = .07$ and $r = .10$, respectively). Because lower effect sizes indicate better adjustment, Rind et al. reported that a major finding of their study was that "self-reported reactions to and effects from CSA indicated that . . . men reacted much less negatively than women" (p. 22). After correcting for attenuation due to base rate differences, Dallam et al. reported that effect sizes for males corresponded to $r = .11$, which is practically identical to the corrected effect size for females, $r = .12$.

6. The special issue was simultaneously issued as a book (see Sandfort, Brongersma, & van Naerssen, 1991).

7. SafeHaven refers self-described "boy-lovers" to the False Memory Syndrome Foundation (an organization which advocates for those claiming to be falsely accused of abusing children) for information and support.

8. Dr. Edward Brongersma is a former member of the Dutch Parliament whose career was interrupted by his arrest in the 1950s for sexual contact with an adolescent boy. After serving less than a year in prison, he was re-elected to the Senate and served as Chair of the Judiciary Committee. He subsequently traveled the world writing about and campaigning for the acceptance of pedophilia. He died in 1998.

9. *Paidika: The Journal of Paedophilia* was founded in 1987. A multidisciplinary coalition of academicians from the United States and Europe sit on its advisory board. In the journal's first issue, the editors outlined their goals by stating:

> The starting point of *Paidika* is necessarily our consciousness of ourselves as paedophiles. . . . But to speak today of paedophilia, which we understand to be consensual intergenerational sexual relationships, is to speak of the politics of oppression. . . . This is the milieu in which we are enmeshed, the fabric of our daily life and struggle. . . . Through publication of scholarly studies, thoroughly documented and carefully reasoned, we intend to demonstrate that paedophilia has been, and remains, a legitimate and productive part of the totality of human experience. ("Statement of Purpose," pp. 2-3)

10. The organization International Pedophile and Child Emancipation (IPCE) was founded in the mid-1990s to encourage cooperation between pedophile advocacy organizations from around the world. NAMBLA is its largest member, and Australia along with every major European country is represented in its membership. According to its website, IPCE's purpose is to exchange opinions and ideas, to share information and to coordinate political and other strategies for the emancipation of pedophiles and the decriminalization of consensual intergenerational relationships. <http://www.humanbeing.demon. nl/ipceweb/Newsleteers/>.

11. The conference also coincided with the release of a book edited by Visser titled, *De Andere Kant van de Medaille. Over de Vraag: Is Pedofilie Misbruik van Kinderen?* [*The Other Side of the Coin. About the Question: Is Pedophilia Child Abuse?*], which devotes a section to describing the results of Rind et al.'s (1998) research. See also, Visser, H. (1998, December 18). *Pastorate and pedophilia.* Symposium sponsored by the Paulus Kerk. De Andere Kant van de Medaille (The Other Side of the Coin), Rotterdam, The Netherlands. Retrieved July 3, 2001 from the World Wide Web: <http://www.humanbeing.demon.nl/ipceweb/Newsletters/NL%20E5.html>.

12. It is interesting to note that in their address, Rind et al. (December 12, 1998) suggested that their views on child sexual abuse were consistent with those of then current APA president Martin Seligman: "In one of his recent books, Seligman reviewed some of the research on the correlates of CSA and concluded, as we have, that mental health researchers have vastly overstated the harmful potential of CSA. He commented that "it is time to turn down the volume" on this issue that has risen to histrionic proportions. . . . We concur completely with Seligman's observations." The passages described come from Seligman's 1994 book, *What You Can Change & What You Cannot,* published by Alfred A. Knopf, Inc.

13. In addition, pedophile groups such as NAMBLA and SafeHaven have promoted Rind et al.'s findings on their websites, and their study has been prominently featured in numerous pedophile publications (e.g., Fergusson, 1999; Goslinga, 1998; Riegel, 2000).

14. Rind et al.'s (1998) proposed redefinition has not been supported by mainstream researchers in the field of child maltreatment (e.g., Ondersma et al., 1999; Ondersma et al., in press) or by the APA (see American Psychological Association, 1999). The consensus opinion in the field is that sexual contact between an adult and a child involves an abuse of adult's position and power (e.g., Courtois, 1988; "Psychiatric Association Criticizes," 1999). Thus a demonstration of harm is not viewed as necessary to make a determination of abuse.

15. Although Rind et al. (1998) failed to credit Jones' work, it is clear that both Rind and Bauserman were familiar with his paper as they had favorably cited it in a previous publication (see Rind & Bauserman, 1993). Bauserman (1990) was also published in the same special issue of the *Journal of Homosexuality* dedicated to "Male Intergenerational Intimacy" as Jones (1990).

REFERENCES

American Psychological Association. (1999). *Statement on childhood sexual abuse: Childhood sexual abuse causes serious harm to its victims.* Washington, DC: Author. Retrieved July 3, 2001 from the World Wide Web: <http://www.apa.org/releases/childsexabuse.html>.

Bauserman, R. (1989). Man-boy sexual relationships in a cross-cultural perspective. *Paidika: The Journal of Paedophilia, 2*, (Issue 5), 28-40.

Bauserman, R. (1990). Objectivity and ideology: Criticism of Theo Sandfort's research on man-boy sexual relations. *Journal of Homosexuality, 20*, 297-312.

Bauserman, R., & Rind, B. (1997). Psychological correlates of male child and adolescent sexual experiences with adults: A review of the nonclinical literature. *Archives of Sexual Behavior, 26*, 105-141.

Berry, K. K. (2000, Jan./Feb.). The Congressional censure of a research paper: Return of the inquisition? *Skeptical Inquirer*, p. 20.

Boney-McCoy, S., & Finkelhor, D. (1995). Psychosocial sequelae of violent victimization in a national youth sample. *Journal of Consulting and Clinical Psychology, 63*, 726-736.

Boney-McCoy, S., & Finkelhor, D. (1996). Is youth victimization related to trauma symptoms and depression after controlling for prior symptoms and family relationships? A longitudinal, prospective study. *Journal of Consulting and Clinical Psychology, 64*, 1406-1416.

Brongersma, E. (1986). *Loving boys: A multidisciplinary study of sexual relations between adult and minor males* (Vol. 1). New York: Global Academic Publishers.

Brongersma, E. (1990). Boy-lovers and their influence on boys: Distorted research and anecdotal observations. *Journal of Homosexuality, 20*, 145-173.

Burling, S. (1999, November 17). Despite stir, sex-abuse study won't be reviewed. *Philadelphia Inquirer*. Retrieved November 27, 1999 from the World Wide Web: <http://www.phillynews.com/inquirer/99/Nov/17/international/PEDO17.htm>.

Chandy, J. M., Blum, R.W., & Resnick, M. D. (1996). Gender-specific outcomes for sexually abused adolescents. *Child Abuse and Neglect, 20*, 1219-1231.

Courtois, C. A. (1988). *Healing the incest wound: Adult survivors in therapy*. New York: W. W. Norton.

Dallam, S. J., Gleaves, D. H., Cepeda-Benito, A., Silberg, J., Kraemer, H. C., & Spiegel, D. (in press). The effects of childhood sexual abuse: A critique of Rind, Tromovitch and Bauserman. (1998). *Psychological Bulletin*.

De Young, M. (1989). The world according to NAMBLA: Accounting for deviance. *Journal of Sociology & Social Welfare, 16*, 111-126.

Dinwiddie, S., Heath, A. C., Dunne, M. P., Bucholz, K. K., Madden, P. A., Slutske, W. S., Bierut, L. J., Statham, D. B., & Martin, N. G. (2000). Early sexual abuse and lifetime psychopathology: A co-twin-control study. *Psychological Medicine, 30*, 41-52.

Dominee Visser pleit voor het aanvaarden van pedofilie. [Reverend Visser pleads for the acceptance of pedophilia]. (1998, December 18). *Rotterdam Dagblad* (Netherlands).

Duin, J. (1999, March 23). Critics assail study affirming pedophilia. *Washington Times*, p. A1.

Duncan, R. D. (2000). Childhood maltreatment and college drop-out rates: Implications for child abuse researchers. *Journal of Interpersonal Violence, 15*, 987-995.

Erikson, J. A. (2000). Sexual liberation's last frontier. *Society, 4*, 21-15.

Ferguson, B. (1999, January). Youthful sexual experience and well-being: Important conference in Rotterdam. *Koinos Magazine, 21*, 5-12. Retrieved July 3, 2001 from the World Wide Web: <http://home.zonnet.nl/koinos/>.

Fergusson, D. M., Horwood, L. J., & Lynskey, M. T. (1996). Childhood sexual abuse and psychiatric disorder in young adulthood: II. Psychiatric outcomes of childhood sexual abuse. *Journal of the American Academy of Child and Adolescent Psychiatry, 34*, 1365-1374.

Fleming, J., Mullen, P. E., Sibthorpe, B., & Bammer, G. (1999). The long-term impact of childhood sexual abuse in Australian women. *Child Abuse and Neglect, 23*, 145-159.

Fowler, R. (1999, May 25). *Controversy regarding APA journal article.* [Email sent to APA division officers: DIVOFFICERS@LISTS.APA.ORG].

Fowler, R. (1999, June 9). *Letter to Hon. Tom Delay.* Retrieved July 3, 2001 from the World Wide Web: <http://www.apa.org/releases/delay.html>.

Fowler, R. (1999, June 10). CSA update. [Email sent to members of the APA Council of Representatives].

Garnefski, N., & Arends, E. (1998). Sexual abuse and adolescent maladjustment: Differences between male and female victims. *Journal of Adolescence, 21*, 99-107.

Geraci, J. (1994). Interview: Gilbert Herdt. *Paidika: The Journal of Paedophilia, 3*(2), 2-17.

Goodyear-Smith, F. (1993). *First do no harm: The sexual abuse industry.* New Zealand: Benton-Guy Publishing Ltd.

Goslinga, G. (1998, January). Bauserman and Rind: Boys' sexual experiences. *Koinos Magazine, 17*, 5-8. Retrieved July 3, 2001 from the World Wide Web: <http://home.zonnet.nl/koinos/>.

Graupner, H. (1999). Love versus abuse: Crossgenerational sexual relations of minors: A gay rights issue? *Journal of Homosexuality, 37*, 23-56.

Holmes, W. C., & Slap, G. B. (1999). Reply to editor. *JAMA, 281*, 2186.

Johnson, J. G., Cohen, P., Brown, J., Smailes, E. M., & Bernstein, D. P. (1999). Childhood maltreatment increases risk for personality disorders during early adulthood. *Archives of General Psychiatry, 56*, 600-606.

Jones, G. P. (1990). The study of intergenerational intimacy in North America: Beyond politics and pedophilia. *Journal of Homosexuality, 20*(1-2), 275-95.

Jumper, S. A. (1995). A meta-analysis of the relationship of child sexual abuse to adult psychological adjustment. *Child Abuse & Neglect, 19*, 715-728.

Kendler, K. S., Bulik, C. M., Silberg, J., Hettema, J. M., Myers, J., & Prescott, C. A. (2000). Childhood sexual abuse and adult psychiatric and substance use disorders in women: An epidemiological and cotwin control analysis. *Archives of General Psychiatry, 57*, 953-959.

Leadership Council on Mental Health, Justice and the Media. (1999, March). Mission statement. Bala Cynwyd, PA: Author.

Leadership Council for Mental Health, Justice and the Media. (1999, May 24). *Mental health leaders suggest flawed research may promote pedophilia.* Bala Cynwyd, PA: Author.

McCarty, R. C. (1999, November/December). AAAS responds to APA's request for review. *Psychological Science Agenda (Bulletin of American Psychological Association Science Directorate) 12*, 2-3.

Merrill, L. L., Thomsen, C. J., Gold, S. R., & Milner, J. S. (2001). Childhood abuse and premilitary sexual assault in male navy recruits. *Journal of Consulting and Clinical Psychology, 69*, 252-261.

Mirkin, H. (1999). The pattern of sexual politics: Feminism, homosexuality and pedophilia. *Journal of Homosexuality, 37*, 1-24.

Mrazek, D. (1990). Response to the Bauserman critique. *Journal of Homosexuality, 20*, 317-318.

Mullen, P. E., Martin, J. L., Anderson, J. C., Romans, S. E., & Herbison, G. P. (1993). Childhood sexual abuse and mental health in adult life. *British Journal of Psychiatry, 163*, 721-732.

Myers, J. (1999, June 2). Coburn condemns psychological study. *Tulsa World*, p. 11.

Neuman, D. A., Houskamp, B. M., Pollock, V. E., & Briere, J. (1996). The long-term sequelae of childhood sexual abuse in women: A meta-analytic review. *Child Maltreatment, 1*, 6-16.

Oddone, E., & Genuis, M. L. (1996). *A meta-analysis of the published research on the effects of child sexual abuse.* Calgary, Canada: National Foundation for Family Research and Education.

Ondersma, S. J., Chaffin, M., & Berliner, L. (1999). Comments on Rind et al. meta-analysis controversy. *The APSAC Advisor, 12*, 2-5.

Ondersma, S. J., Chaffin, M., Berliner, L., Cordon, I., Goodman, G. S., & Barnett, D. (in press). Sex with children is abuse: The Rind et al. meta-analysis controversy. *Psychological Bulletin.*

Paolucci, E. O., Genuis, M. L., & Violato, C. (2001). A meta-analysis of the published research on the effects of child sexual. *Journal of Psychology, 135*, 17-36.

Paidika: Statement of purpose. (1987). *Paidika: The Journal of Paedophilia, 1*(Issue 1), 1-2.

Psychiatric Association Criticizes Other APA for Pedophilia Paper. (1999, June 3). *CultureFacts.* (Online Newsletter by Family Research Council). Retrieved July 3, 2001 from the World Wide Web: <http://www.frc.org/culture/cu99f1.html>.

Riegel, D. (2000). *Understanding loved boys and boy lovers.* Philadelphia PA: SafeHaven Foundation Press.

Rind, B. (1995a). First do no harm: The sexual abuse industry [Review of the book]. *Paidika: The Journal of Paedophilia, 3* (Issue 12), 79-83.

Rind, B. (1995b). An analysis of human sexuality textbook coverage of the psychological correlates of adult-nonadult sex. *The Journal of Sex Research, 32*, 219-233.

Rind, B. (1998). Biased use of cross-cultural and historical perspectives on male homosexuality in human sexuality textbooks. *Journal of Sex Research, 35*, 397-407.

Rind, B., & Bauserman, R. (1993). Biased terminology effects and biased information processing in research in adult-nonadult sexual interactions: An empirical investigation. *Journal of Sex Research, 30*, 260-269.

Rind, B., Bauserman, R., & Tromovitch, P. (1998, December 18). *An examination of assumed properties of child sexual abuse based on nonclinical samples.* Paper presented at symposium sponsored by the Paulus Kerk called De Andere Kant van de Medaille (The Other Side of the Coin), Rotterdam, The Netherlands. Retrieved July 3, 2001 from the World Wide Web: <http://www.humanbeing.demon.nl/ipceweb/Library/Examinatio.htm#Discussion>.

Rind, B., Bauserman, R., & Tromovitch, P. (1999). Interpretation of research on sexual abuse of boys. *Journal of the American Medical Association, 281*, 2185.

Rind, B., Tromovitch, P., & Bauserman, R. (1998). A meta-analytic examination of assumed properties of child sexual abuse using college samples. *Psychological Bulletin, 124*, 22-53.

Rind, B., Tromovitch, P., & Bauserman, R. (1999, May 12). *Authors' statement.* Washington, DC: American Psychological Association.

Rind, B., Tromovitch, P., & Bauserman, R. (1999, November 6). *The clash of media, politics, and sexual science: An examination of the controversy surrounding the Psychological Bulletin meta-analysis on the assumed properties of child sexual abuse.* Paper presented at the 1999 Joint Annual meeting of the Society for the Scientific Study of Sexuality and the American Association of Sex Educators, Counselors, and Therapists.

Rivas, T. (1997, October). A new approach to the societal emancipation of affectionate relationships between minors and adults *IPCE (International Pedophile and Child Emancipation) Newsletter*, Number E 2. Retrieved July 3, 2001 from the World Wide Web: <http://www.humanbeing.demon.nl/ipceweb/Newsletters/NL%20E2.html>.

Saunders, D. J. (1999, March 28). Lolita nation. *The San Francisco Chronicle*, p. 7.

SafeHaven Foundation. (2001). Boylove, truth versus myth. Retrieved March 28, 2001 from the World Wide Web: <http://www.safet.net/info/index.html>.

Sandfort, T. (1987). *Boys on their contacts with men.* Elmhurst, NY: Global Academic Publishers.

Sandfort, T., Brongersma, E. & van Naerssen, A. (1990). Man-boy relationships: Different concepts for a diversity of phenomena. *Journal of Homosexuality, 20*(1-2), 5-12.

Sandfort, E. Brongersma & A. van Naerssen (Eds.) (1991). *Male intergenerational intimacy: Historical, socio-psychological, and legal perspectives.* Binghamton, New York: Harrington Park Press.

Schuijer, J. (1990). Tolerance at arm's length: The Dutch experience. *Journal of Homosexuality, 20*, 199-229.

Spiegel, D. (2000). The price of abusing children and numbers. *Sexuality and Culture, 4*, 63-66.

Stein, J. A., Golding, J. N., Siegel, J. M., Burnam, M. A., & Sorenson, S. B. (1988). Long-term psychological sequelae of child sexual abuse. In G. E. Wyatt & G. J. Powell (Eds.), *Lasting effects of child sexual abuse* (pp. 135-154). Newbury Park, CA: Sage Publications.

Tavris, C. (1999, July 19). Uproar over sexual abuse study muddies the water. *Los Angeles Times*, p. B5.

The other side of the coin. (September 1998). *IPCE (International Pedophile and Child Emancipation) Newsletter*, Number E 3. Retrieved July 3, 2001 from the World Wide Web: <http://www.humanbeing.demon.nl/ipceweb/Newsletters/NL%20E3.html#The Other Side>.

When politics clashes with science: An Examination of the controversy surrounding the Psychological Bulletin article meta-analysis on the assumed properties of child sexual abuse. (2000). Flyer for symposium lead by Bruce Rind and Carol Tavris, University of Tennessee-Knoxville.

Whitely, W. P., Rennie, D., & Hafner, A. W. (1994, July 13). The scientific community's response to evidence of fraudulent publication. The Robert Slutsky case. *JAMA, 272*(2), 170-173.

Woll, S. (1999, July 26). Child sexual abuse study [letter to the editor]. *Los Angeles Times*, p. B4.

A Critical Appraisal
of the 1998 Meta-Analytic Review
of Child Sexual Abuse Outcomes
Reported by Rind, Tromovitch,
and Bauserman

John A. Whittenburg
Pamela Paradis Tice
Gail L. Baker
Dorothy E. Lemmey

SUMMARY. The goal of this article is to present a methodological critique of the 1998 meta-analysis of child sexual abuse outcomes by Rind,

John A. Whittenburg, PhD, is Research Psychologist, SSTAR (Social Systems Training and Research), Inc., 7602 Del Rey Lane, Houston, TX 77071 (E-mail: jwhittenburg@go.com). Pamela Paradis Tice, BA, ELS, is Research Associate, Department of Family and Community Medicine, Baylor College of Medicine, Houston, TX, USA. Gail L. Baker, MA, is Research Psychologist, SSTAR (Social Systems Training and Research), Inc., 7602 Del Rey Lane, Houston, TX 77071 (E-mail: sstarinc@wt.net). Dorothy E. Lemmey, PhD, RN, Department of Maternity Nursing, Lakeland Community College, 7700 Clocktower Drive, Kirtland, OH 44094 (E-mail: Dotlemmey@aol.com).

Address correspondence to: Pamela Paradis Tice, BA, ELS, Department of Family and Community Medicine, Baylor College of Medicine, 5615 Kirby Drive, Suite 610, Houston, TX 77005 (E-mail: pptice@bcm.tmc.edu).

The authors thank Doris Georgiou, PhD, for her critical comments throughout the preparation of this manuscript.

[Haworth co-indexing entry note]: "A Critical Appraisal of the 1998 Meta-Analytic Review of Child Sexual Abuse Outcomes Reported by Rind, Tromovitch, and Bauserman." Whittenburg, John A. et al. Co-published simultaneously in *Journal of Child Sexual Abuse* (The Haworth Maltreatment & Trauma Press, an imprint of The Haworth Press, Inc.) Vol. 9, No. 3/4, 2001, pp. 135-155; and: *Misinformation Concerning Child Sexual Abuse and Adult Survivors* (ed: Charles L. Whitfield, Joyanna Silberg, and Paul Jay Fink) The Haworth Maltreatment & Trauma Press, an imprint of The Haworth Press, Inc., 2001, pp. 135-155. Single or multiple copies of this article are available for a fee from The Haworth Document Delivery Service [1-800-HAWORTH, 9:00 a.m. - 5:00 p.m. (EST). E-mail address: getinfo@haworthpressinc.com].

Tromovitch, and Bauserman. Seven major concerns are addressed. Rind et al.'s view is, at best, extremely limited. By restricting a supposedly broad meta-analysis to only some of the population in question, the conclusions they drew regarding this complex topic, primarily that adult-child sex is not necessarily harmful, are invalid. *[Article copies available for a fee from The Haworth Document Delivery Service: 1-800-HAWORTH. E-mail address: <getinfo@haworthpressinc.com> Website: <http://www.HaworthPress.com> © 2001 by The Haworth Press, Inc. All rights reserved.]*

KEYWORDS. Child sexual abuse, outcomes, meta-analysis, study methodology, critique

In 1998, "A Meta-Analytic Examination of Assumed Properties of Child Sexual Abuse Using College Samples," by Bruce Rind, Philip Tromovitch, and Robert Bauserman was published in the *Psychological Bulletin*. The topic is, undeniably, of great import to all concerned with the welfare of children throughout the world. However, the research reported was flawed in two critical areas: the methodology used by the authors, and the extant studies supporting quite different conclusions that they ignored. An October 2000 search of the Social Science Citation Index identified only 28 published papers in which the meta-analytic review by Rind et al. has been cited; none of those publications was a formal critique of the authors' work.

We present such a methodological critique in this first article. In this critique, seven major concerns are addressed: (1) the child sexual abuse population selected, (2) the research strategy adopted, (3) the meta-analytic coding used, (4) the statistical techniques applied, (5) the psychological adjustment symptoms of child sexual abuse analyzed, (6) the confounding of gender and age and the underrepresentation of males, and (7) the limitations of the retrospective cross-sectional approach. At the end, conclusions are presented with suggestions to guide future research on child sexual abuse.

The article by Rind et al. is long, consisting of 30-double column pages, which include 12 tables and 191 references, and a two-page Appendix. To aid the reader in identifying specific passages referred to in the present critique, pertinent quotations are included.

CHILD SEXUAL ABUSE POPULATION SELECTED

Our first methodological question concerns the representativeness of the population selected by Rind et al. to examine child sexual abuse, and the identification of the underlying distribution characteristics of the entire child sexual abuse population. Rind et al. defined the population of sexually abused youth as both children and adolescents who have suffered any type of sexual abuse. Included in their study were only individuals whose psychological reactions were classifiable into mutually exclusive negative, neutral, or positive categories. Excluded were the more severe clinical and legal cases, considered by the authors to be nonrepresentative of the general child sexual abuse population. Rind et al. argued that samples of college students are representative of the general population of individuals sexually abused as children, while samples drawn from the more severe clinical and legal cases, especially those individuals suffering adverse physical and mental consequences from child sexual abuse, are anomalous. They presented data from three national samples to support this assertion, noting in their article:

> [T]he top half of Table 1 [p. 30] shows the estimated pervasive rates in the college population for the different types of CSA [child sexual abuse] for SA [sexually abused] women and men separately and combined. To provide a frame of reference for these results, we estimated corresponding prevalence rates for SA persons in the general population [i.e., the population of those individuals who were sexually abused as children] based on reports from 3 national samples (Baker & Duncan, 1985; Laumann, Gagnon, Michael, & Michaels, 1994; López, Carpintero, Hernández, & Fuertes, 1995). Data in these studies were obtained in face-to-face interviews of respondents selected to be representative of their nations (Britain, United States, and Spain, respectively). The strength of face-to-face interviews in obtaining valid data along with the high response rates of these studies (unweighted mean = 83%) suggest that their prevalence rates serve as good population estimates. . . . The bottom half of Table 1 displays the estimated prevalence rates for the different types of CSA for SA persons in the general population. (1998, p. 30)

Rind et al. conducted computerized database searches of PsycLIT, Sociofile, PsycInfo, Dissertation Abstracts International, and ERIC to produce 59 "usable" studies (36 published studies, 21 unpublished dissertations, and two unpublished master's theses) that they included in their meta-analysis. While Rind et al. believe that college samples are representative of the general population of those individuals who were sexually abused, not all investigators involved in child sexual abuse research concur (Haugaard & Emery, 1989; Silverman, Reinherz, & Giacona, 1996).

To determine whether the college samples and the three national samples analyzed by Rind et al. came from what can be considered to be the same population, one of us (J.A.W.) conducted nonparametric χ^2 tests[1] using the data contained in Tables 1 and 2 of the meta-analysis (1998, pp. 30 and 31); the face validity of these data was assumed for all of the tests.[2] The χ^2 values obtained (our Tables 1 and 2) indicated that the college samples differed considerably from the national samples (see below) and that these samples do not come from the same child sexual abuse population as stated by Rind et al.

Based on the sample, J.A.W. converted the percentages of those respondents who had experienced exhibitionism, fondling, oral sex, or intercourse (1998, p. 30, Table 1) into frequencies and performed eight χ^2 tests as shown in our Table 1. The results of the analyses comparing the college samples with the national samples revealed that there are statistically significant differences with regard to two of the four types of child sexual abuse. This indicated that, with regard to two of the four types of child sexual abuse, the college samples are not representative of the child sexual abuse population represented by the national samples. The results of the analyses comparing females and males revealed that there are highly significant gender differences with regard to all four types of child sexual abuse. Specifically, the differences in the observed and the expected frequencies between females and males indicated that females reported relatively more cases of exhibitionism than did the males and that the males reported relatively more cases of fondling, oral sex, and intercourse than did the females. Apparently, more females in the samples were abused but more passively, whereas fewer males were abused but were so more actively.

Rind et al. also compared the college samples and the national samples with regard to relationship information (1998, p. 31, Table 2), such as the close family (e.g., biological parents, stepparents, grandparents, older siblings) and the wider family (both close family and other relatives). The results of our χ^2 analyses (see our Table 2) indicated that the college samples differed considerably from the national samples with regard to child sexual abuse involving both the close and the wider family members. Rind et al.'s inclusion of the close family data as a component of the wider family data in their prevalence rate estimates is questionable; this confounding affected the results of our χ^2 analyses (our Table 2). Nevertheless, since both the wider family and close family entities demonstrated statistically significant differences between the college samples and the national samples, it is reasonable to conclude that our family relationship findings are valid.

To reiterate, our finding that four of the six χ^2 comparisons we made between the college samples and the national samples are statistically significant (our Tables 1 and 2) indicates that for those measures the samples are not from the same population. In view of this finding, we want to emphasize that Rind et

TABLE 1. χ^2 Analyses of Prevalence Rate Estimates of Four Types of Child Sexual Abuse for Population Samples and Gender as Reported in the Meta-Analysis by Rind, Tromovitch, and Bauserman (1998, p. 30, Table 1)

Type of Child Sexual Abuse*	Population/ Gender	Reported Abuse	Frequency O†	E	χ^2 Value	p Value
Exhibitionism						
	College‡	Yes	806	827		
		No	1,872	1,851	2.93 (1 df)	> .05
	National	Yes	316	295		
		No	640	661		
	Female	Yes	919	853		
		No	1,843	1,909	30.80 (1 df)	< .001
	Male	Yes	203	269		
		No	669	603		
Fondling						
	College‡	Yes	1,105	1,292		
		No	1,573	1,386	198.78 (1 df)	< .001
	National	Yes	648	461		
		No	308	495		
	Female	Yes	1,242	1,332		
		No	1,520	1,430	49.14 (1 df)	< .001
	Male	Yes	511	421		
		No	361	451		
Oral sex						
	College‡	Yes	136	199		
		No	2,542	2,479	81.92 (1 df)	< .001
	National	Yes	134	71		
		No	822	885		
	Female	Yes	118	205		
		No	2,644	2,557	165.7 (1 df)	< .001
	Male	Yes	152	65		
		No	720	807		
Intercourse						
	College‡	Yes	449	436		
		No	2,229	2,242	1.77 (1 df)	> .05
	National	Yes	142	155		
		No	814	801		
	Female	Yes	376	449		
		No	2,386	2,313	59.00 (1 df)	< .001
	Male	Yes	215	142		
		No	657	730		

*The combined total number of the four types of sexual abuse for all college samples and all national samples was 3,634.
†Because all of these values were calculated by one of us (J.A.W.) from percentages calculated by Rind et al., rounding errors may exist.
‡For the college population sample (n = 2,678), data for the "combined" values from Rind et al.'s Table 1 (1998, p. 30) were not used to calculate the observed (O) and expected (E) frequencies because the data for males and females were commingled.

TABLE 2. χ^2 Analyses of the Prevalence Rate Estimates of the Relationship Between Sexually Abused Respondents and Their Abusers for Population Samples and for Gender as Reported in the Meta-Analysis by Rind et al. (1998, p. 31, Table 2)

Relationship to Abuser*	Population/ Gender	Reported Abuse	Frequency O†	E	χ^2 Value	p Value
Wider Family	College‡	Yes	1,145	1,080		
		No	2,170	2,235	25.39 (1 df)	< .001
	National	Yes	255	320		
		No	726	661		
	Female	Yes	1,218	1,089		
		No	2,123	2,252	138.32 (1 df)	< .001
	Male	Yes	182	311		
		No	773	644		
Close Family	College‡	Yes	180	149		
		No	882	913	15.63 (1 df)	< .001
	National	Yes	106	137		
		No	875	844		
	Female	Yes	249	196		
		No	1,149	1,202	52.94 (1 df)	< .001
	Male	Yes	37	90		
		No	608	555		

*Calculations were confounded by inclusion of close family data as a component of wider family data in the meta-analysis by Rind et al.
†Because all of these values were calculated by one of us (J.A.W.) from percentages calculated by Rind, Tromovitch, and Bauserman, rounding errors may exist.
‡Data for the "combined" values from Rind et al.'s Table 2 (1998, p. 31) were not used to calculate the observed (O) and expected (E) frequencies because the data for males and females were commingled.

al. neglected to perform a single statistical analysis of the data they presented in their Table 1 and Table 2 (1998, pp. 30-31).

Another concern is the use of the face-to-face interviewer-interviewee method used to collect data from all three national samples. Rind et al. believe such methodology to be very effective. However, it has limitations, particularly when the topic of interest is as emotionally charged as is that of child sexual abuse. An important limitation is the potential risk that the interviewer may transfer to the interviewee whatever biases he or she may have (Babbie, 1973).

With regard to general volunteer bias, investigators of such bias in sexuality research, for example, have pointed out that reliance on college student samples limits the generalizability of study results (Strassberg & Lowe, 1995). Overreliance on college student samples may, in fact, even give us biased views of human social behavior (Sears, 1986). Sears states, "[This is because] college students are likely to have less-crystallized attitudes, less-formulated senses of self, stronger cognitive skills, stronger tendencies to comply with authority, and more unstable peer group relationships" (1986, p. 515). He concludes, "[A] greater effort must be made to conduct research on persons from life stages other than late adolescence" (1986, p. 527).

Before such biases in data collection are addressed, and attempts are made to ensure the selection of an appropriate study population, however, the definition and scope of child sexual abuse must be explicitly identified by any investigator in the field (Itzin, 1997).

RESEARCH STRATEGY ADOPTED

Our second methodological question concerns the appropriateness of the research strategy employed by Rind et al. in their meta-analysis. On the surface, their meta-analytic findings appear to present a very different picture of the problem of sexual abuse and its effects on children's psychological adjustment from that of many other researchers. Upon closer examination, however, it is obvious that they meta-analyzed only a very carefully selected number of the many published studies easily available for examination. They asserted:

> Opinions expressed in the media and by many popular press and professional writers imply that CSA has certain basic properties or qualities irrespective of the population of interest. These implied properties are (a) CSA causes harm, (b) this harm is pervasive in the population of persons with a history of CSA, (c) this harm is likely to be intense, and (d) CSA is an equivalent experience for boys and girls in terms of its widespread and intensely negative effects. (1998, p. 22)

Rind et al. employed a strategy not commonly used in scientific studies: setting up a straw man and then knocking the straw man down. The authors presented what they considered to be the four commonly assumed properties of child sexual abuse and then disputed their significance with the findings from their meta-analysis of other child sexual abuse studies. Most researchers would approach such a complex research problem differently, by either clearly stating hypotheses to be tested within the scope of a study design or by conducting exploratory studies to identify useful information for analysis and possibly for future development of hypotheses. In effect, once Rind et al. removed the more severe clinical and legal studies as being nonrepresentative of the general child sexual abuse population, they made no effort to test their own hypothesis.

As discussed in the preceding section, the college student samples on which Rind et al. based their conclusions cannot be considered to be representative of the general child sexual abuse population. Rind et al. themselves acknowledged that numerous literature reviews published during the preceding 15 years "have attempted to synthesize the growing body of empirical investigations of CSA effects and correlates. . . . These reviews have not been unanimous in their conclusions" (1998, p. 23). In any case, even if the four assumed properties of child sexual abuse identified by Rind et al. were based on more than just opinions offered in both the lay and the professional literature, and the findings were more consistent, the concept of causality cannot be inferred with only correlational data. Rind et al. drew their conclusions from such data.

META-ANALYTIC CODING USED

Our third methodological question concerns the objectivity of the coding procedure used by two of the authors. Rind and Tromovitch reviewed all of the 59 studies they selected as usable and "independently coded" them for subsequent meta-analysis. Rind et al. explained:

> For each study, the following information was coded: (a) all statistics, if provided, on psychological correlates of CSA . . . (b) types of psychological correlates reported; (c) all statistics regarding relations between moderator variables (e.g., force, penetration, frequency of CSA) and psychological correlates; (d) sex of participants; (e) definition of CSA, including ages that defined a 'child' and an older person, whether peer experiences were included, whether CSA experiences were limited to contact sex or also included noncontact sexual experiences, and whether CSA experiences were limited to unwanted sex or also included willing sexual experiences; (f) all reaction data, if provided, including both retrospectively recalled reactions to and current reflections on the CSA experiences; (g) all self-reported effects data, if provided, including responses to how these experiences affected participants overall and how they affected their sex lives; (h) types of family environment measures used; and (i) all statistics on family environment measures, including their relations with CSA and with psychological correlates (1998, p. 27)

To establish interrater coding reliability, Rind and Tromovitch "independently" coded six different measures: psychological correlates; reactions of students to their child sexual abuse experiences; self-reported effects of child sexual abuse; relationships between family environment and child sexual abuse; relationships between family environment and psychological adjustment; and results of statistical control. The interrater agreement for these codings ranged from 85% to 100%, and all disagreements were resolved by discussion. However, because the two authors are colleagues who undoubtedly share similar attitudes regarding child sexual abuse (e.g., Rind & Tromovitch, 1997), it is unlikely that they can be considered to be truly independent judges. Anything less than high interrater reliability in this case would be surprising.

In addition, the raters classified the students' retrospectively recalled reactions and current reflections into three mutually exclusive categories: negative, neutral, or positive. Child sexual abuse experiences, especially those believed to be negative, however, are known to be complex and diverse (e.g., Ronai's personal account [Ronai, 1995]). Compared with the relatively narrow ranges of positive and neutral experiences, such a limited classification system accounts for neither the type nor the intensity of the much broader range of negative experiences. Reduction of the broad range of negative abuse experiences into a single category increases the likelihood that statistical correlations involving these experiences will be artificially reduced as well. In addition, abusive childhood experiences believed to be positive may actually represent a developed coping strategy that generally fails in interpersonal relationships (Styron & Janoff-Bulman, 1997). The eventual failure of such coping strategies also calls self-reports of willing or consensual participation in adult-child sexual relations into question.[3] The perception of willing or consensual participation might simply be a component of the developed coping strategy.

STATISTICAL TECHNIQUES APPLIED

Our fourth methodological question concerns the defensibility for Rind et al.'s use of parametric statistics. In their meta-analysis, they used a parametric statistic, Pearson correlation coefficient r, to determine direction (negative or positive) and strength of relationships between variables. They also used a nonparametric statistic, χ^2, in their test of the homogeneity of variance among the 54 independent samples of individuals who had been sexually abused as children for whom psychological effects or correlates could be computed. As Rind et al. described:

> The effect size used in this review was r, the Pearson correlation coefficient. For CSA-psychological adjustment relations, positive rs indicted poorer adjustment for CSA participants compared to control participants. For CSA-family environment relations, positive rs indicated poorer family functioning for CSA subjects. For family environment-ad-

justment relations, positive rs indicated that poorer family functioning was associated with poorer adjustment. Pearson rs were also computed to assess the magnitude of the relation between various moderating variables (e.g., force) and outcome measures (i.e., psychological adjustment and self-reported reactions). Positive rs indicated that higher levels of moderators were associated with higher levels of symptoms or more negative reactions to the CSA. Finally, Pearson rs were computed to assess the size of the differences in reactions and self-reported effects between men and women who had CSA experiences. In this case, positive rs indicated that men reported fewer negative reactions or effects than [did] women, or conversely, that they reported more positive reactions or effects than [did] women. (1998, p. 29)

In addition, Rind et al. pointed out, "To examine the intensity of CSA psychological effects or correlates, we first meta-analyzed the sample-level effect sizes from the 54 [independent] samples for which these could be computed . . . The resulting unbiased effect size estimate, based on 15,912 participants, was r_u = .09, with a 95% confidence interval from .08 to .11" (1998, p. 31). They continued, "In an attempt to achieve homogeneity, we examined the distribution of sample-level effect sizes to determine whether outliers existed. We defined outliers to be effect sizes that were at least 1.96 standard deviations away from the unweighted mean effect size (i.e., falling in the extreme 5% of the distribution). Three outliers were found" (1998, p. 31).

The primary advantage of the meta-analytic method is that by combining the data for different sample sizes from several similar studies into a single larger sample group, greater statistical power can be attained. But use of this method in the examination of child sexual abuse has drawbacks. Individuals react quite differently to their different abuse experiences; the technical soundness of study designs varies widely; the utility and the consistency of the procedures followed in the studies also varies; and study outcomes reveal wide variability among the dependent variables, both within a specific study and across studies (Haugaard & Emery, 1989).

Large samples, such as those used by Rind et al., often produce statistically significant findings that have no practical and little theoretical value. For example, based on the 54 independent samples that contained data that could be correlated (N = 15,912 participants), Rind et al. found a statistically significant r value of .09 between the intensity of child sexual abuse and psychological adjustment effects. Although this suggested that students who had been sexually abused as children were less well adjusted than those who had not been abused, such a low correlation accounted for less than 1% of the total adjusted variance in Rind et al.'s meta-analysis (in other words, unknown variables accounted for more than 99% of the reasons for the lower psychological adjustment of sexually abused individuals).

Parametric statistics, which use the actual data values obtained, are more powerful for obtaining statistically significant findings involving two samples than are nonparametric statistics, which use rank-order data (Siegel, 1956). The use of parametric statistics, however, requires that two assumptions be met: the population must be normally distributed, and the intervals must be equal (Edwards, 1960). Rind et al. provided information about neither the shape nor the nature of the population of individuals who had been sexually abused as children with regard to either the intensity of the abuses or the nature of the effects. Researchers investigating the complexities of child sexual abuse have recognized for some time that, given such an ill-defined population, it is essential that appropriate statistical techniques be selected and applied (Plunkett & Oates, 1990).

For example, investigators will usually establish a priori a statistically significant probability figure for stating that a null hypothesis is rejected or that a statistically significant relationship exists between two samples. Rind et al. used two different probability values for determining statistical significance: .05 with the nonparametric χ^2 statistic, and .10 with the parametric Pearson correlation coefficient r statistic. However, they provided no rationale for why they chose two different probability values.

When several studies are combined to obtain a larger sample size, heterogeneity of variance is also a potential problem. Any comparisons involving Pearson correlations that contain heterogeneous variances will not yield accurate estimates of the true relationships. For example, 10 of the 18 symptom-level meta-analyses (paper-and-pencil instruments were used to measure psychological adjustment) yielded heterogeneous results; repeated removal of the supposedly anomalous outliers increased the number of homogenous sets to 15 of the 18.

Thus, given the ill-defined child sexual abuse population, together with the wide variability within the samples and the heterogeneity of variances between the samples, the appropriateness of using parametric statistics and applying the meta-analytic technique is questionable.

PSYCHOLOGICAL ADJUSTMENT SYMPTOMS OF CHILD SEXUAL ABUSE ANALYZED

Our fifth methodological question concerns the absence both of a rationale for giving all 18 psychological adjustment symptoms equal weight with regard to child sexual abuse and of any relevance of low, albeit statistically significant, correlations. In the 59 usable studies examined by Rind et al., standardized tests, inventories, checklists, questionnaires, scales, a diagnostic instrument, a grid, surveys, schedules, and investigator-authored items were used to identify and measure what, if any, negative attitudinal and behavioral consequences might be correlated with child sexual abuse.

Rind et al. "[coded] the studies [that] resulted in 18 categories of psychological correlates of CSA; several additional correlates were infrequently reported and were therefore not considered in the meta-analyses" (1998, p. 28). At least one of the 18 different types of psychological adjustment "symptoms" was reported in each of the 54 independent samples analyzed: alcohol problems, anxiety, depression, dissociation, eating disorders, hostility, interpersonal sensitivity, locus of control, obsessive-compulsive symptomatology, paranoia, phobia, psychotic symptoms, self-esteem, sexual adjustment, social adjustment, somatization (which reflects bodily related distress), suicidal ideation and behavior, and wide adjustment (which is a general measure of psychological adjustment or symptomatology). It would have been desirable for the frequency with which each of the symptoms was identified in the 54 independent samples and their relevance in each sample to have been presented.

Rind et al.'s meta-analysis produced small but positive correlations, ranging from $r_u = .04$ to $.13$ (1998, p. 32, Table 3); all effect size estimates except one, locus of control, were statistically significant. According to Rind et al., the 17 statistically significant findings indicate that, for all symptoms except one, child sexual abuse participants as a group were slightly less well adjusted than the control participants. As discussed earlier, however, large samples often produce low albeit statistically significant correlations that have no practical value; the sample sizes for each of the 18 symptoms ranged from a low of 1,324 to a high of 7,949 (1998, p. 32, Table 3). Rind et al. interpreted the small correlations between psychological symptoms and child sexual abuse experiences to be supportive of their argument that CSA is not necessarily harmful. A simpler explanation for the small correlations is that many mediating factors degrade their sizes.

Specifically with regard to the relationship between child sexual abuse and psychological adjustment, Rind et al. concluded that "[t]he small magnitude of all effect size estimates implied that CSA effects or correlates in the college population are not intense for any of the 18 meta-analyzed symptoms" (1998, p. 32). Later in their paper, when they "analyzed the relationship between family environment and CSA in the college samples to determine whether they were confounded as a first step in examining whether CSA caused symptoms" (1998, p. 38), Rind et al. concluded that "the majority of significant CSA-symptom relations examined . . . may have been spurious. These results imply that significant CSA-symptom relations in studies based on college samples cannot be assumed to represent effects of CSA" (1998, p. 40). They summarized, "CSA-symptom relations could be underestimated relative to family environment-symptom relations because of unreliability of CSA measures, low base rates for CSA, and artificial dichotomization of CSA" (1998, p. 41). Underestimation appears to be quite likely; several earlier studies found the family environment to be significant as an influence on the behavioral and emotional life of individuals sexually abused as children; moreover, knowledge of the family environment can be invaluable to supplement information obtained from the victims themselves (Bushnell, Wells, & Oakley-Browne, 1992; Finkelhor, Moore, Hamby, & Straus, 1997).

Rind et al. failed to hypothesize a priori that, for example, certain psychological problems should show statistically significant correlations with child sexual abuse based on a stated theoretical construct; instead, they treated all 18 psychological adjustment correlates as if they were of equal weight, which suggests that they were simply noting that 17 of the 18 indicators supported their position that child sexual abuse had few statistically significant, even marginally negative effects. Nor did they offer a posteriori any hypotheses regarding future, more detailed study of any of the indicators. Essentially, their investigation of the 18 psychological adjustment indicators lacked theoretical focus. Some psychological adjustment symptoms have been found to be common across a number of studies: anxiety disorder, depression, self-esteem, sexual problems, and suicidal behaviors, as well as conduct disorder, sleep and somatic disorders, and substance abuse disorder (Fergusson, Horwood, & Lynskey, 1996; Kendall-Tackett, Williams, & Finkelhor, 1993; Swanston, Tebbutt, O'Toole, & Oates, 1997).

The wide variability in the types of psychological adjustment symptoms identified in the samples Rind et al. examined (1998, p. 32, Table 3) overlap with the symptoms identified by other researchers. Least often found are hostility and phobia (five studies), while most often found is depression (23 studies); seven types of symptoms (anxiety, depression, low self-esteem, poor sexual adjustment, poor social adjustment, somatization, and poor general psychological adjustment) were found in 15 or more of the studies. Rind et al. failed to consider these findings either in their study design or in their discussion of their own meta-analytic findings.

CONFOUNDING OF GENDER AND AGE AND UNDERREPRESENTATION OF MALES

From their meta-analytic study, Rind et al. concluded that young women experienced more severe negative reactions to and effects from earlier child sexual abuse than did young men. In fact, according to the authors, the reactions of many of the young men in their college samples who had experienced earlier abuse were either neutral or positive. This finding, Rind et al. acknowledged, disputes the findings of other investigators who have asserted that child sexual abuse is an equivalently negative experience for both males and females in both scope and effect.

Our sixth methodological question concerns inadequacy of the gender sampling reported, the confounding of gender and age in the meta-analysis, and the underrepresentation of males relative to females in the child sexual abuse literature. Rind et al. emphasized that their "[meta-analytic review] goal was to address the question: In the population of persons with a history of CSA, does this experience cause intense psychological harm on a widespread basis for both genders?" (1998, p. 22). They indicated:

> Bauserman and Rind (1997), on the basis of a review of college, national, and convenience samples, concluded that reactions and outcomes for boys are more likely to be neutral or positive than for girls. Many reviewers, however, have concluded or implied that CSA is an equivalent experience for boys and girls in terms of its negative impact (e.g., Black & DeBlassie, 1993; Briere & Runtz, 1993; Mendel, 1995; Urquiza & Capra, 1990; Watkins & Bentovim, 1992). Black and DeBlassie stated that CSA 'has, at the very least, an equivalent impact on males and females' (p. 128). Watkins and Bentovim claimed that one prevalent myth about CSA is that boys are less psychologically affected than girls. Mendel dismissed as an 'exercise in futility' efforts to determine whether boys or girls are more adversely affected by CSA, and concluded that CSA 'has pronounced deleterious effects on its victims, regardless of their gender' (p. 101). (1998, p. 24)

Concerning comparability of male and female reactions, Rind et al. reviewed 15 studies of self-reported effects of child sexual abuse experiences (1998, p. 36, Table 7). Ten studies involved 1,421 females; 11% considered their child sexual abuse to have been a positive experience, 18% considered it to have been neutral, and 72% considered it to have been negative. Nine studies involved 606 males; 37% considered their abuse to have been positive, 29% considered it to have been neutral, and 33% considered it to have been negative. (Rind et al. noted that the percentages do not total exactly 100 because of rounding.) Nevertheless, while the gender differences reported in these studies regarding negative effects from child sexual abuse are great, that one-third of the reporting males indicated the effects to be negative is not an insignificant number.

In order for Rind et al. to validly compare effects of child sexual abuse on females with its effects on males, it is essential that at least three methodological prerequisites of population sampling be comparable in the studies of both genders, specifically, the definition of child sexual abuse, the measurement of abuse prevalence rate, and the sampling method. One way of testing for comparability would be to determine whether the same type of relationship exists between sample sizes and abuse prevalence rates within the gender samples; to determine these relationships the senior author of the present article (J.A.W.) calculated Spearman rank correlation coefficients, a nonparametric statistic.

Of the 70 independent samples listed in the Rind et al. Appendix (1998, pp. 52-53) that provided data usable for meta-analytic estimation, 45 (64%) involved only female college students, whereas 25* (36%) involved only male college students. In these samples, 5,851 (27%) of the 21,999 women self-reported reactions to and effects from child sexual abuse as compared with 1,903 (14%) of the 13,651* men. (The two asterisks note numerical discrepancies. In their Results section [1998, p. 29], Rind et al. indicated that the male samples totaled 26. Apparently, one study [$N = 53$] was not included in the Appendix. When sample sizes are calculated from the percentages listed in the Appendix, therefore, the total is not 13,704. Rounding is not the cause; there are no discrepancies in the female figures.)

The 45 female samples revealed a statistically significant positive relationship between sample sizes and abuse prevalence rates ($r = .60$, 43 df, $p < .005$ [1-tail test]). In contrast, the 25 male samples revealed a nonsignificant relationship ($r = .21$, 23 df, $p > .05$ [1-tail test]).

These findings indicate that at least one methodological prerequisite was not met. The definition of child sexual abuse, as well as the measurement of its prevalence rate, might have differed for females and for males. The sampling method for the males might also have differed from study to study; some investigators might have explicitly sought individuals who had experienced child sexual abuse, others might have used random sampling strategies, and still others might have simply relied upon convenient availability of subjects. Thus, in addition to the inappropriateness of sampling only college students when attempting to assess the prevalence rate of child sexual abuse in the general population, which we have already addressed, basic differences between the gender samples themselves make even conclusions regarding college students inappropriate.

Moreover, concerning gender and age, the two measures were confounded in the meta-analysis. Rind et al. did not present the ages of the individual males and females who were sexually abused as children, only their upper ages are given in the Appendix (1998, p. 53). Because many researchers have found that girls are younger than boys when they are initially abused sexually, confounding of gender and age is likely (Fergusson, Lynskey, & Horwood, 1996; Silverman, Reinherz, & Giacona, 1996). Besides the basic biological and developmental differences between males and females, today's social norms regarding the sexually related behavior of females, including peer pressure, still differ substantially from those regarding the sexually related behavior of males, particularly during adolescence (De Gaston, Weed, & Jensen, 1996; Lab, Feigenbaum, & De Silva, 2000).

Concerning the underrepresentation of males relative to females in the child sexual abuse literature, Lab, Feigenbaum, and De Silva (2000) discuss the fact that for various cultural and social reasons far less research has been done on males than on females who experienced sexual abuse as children. When queried about their experiences, for example, males tend either to volunteer less frequently than females do or to respond less frankly than females do (Widom & Morris, 1997; Williams, 1994). Such underrepresentation is borne out in the studies sampled by Rind et al. As noted earlier, of the 70 independent samples identified for estimating prevalence rates, 64% involved women and 36% involved men (of the total of 35,650 college students, 62% were women and 38% were men, a ratio of approximately 3 to 2); 27% of the women and 14% of the men self-reported child sexual abuse. From the 59 usable studies examined by the authors, effect size data were based on 15,824 participants (3,254 men from 18 samples and 12,570 women from 40 samples), a ratio of almost 4 to 1.

LIMITATIONS OF THE RETROSPECTIVE
CROSS-SECTIONAL APPROACH

Retrospective cross-sectional studies, in which descriptive data are collected at a single point in time from a specific population regarding events that occurred during one or more earlier time periods, have dominated child sexual abuse research. They are inexpensive and easy to conduct, and they can be initiated and completed within a relatively short time. Compared with long-term, scientifically rich longitudinal studies that are far more expensive and demanding, however, they are limited to information collection, descriptive analyses, and the development of theoretical constructs and hypotheses; it is difficult to test hypotheses in retrospective cross-sectional studies.

Our seventh and most important methodological question concerns the major limitation of the retrospective cross-sectional approach used by Rind et al. Reliance on but a single human source, the victim, to accurately depict events and emotions associated with a probably traumatic experience that occurred many years earlier, as well as the present psychological adjustment of that individual, raises issues regarding both validity and reliability. Rind et al. reported that "[f]or each study . . . information . . . coded [included] (f) all reaction data, if provided, including both retrospectively recalled reactions to and current reflections on the CSA experiences; (g) all self-reported effects data, if provided, including responses to how these experiences affected participants overall and how they affected their sex lives . . . " (1998, p. 27).

All of the college samples included in the meta-analysis used the retrospective cross-sectional approach. The students had been asked to recall their child sexual abuse experiences and their reactions to them then, as well as their current reflections about the earlier experiences. The limitations of this type of research are well documented. Three specific limitations (distortion of information, absence of information, and personal maturation) affect the conclusions that can be drawn in child sexual abuse research.

With regard to the distortion of information, recall of earlier events and potentially emotionally and physically traumatic reactions to them have been found to be incomplete and inaccurate. People forget, especially events in the distant past; they tend to remember events as having occurred earlier than the actual dates; and they often reinvent the past to suit their current circumstances and needs (Briere, 1992; Henry, Moffitt, Caspi, Langley, & Silva, 1994). Rind et al. cited a controlled classroom study conducted earlier by two of them, which illustrates the problem of fallibility in retrospective recall. Rind and Bauserman (1993) found that students' judgments concerning adult-child sexual relations were biased negatively in their experiment by the simple use of negative terminology as opposed to neutral terminology.[4]

With regard to the absence of information, the only source of information regarding whether the college students experienced sexual abuse as children and subsequent effects later was the students themselves. Apparently, no other sources were checked for corroboration, such as family members, friends, peer groups, coworkers, and medical, educational, clinical, and legal records. This is a significant oversight.

With regard to personal maturation, the behavioral and emotional development of the sexually abused individual from childhood to adulthood is strongly influenced by numerous factors. Specific socioeconomic, demographic, and cultural circumstances of the abuse as well as the amount and type of familial support that was available are particularly important. Myriad experiences during the time between abuse and recall also affect that recall. Perceptions and attitudes about the earlier child sexual abuse may be altered by the experiences that occur in the intervening years, such that as a young adult an individual's reactions may be quite different (Briere, 1992). For example, if negative terminology as compared with neutral terminology could impact the results of the Rind and Bauserman (1993) classroom study, it goes without saying that many years of diverse cultural, social, and emotional experiences in the real world could have an even greater impact on the validity and reliability of the college students' self-reports of sexual abuse experienced much earlier. Retrospective studies are extremely limited in their ability to collect information regarding these critical interactive variables.

During the past decade organizational structures have been developed for the long-term planning, coordination, and conduction of longitudinal research (Herrenkohl, Herrenkohl, Egolf, & Wu, 1991; Runyan et al., 1998). In fact, several notable longitudinal studies have been conducted (e.g., Bagley & Mallick, 2000; Fergusson, Horwood, & Lynskey, 1997; Herrenkohl, Egolf, & Herrenkohl, 1997). While longitudinal studies are limited by such factors as economics and the participation of different corroborating informants such as parents and teachers (Briere, 1992; Frothingham et al., 2000), the methodological and scientific obstacles are fewer than those that are found in retrospective cross-sectional studies.

CONCLUSION

In this critical appraisal, seven major concerns have been identified and discussed with regard to the methodology used by Rind et al. in their meta-analytic review of child sexual abuse outcomes. Child sexual abuse is a pressing public problem that demands defensible research that can lead to better ways of identifying such abuse and, consequently, to better intervention and prevention procedures.

In particular, valid conclusions about the nonharmfulness of CSA cannot be drawn from Rind et al.'s poorly supported findings. The fact that this problem area is so very difficult to adequately investigate makes solid research design and conduct even more important. One obstacle has been and continues to be the development of a meaningful definition of child sexual abuse (Haugaard, 2000). A broader conceptualization of child sexual abuse to include all forms of child and adolescent sexual exploitation is needed (Itzin, 1997); this will facilitate articulation of the researchable definition.

A literature review of child sexual abuse research not cited by Rind et al. in their 1998 meta-analysis is presented in our second article in this volume. While some of the studies cited in our second article were published after Rind et al.'s meta-analysis, many papers published earlier could and should have been reviewed by Rind et al. before they undertook their massive effort. Their methodology and conclusions would have been different if they had included the omitted research.

NOTES

1. In χ^2 analyses, expected frequencies are determined from the marginal totals in a 2×2 design. When the expected and the observed frequencies are close in size, the resulting χ^2 values will not be statistically significant; as the size of the differences increases, the probability of obtaining statistical significance increases. The direction of

the differences is also important; when the observed frequencies are larger than the expected frequencies, that group is reporting more abuses than the comparison group, and when the observed frequencies are smaller, that group is reporting fewer abuses than the comparison group.

2. Specific problems with Rind et al.'s representation of the data from the three national studies are described in Dallam, S. J., Gleaves, D. H., Cepeda-Benito, A., Silberg, J., Kraemer, H. C., & Spiegel, D. (in press). The effects of childhood sexual abuse: A critique of Rind, Tromovitch and Bauserman (1998). *Psychological Bulletin*.

3. Our concerns about Rind et al.'s emphasis on perceived willingness as a factor in psychological outcome are addressed in our second article in this volume (pp. 157-182).

4. Our concerns about Rind et al.'s preference for using neutral terminology in child sexual abuse research are addressed in our second article in this volume (pp. 157-182).

REFERENCES

Babbie, E. R. (1973). *Data collection II: Interviewing. Survey research methods* (pp. 171-185). Belmont, CA: Wadsworth Publishing Company, Inc.

Bagley, C., & Mallick, K. (2000). Prediction of sexual, emotional, and physical maltreatment and mental health outcomes in a longitudinal cohort of 290 adolescent women. *Child Maltreatment, 5*(3), 218-226.

Briere, J. (1992). Methodological issues in the study of sexual abuse effects. *Journal of Consulting and Clinical Psychology, 60*(2), 196-203.

Bushnell, J. A., Wells, J. E., & Oakley-Browne, M. A. (1992). Long-term effects of intrafamilial sexual abuse in childhood. *Acta Psychiatrica Scandinavica, 85*(2), 136-142.

De Gaston, J. F, Weed, S., & Jensen, L. (1996). Understanding gender differences in adolescent sexuality. *Adolescence, 31*(121), 217-231.

Edwards, A. L. (1960). *Experimental design in psychological research. Revised edition.* New York, NY: Rinehart & Company, Inc.

Fergusson, D. M., Horwood, L. J., & Lynskey, M. T. (1996). Childhood sexual abuse and psychiatric disorder in young adulthood: II. Psychiatric outcomes of childhood sexual abuse. *Journal of the American Academy of Child and Adolescent Psychiatry, 35*(10), 1365-1374.

Fergusson, D. M., Horwood, L. J., & Lynskey, M. T. (1997). Childhood sexual abuse, adolescent sexual behaviors and sexual revictimization. *Child Abuse & Neglect, 21*(8), 789-803.

Fergusson, D. M., Lynskey, M. T., & Horwood, L. J. (1996). Childhood sexual abuse and psychiatric disorder in young adulthood: I. Prevalence of sexual abuse and factors associated with sexual abuse. *Journal of the American Academy of Child and Adolescent Psychiatry, 35*(10), 1355-1364.

Finkelhor, D., Moore, D., Hamby, S. L., & Straus, M. A. (1997). Sexually abused children in a national survey of parents: Methodological issues. *Child Abuse & Neglect, 21*(1), 1-9.

Frothingham, T. E., Hobbs, C. J., Wynne, J. M., Yee, L., Goyal, A., & Wadsworth, D. J. (2000). Follow up study eight years after diagnosis of sexual abuse. *Archives of Disease in Childhood, 83*(2), 132-134.

Haugaard, J. J. (2000). The challenge of defining child sexual abuse. *American Psychologist, 55*(9), 1036-1039.

Haugaard, J. J., & Emery, R. E. (1989). Methodological issues in child sexual abuse research. *Child Abuse & Neglect, 13*(1), 89-100.

Henry, B., Moffitt, T. E., Caspi, A., Langley, J., & Silva, P. A. (1994). On the "remembrance of things past": A longitudinal evaluation of the retrospective method. *Psychological Assessment, 6*(2), 92-101.

Herrenkohl, R. C., Egolf, B. P., & Herrenkohl, E. C. (1997). Preschool antecedents of adolescent assaultive behavior: A longitudinal study. *American Journal of Orthopsychiatry, 67*(3), 422-432.

Herrenkohl, R. C., Herrenkohl, E. C., Egolf, B. P., & Wu, P. (1991). The developmental consequences of child abuse: The Lehigh longitudinal study. In R. H. Starr, Jr., & D. A. Wolfe (Eds.), *The effects of child abuse and neglect: Issues and research* (pp. 57-81). New York: Guilford Press.

Itzin, C. (1997). Pornography and the organization of intra-and extrafamilial child sexual abuse: A conceptual model. In G. K. Kantor & J. L. Jasinski (Eds.), *Out of the darkness: Contemporary perspectives on family violence* (pp. 58-79). Thousand Oaks, CA: Sage Publications, Inc.

Kendall-Tackett, K. A., Williams, L. M., & Finkelhor, D. (1993). Impact of sexual abuse on children: A review and synthesis of recent empirical studies. *Psychological Bulletin, 113*(1), 164-180.

Lab, D. D., Feigenbaum, J. D., & De Silva, P. (2000). Mental health professionals' attitudes and practices towards male childhood sexual abuse. *Child Abuse & Neglect, 24*(3), 391-409.

Plunkett, A., & Oates, R. K. (1990). Methodological considerations in research on child sexual abuse. *Paediatric and Perinatal Epidemiology, 4*(3), 351-360.

Rind, B., & Bauserman, R. (1993). Biased terminology effects and biased information processing in research on adult-nonadult sexual interactions: An empirical investigation. *Journal of Sex Research, 30*(3), 260-269.

Rind, B., & Tromovitch, P. (1997). A meta-analytic review of findings from national samples on psychological correlates of child sexual abuse. *Journal of Sex Research, 34*(3), 237-255.

Rind, B., Tromovitch, P., & Bauserman, R. (1998). A meta-analytic examination of assumed properties of child sexual abuse using college samples. *Psychological Bulletin, 124*(1): 22-53.

Ronai, C. R. (1995). Multiple reflections of child sexual abuse: An argument for a layered account. *Journal of Contemporary Ethnography, 23*(4), 395-426.

Runyan, D. K., Curtis, P. A., Hunter, W. M., Black, M. M., Kotch, J. B., Bangdiwala, S., Dubowitz, H., English, D., Everson, M. D., & Landsverk, J. (1998). LONGSCAN [Longitudinal Studies of Child Abuse and Neglect]: A consortium for longitudinal studies of maltreatment and the life course of children. *Aggression and Violent Behavior, 3*(3), 275-285.

Sears, D. O. (1986). College sophomores in the laboratory: Influences of a narrow data base on social psychology's view of human nature. *Journal of Personality and Social Psychology, 51*(3), 515-530.

Siegel, S. (1956). *Nonparametric statistics for the behavioral sciences.* New York, NY: McGraw-Hill Book Company, Inc.

Silverman, A. B., Reinherz, H. Z., & Giaconia, R. M. (1996). The long-term sequelae of child and adolescent abuse: A longitudinal community study. *Child Abuse & Neglect, 20*(8), 709-723.

Strassberg, D. S., & Lowe, K. (1995). Volunteer bias in sexuality research. *Archives of Sexual Behavior, 24*(4), 369-382.

Styron, T., & Janoff-Bulman, R. (1997). Childhood attachment and abuse: Long-term effects on adult attachment, depression, and conflict resolution. *Child Abuse & Neglect, 21*(10), 1015-1023.

Swanston, H. Y., Tebbutt, J. S., O'Toole, B. I., & Oates, R. K. (1997). Sexually abused children 5 years after presentation: A case-control study. *Pediatrics, 100*(4), 600-608.

Widom, C. S., & Morris, S. (1997). Accuracy of adult recollections of childhood victimization: Part 2. Childhood sexual abuse. *Psychological Assessment, 9*(1), 34-46.

Williams, L. M. (1994). Recall of childhood trauma: A prospective study of women's memories of child sexual abuse. *Journal of Consulting and Clinical Psychology, 62*(6), 1167-1176.

The Real Controversy About Child Sexual Abuse Research: Contradictory Findings and Critical Issues Not Addressed by Rind, Tromovitch, and Bauserman in Their 1998 Outcomes Meta-Analysis

Pamela Paradis Tice
John A. Whittenburg
Gail L. Baker
Dorothy E. Lemmey

SUMMARY. This article presents a review of all types of child sexual abuse research ignored by Rind, Tromovitch, and Bauserman in their

Pamela Paradis Tice, BA, ELS, is Research Associate, Department of Family and Community Medicine, Baylor College of Medicine, Houston, TX. John A. Whittenburg, PhD, is Research Psychologist, SSTAR (Social Systems Training and Research), Inc., 7602 Del Rey Lane, Houston, TX 77071 (E-mail: jwhittenburg@go.com). Gail L. Baker, MA, is Research Psychologist, SSTAR (Social Systems Training and Research), Inc., 7602 Del Rey Lane, Houston, TX 77071 (E-mail: sstarinc@wt.net). Dorothy E. Lemmey, PhD, RN, is affiliated with the Department of Maternity Nursing, Lakeland Community College, 7700 Clocktower Drive, Kirtland, OH 44094 (E-mail: Dotlemmey@aol.com).

Address correspondence to: Pamela Paradis Tice, BA, ELS, Department of Family and Community Medicine, Baylor College of Medicine, 5615 Kirby Drive, Suite 610, Houston, TX 77005 (E-mail: pptice@bcm.tmc.edu).

The authors thank Doris Georgiou, PhD, for her critical comments throughout the preparation of this manuscript.

[Haworth co-indexing entry note]: "The Real Contoversy About Child Sexual Abuse Research: Contradictory Findings and Critical Issues Not Addressed by Rind, Tromovitch, and Bauserman in Their 1998 Outcomes Meta-Analysis." Tice, Pamela Paradis et al. Co-published simultaneously in *Journal of Child Sexual Abuse* (The Haworth Maltreatment & Trauma Press, an imprint of The Haworth Press, Inc.) Vol. 9, No. 3/4, 2001, pp. 157-182; and: *Misinformation Concerning Child Sexual Abuse and Adult Survivors* (ed: Charles L. Whitfield, Joyanna Silberg, and Paul Jay Fink) The Haworth Maltreatment & Trauma Press, an imprint of The Haworth Press, Inc., 2001, pp. 157-182. Single or multiple copies of this article are available for a fee from The Haworth Document Delivery Service [1-800-HAWORTH, 9:00 a.m. - 5:00 p.m. (EST). E-mail address: getinfo@haworthpressinc.com].

1998 meta-analytic study. Eight major findings are addressed. Altogether, these findings demonstrate the narrow focus of the Rind et al. meta-analysis. By restricting a supposedly broad meta-analysis to only some of the research and population in question, the conclusions Rind et al. drew regarding this complex topic (primarily, that adult-child sex is not necessarily harmful to children) are invalid. *[Article copies available for a fee from The Haworth Document Delivery Service: 1-800-HAWORTH. E-mail address: <getinfo@haworthpressinc.com> Website: <http://www.HaworthPress.com> © 2001 by The Haworth Press, Inc. All rights reserved.]*

KEYWORDS. Child sexual abuse, long-term effects, outcomes, meta-analysis, methodology, critique

The articles and studies selected and cited by Rind, Tromovitch, and Bauserman (1998) in their meta-analysis of child sexual abuse effects (see our methodological critique and the critique by Dallam in this volume) presented but a limited view of recent thinking regarding child sexual abuse. Their major meta-analytic effort included studies of child sexual abuse that involved the recall of such experiences only by college students, a study population that is known to be problematic (Sears, 1986; Strassberg & Lowe, 1995). We believe that their decision to exclude the more severe clinical and legal cases and to examine this extremely controversial topic as conservatively as possible significantly biased their meta-analytic findings.

To support this contention, we discuss in this article some of the more adverse physical and mental consequences of child sexual abuse; we provide sound reasons why we believe these consequences cannot simply be dismissed as exceptional or extraordinary. We also discuss some significant gaps other investigators have discovered in our understanding of child sexual abuse and its outcomes as well as in certain national statistics, gaps that suggest the conclusions drawn by Rind et al. from their meta-analysis are more subjective than objective since the study design itself did not permit methodologically valid conclusions to be drawn. In the literature review[1] of child sexual abuse research papers not cited by Rind et al., and others published since 1998, eight major findings are addressed in the present article: (1) children are physically harmed by sexual relations with adults; (2) children are also psychologically and behaviorally harmed; (3) child sexual abuse is often intrusive and can be violent; (4) the different forms of sexual exploitation blur the boundaries between childhood and adolescence; (5) unhealthy sexual behaviors in young adulthood suggest previous exploitation; (6) the use of neutral language absolves adult responsibility for child harm; (7) the criterion of child willingness avoids adult ethical concerns about sexual behavior; and (8) statistics on child sexual abuse and its outcomes remain quite incomplete. These are discussed below.

CHILDREN ARE PHYSICALLY HARMED
BY SEXUAL RELATIONS WITH ADULTS

More than 50 years ago, Kinsey and his colleagues (Kinsey, Pomeroy, & Martin, 1948) claimed that adult-child sexual relations harmed children only when authority figures (parents, teachers, and the police, for example) became hysterical and overreacted. They completely ignored the possibility of physical harm, as did Rind et al. in 1998.

Although physical injuries in sexually abused children are often apparently absent or are undetectable because they have completely healed (De Jong, 1992), the pathology of sexual activity, including lacerations of the genitals, rectal damage, collapse of the anal sphincter muscle, internal bleeding, and asphyxiation, has been and continues to be an important issue in pediatric medicine (Kadish, Schunk, & Britton, 1998; Pokorny, Pokorny, & Kramer, 1992) and, more specifically, in pediatric forensic medicine (Banaschak & Brinkmann, 1999; McCann, Reay, Siebert, Stephens, & Wirtz, 1996). Many circumstances exist under which a child or an adolescent can be the victim of sexual exploitation; in many of these situations, the possibility of physical harm can indeed be great. For example, adolescent and adult prostitutes have been beaten by their clients, sometimes to the point that they required hospitalization (Farley & Barkan, 1998).

The possibility that adult-child sexual relations can cause child death also should not be ignored, nor should deliberate acts of child sexual homicide. Although child sexual homicide is the rarest form of child sexual abuse, the fact remains that more than 25% of sexual assault murder victims are under 18 years of age (Greenfeld, 1997). Other investigators have further emphasized that many child homicide cases involving abducted children lack the forensic testing needed to establish sexual assault before death, even though children 5 to 17 years of age are often abducted for this expressed purpose (Rodreguez, Nahirny, Burgess, & Burgess, 1998), and usually by a stranger or a nonfamily member (Finkelhor, Hotaling, & Sedlak, 1992).

Furthermore, the possibility of children and adolescents acquiring sexually transmitted diseases (STDs) from sexual relations with adults should never be ignored; children are especially susceptible to these diseases (Moscicki, Winkler, Irwin, & Schachter, 1989), some of which can cause significant morbidity and can be fatal (Holmes et al., 1999). While the risk of children acquiring STDs through sexual abuse is seemingly minimal, only 2% of reported cases each year occur in children (Centers for Disease Control and Prevention [CDC], 1998a), these national statistics are incomplete, because the only STDs for which the CDC collect notification data are syphilis, gonorrhea, chlamydia, and human immunodeficiency virus (HIV) infection (CDC, 1998a; CDC, 1998b). Although the CDC has investigated sexual abuse as a risk factor in the transmission of STDs in children and adolescents (Beck-Sague & Solomon, 1999), quantifiable estimates of the numbers of children and adolescents who acquired the different diseases through sexual abuse, prostitution, or survival sex while homeless on the streets are unavailable.

The pervasiveness of child sexual abuse, the potential for physical damage, and the possibility of infection with STDs were sufficient for child sexual abuse to be declared a significant public health problem more than a decade ago by then Surgeon General C. Everett Koop (1989) and reemphasized as such more recently by child sexual abuse researchers (McMahon & Puett, 1999). A committed medical research agenda is required to address such a major risk to all of those children and adolescents who are sexually exploited (Kerns, 1998).

CHILDREN ARE ALSO PSYCHOLOGICALLY AND BEHAVIORALLY HARMED

The psychological and behavioral consequences of child sexual abuse are well established (Kendall-Tackett, Williams, & Finkelhor, 1993; Roesler & McKenzie, 1994). Some are severe and irreversible (Perry, Pollard, Blakley, Baker, & Vigilante, 1995). The most common symptoms among sexually abused individuals are depression, anxiety, aggression, sexual acting-out, and poor self-esteem (Kendall-Tackett et al., 1993; Roesler & McKenzie, 1994). The more extreme symptoms include self-mutilation, suicidal ideation, repeated suicide attempts, and suicide (Briere & Gil, 1998; Brown, Cohen, Johnson, & Smailes, 1999; Santa Mina & Gallop, 1998).

Having sex as a child, irrespective of abuse, appears to be predictive of coerciveness in later sexual relations (Lodico, Gruber, & DiClemente, 1996). In addition, there is evidence that abusive sexual relations might predispose both girls and boys not only to victimizing sexual behavior in childhood and adolescence (Gray, Pithers, Busconi, & Houchens, 1999; Hall, Mathews, & Pearce, 1998; Skuse et al., 1998) but also to revictimization in adolescence (Fergusson, Horwood, & Lynskey, 1997; Lodico et al., 1996) as well as in adulthood (Muehlenhard, Highby, Lee, Bryan, & Dodrill, 1998). In some sexually abused boys, there might also be a predisposition to continual reenactment of the abuse and to subsequent repetition of sexually aggressive behaviors such as serial rape (Burgess, Hazelwood, Rokous, Hartman, & Burgess, 1988). It is noteworthy that, of the 88,100 convicted sex offenders imprisoned in state facilities throughout the United States in 1994, the most recent year for which data are available, more than one-third had, themselves, been physically or sexually abused as children, and one in seven had been previously convicted of a violent sex crime (Greenfeld, 1997). When these sex offenders had lone victims, 78% of the victims were under 18 years of age and 45% were under 12 years of age; the median age of all reported victims of sexual assault was under 13 years of age (Greenfeld, 1997).

Given such documented negative psychological and behavioral consequences among those who had been sexually abused as children, it is surprising and puzzling that Rind et al. limited their meta-analysis to a different population, college student samples alone, and instead, emphasized positive outcomes. For example, the authors cited, but did not analyze, a study by McMillen, Zuravin, and Rideout (1995) in which the benefits perceived among a group of adult women who were sexually abused as children included the desire to protect children from abuse, the desire to protect oneself from further abuse, greater knowledge of child sexual abuse, and a stronger personality. Only anecdotal evidence of perceived benefit has been presented in other reports of childhood sexual abuse outcomes (Brongersma, 1990). Rind et al. made no attempt to ascertain the reasons why some college students expressed positive perceptions. They also neglected to even consider that a positive attitudinal response toward past child sexual abuse might be simply a ubiquitously human, self-protective reaction; so often, individuals who have endured adverse life experiences try to find at least some redemption in those experiences.

Studies of cognitive coping strategies and postabuse resilience in children (Herrenkohl, Herrenkohl, & Egolf, 1994; Spaccarelli & Kim, 1995), in adolescents (Johnson & Kenkel, 1991; Shapiro & Levendosky, 1999), and in young and older adults (Liem, James, O'Toole, & Boudewyn, 1997; Sigmon, Greene, Rohan, & Nichols, 1996) have elucidated how seemingly positive outcomes of child sexual abuse could be possible. Nevertheless, individuals truly resilient to child sexual abuse experiences actually comprise but a small minority of people who have experienced such abuse, and identifying them unequivocally is fraught with methodological problems.

The first and foremost problem is that the definition of resilience to child sexual abuse, and other forms of child maltreatment, varies from study to study; such variance makes comparisons across studies tenuous at best (Heller, Larrieu, D'Imperio, & Boris, 1999). The validity of resilience studies is also compromised by the reliance, typically, on a single source of data rather than on multiple sources; the need for multiple informants in comprehensive evaluations of the outcomes of child sexual abuse has been well documented (Kaufman, Jones, Stieglitz, Vitulano, & Mannarino, 1994; Spaccarelli & Kim, 1995). Furthermore, most of the resilience studies of child sexual abuse survivors have been cross-sectional. This methodology does not permit evaluation of potential delayed effects of sexual abuse that can occur either in adolescence or in adulthood (Briere, 1992); because of the limited time span, it is also insufficient to permit the labeling of youths in particular as resilient (Luthar & Zigler, 1991). For example, in a 16-year longitudinal study (Herrenkohl et al., 1994), only 25 (5.5%) of 457 children could be characterized as resilient. For obvious reasons, few truly longitudinal studies such as this have been conducted.

As we attempt to establish the relationship between coping strategies and child sexual abuse outcomes, we must proceed with caution. We cannot assume that individuals who have not been referred for psychotherapy for childhood sexual abuse are resilient or are coping well with their immediate or past experiences of such abuse. Many individuals who need psychotherapy never enter the mental health system (Green, 1993); many who do enter it are not followed long enough (usually two years or less in most published studies) to ascertain delayed negative outcomes. Claiming positive outcomes prematurely and without some form of objective corroboration can only serve to distort the true effects of child sexual abuse.

CHILD SEXUAL ABUSE IS OFTEN INTRUSIVE AND CAN BE VIOLENT

The physically and emotionally intrusive and sometimes violent nature of child sexual abuse is supported by historical evidence (e.g., deMause, 1991; Lascaratos & Poulakou-Rebelakou, 2000) as well as contemporary evidence (e.g., Emmert & Kohler, 1998; Finkelhor & Dziuba-Leatherman, 1994; Fischer & McDonald, 1998). Child sexual abuse can easily become a part of a global pattern of victimization in families rife with domestic violence (Bowen, 2000). In fact, the abuse itself can be an act of family violence (Alpert, Cohen, & Sege, 1997; Fischer & McDonald, 1998; Kaplan, 2000). That some children are both physically and sexually abused is well documented (e.g., Gray et al., 1999; Reinhart, 1987; Schaaf & McCanne, 1998). While some investigators prefer to distinguish these children from those who have been only sexually or only physically abused (Schaaf & McCanne, 1998), others believe that signs of physical abuse should automatically raise the suspicion of sexual abuse

(Reinhart, 1987). Given the retrospective realization by historians of the psychosexual dynamics involved in the once-ritualized corporal punishment of children (Benthall, 1991), we should be seeking to discover the ways in which physical and sexual abuse overlap, and to identify those forms of physical abuse (e.g., violence to genitals as reported by Finkelhor & Dziuba-Leatherman, 1994) from which the perpetrator may derive psychosexual gratification.

Child sexual abuse can also be an act of extrafamilial sexual assault (Emmert & Kohler, 1998; Fischer & McDonald, 1998; Greenfeld, 1997) or a component of cumulative trauma through revictimization in adulthood (Follette, Polusny, Bechtle, & Naugle, 1996; Muehlenhard et al., 1998). Some investigators have even suggested that what we now know about the acute and chronic effects of child sexual abuse is sufficient for it to be used as a model of chronic trauma in children (Putnam & Trickett, 1993). Others have identified specific traumagenic dynamics of child sexual abuse (traumatic sexualization, betrayal, stigmatization, and powerlessness) that undoubtedly affect outcomes (Finkelhor & Browne, 1985).

An adverse family environment can contribute to negative outcomes following adult-child sexual relations, but Rind et al. ignored the report by Finkelhor (1993) that no specific demographic or family characteristics that have been found to be predictive of child sexual abuse have also been found to be predictive of outcomes. They also ignored the many consequences of at least five documented factors: incestuousness (Bachmann, Moggi, & Stirnemann-Lewis, 1994; Rudd & Herzberger, 1999), the extrafamilial sexual abuse that occurs among children in higher socioeconomic strata (Basta & Peterson, 1990; Garnefski & Arends, 1998), the intrafamilial and extrafamilial sexual abuse perpetrated by some sex offenders (Abel, Becker, Cunningham-Rathner, Mittelman, & Rouleau, 1988), the high-level physical and emotional intrusiveness of both intrafamilial and extrafamilial sexual abuse (Fischer & McDonald, 1998), and the sexual exploitation many adolescents often encounter as they try to survive on the streets after escaping abusive family environments by running away (e.g., Greene, Ennett, & Ringwalt, 1999; Kral, Molnar, Booth, & Watters, 1997).

That child sexual abuse should be considered to be a form of trauma is substantiated by neurobiological studies. Perry and colleagues (Perry et al., 1995) have found permanent physical and biochemical changes in the brains of both boys and girls who have endured prolonged physical or sexual abuse. These changes have long-term physical, emotional, behavioral, cognitive, and social effects that can result in persistent, maladaptive traits; such changes in a child's developing brain cannot be reversed in later life, even with intense psychotherapy.

The findings of Perry and colleagues are not spurious. Other investigators have also documented specific changes in the brains of sexually abused individuals, such as a significantly reduced left-sided hippocampal volume (Bremner et al., 1997; Stein, Koverola, Hanna, Torchia, & McClarty, 1997) and abnormal cerebral cortical development (Ito, Teicher, Glod, & Ackerman, 1998; Teicher et al., 1997). In some abused individuals, who might have been predisposed to epileptic seizures, the effects of child sexual abuse on their brains have been so potent that seizures were triggered (Greig & Betts, 1992).

What is being made clear by these neurobiological studies is that some of the devastating long-term behavioral consequences of child sexual abuse can also be biologically expressed. Additional research is needed before all of the ramifications of neurological findings in the context of child sexual abuse can be fully appreciated.

DIFFERENT FORMS OF SEXUAL EXPLOITATION BLUR BOUNDARIES BETWEEN CHILDHOOD AND ADOLESCENCE

Age is an established critical variable with regard to outcomes of child sexual abuse (Feiring, Taska, & Lewis, 1999; Mraovich & Wilson, 1999). Rind et al. stated that "[a]dolescents are different from children in that they are more likely to have sexual interests, to know whether they want a particular sexual encounter, and to resist an encounter that they do not want" (1998, p. 46). When we consider the variations of sexual exploitation that occur among both girls and boys in both of these age groups (for example, incestuousness and nonincestuousness, organized child sex rings, child pornography, and child prostitution; Itzin, 1997), these differences and the developmental boundaries between childhood and adolescence become less distinct. While they are more developmentally mature than children, adolescents (not unlike adults) can still be sexually exploited. The strategies used to seduce them, which are often very sophisticated, take blatant advantage of adolescent sexual curiosity (Singer, Hussey, & Strom, 1992).

Sexual exploitation of adolescents occurs whether they live at home (Council on Scientific Affairs, 1993; Gardner & Cabral, 1990) or whether they are homeless on the streets (Greene et al., 1999; Kral et al., 1997). The most recent estimates available of homeless youths in the United States, ranging from 250,000 to 2 million (Council on Scientific Affairs, 1989; Robertson, 1992), suggest that the potential number of adolescents who could be sexually exploited is quite large. In fact, according to the most recent estimate that could be found, approximately 75% of the youths involved in prostitution in the

United States are homeless or have run away from home because of an abusive environment (Cohen, 1987). For those who engage in survival sex or prostitution, abuse undoubtedly continues.

The high-risk sexual behaviors of adolescents that result from such exploitation, or that are representative of re-victimization subsequent to sexual abuse in childhood, must be taken seriously; the infection with STDs discussed above of some three million adolescents in the United States each year is one of the major reasons (Eng & Butler, 1997). How these infections are introduced into the adolescent population has become such a serious public health issue that the CDC now offers supplemental funding to facilities, which have already been awarded a Comprehensive STD Prevention Systems grant, that serve high-risk adolescents (e.g., school-based clinics, drug treatment centers, juvenile detention centers, and clinics for homeless youths) (2000 funding announcement posted at http://www.cdc.gov/od/pgo/funding/STDSupp.htm).

UNHEALTHY SEXUAL BEHAVIORS IN YOUNG ADULTHOOD SUGGEST PREVIOUS EXPLOITATION

An important indicator of positive outcomes following childhood sexual experiences would be the eventual ability to form lasting, intimate relationships. Even in many college student samples, however, negative attitudinal and behavioral outcomes are evident.

For example, some college students consider homosexual adult-adolescent sexual relations to be exploitative but perceive heterosexual adult-adolescent sexual relations to be nonexploitative (Maynard & Wiederman, 1997). In particular, some college men regard sexual relations between an adult female and an adolescent male to be nonrepresentative of child sexual abuse but sexual relations between an adult male and an adolescent female to be representative of such abuse (Broussard, Wagner, & Kazelskis, 1991; Smith, Fromuth, & Morris, 1997). Others have misconceptions about what acts constitute sexual relations; even today, some believe that fellatio, cunnilingus, and penal-anal intercourse are not sexual behaviors (Sanders & Reinisch, 1999). Perceptions about childhood sexual experiences might well influence such misconceptions. For example, many young men and some young women with court-substantiated histories of child sexual abuse do not recall or report having had the experiences (Widom & Morris, 1997; Williams, 1994), and some college men and women acknowledge sexual interest in children (Smiljanich & Briere, 1996). Some college students who engage in risky sexual behaviors and use drugs have misconceptions about their own risk of HIV infection (Brown, 1998). Even when college students do engage in safer sexual behaviors, however, their attitudes can still remain supportive of casual or experimental sex (Feigenbaum, Weinstein, & Rosen, 1995; Netting, 1992). Later casual college sex might even lead some students to overlook earlier potentially negative sexual experiences.

Specific problems involving sexual behavior are often found among college students. Coerciveness in sexual relations is one common example (e.g., Biglan, Noell, Ochs, Smolkowski, & Metzler, 1995; Struckman-Johnson & Struckman-Johnson, 1994). Rape is another (e.g., Abbey, McAuslan, & Ross, 1998; Rickert & Wiemann, 1998).

In addition, having had forced sexual relations in adolescence predisposes young adults to health-risk behaviors (Brener, McMahon, Warren, & Douglas, 1999). In one sample of male college students included by Rind et al. in their meta-analytic review, only 7.3% of the 2,972 18- to 24-year-olds reported an abusive sexual experience such as exhibition, fondling, and penetration before the age of 14 years (Risin & Koss, 1987). A separate part of this study, however, which involved the same sample of 2,972 young men but instead addressed predictors of sexual aggression, was not included in Rind et al. review. In this second part, Koss and Dinero (1988) discovered that after the age of 14 years, 4.4% of the young men admitted to perpetrating acts legally defined as rape, 3.3% to acts legally defined as attempted rape, 7.2% to acts of sexual coercion (that is, intercourse subsequent to the use of menacing verbal pressure or misuse of authority), and 10.2% to forced fondling and kissing; all are accepted to be acts of nonconsensual sexual contact. Although Koss and Dinero (1988) did not indicate how many of the young men who made these admissions had also had childhood sexual experiences, they did state that their overall results "[provide] support for a developmental sequence for sexual aggression in which early experiences [i.e., before 14 years of age] and psychological characteristics establish preconditions for sexual violence" (1998, p. 144); this developmental sequence occurs whether the early sexual experiences were voluntary or involuntary.

As Rind et al. stated, "Reviewers who are convinced that CSA [child sexual abuse] is a major cause of adult psychopathology may fall prey to confirmation bias by noting and describing study findings indicating harmful effects but ignoring or paying less attention to findings indicating nonnegative outcomes" (1998, p. 24). The converse is just as true. That Rind et al., themselves, overlooked the report by Koss and Dinero (1988) is disquieting: "Mendel (1995) focused on results from Fromuth and Burkhart's (1989) midwestern sample of [university] males to argue that boys are harmed by their CSA [child sexual abuse] experiences but paid little attention to the southeastern sample of males reported in the same article, for whom all CSA-adjustment correlates were nonsignificant" (1998, p. 24). Perhaps the study by Koss and Dinero (1988) simply did not meet the inclusion criteria of the meta-analytic review; nevertheless, ignoring even the mention of such conflicting data casts doubt on the objectivity of Rind et al.

USE OF NEUTRAL LANGUAGE
ABSOLVES ADULT RESPONSIBILITY FOR CHILD HARM

Rind et al. reluctantly accept the general definition of child sexual abuse to be "a sexual interaction involving either physical contact or no contact (e.g., exhibitionism) between either a child or adolescent and someone significantly older, or between two peers who are children or adolescents when coercion is used" (1998, p. 23). They prefer that neutral language be used in all professional discourse concerning child sexual abuse, however, which had been defended in more detail in an earlier publication (Rind & Bauserman, 1993).

In recent years, use of neutral language has become commonplace among some investigators with regard to human sexual behaviors; prostitution is now commercial sex work, sexual promiscuity or addiction has become a lifestyle, rape might be an evolutionary adaptation for procreative purposes, pedophilia could be a sexual preference. Children are simply sexual outlets for adults and for each other. The intention of investigators has been to introduce neutrality into human sexuality research.

While such neutralization may appear inconsequential, it definitely is not. Instead, this practice has tended to neutralize human sexual behaviors themselves, from innocent flirtation to tragic sexual homicide. But even sexual behaviors that now have greater social acceptance carry certain risks. For example, the increased practice of anal intercourse among heterosexuals during the past 50 years has led to a significantly increased incidence of anorectal cancer (a rare cancer that was once most common in homosexual and bisexual men) among women (e.g., Melbye, Rabkin, Frisch, & Biggar, 1994). In other words, a child or an adolescent who has had anal intercourse not only is at risk for infection with a sexually transmitted disease but also is at risk for developing anorectal cancer.

There is another reason why the use of neutral language acts to absolve adults from their responsibility for sexual harm to children. Given the neutralization techniques known to be used by pedophile organizations in their publications (e.g., de Young, 1988), the language preference of Rind et al. is inappropriate in their meta-analytic review.

CRITERION OF CHILD WILLINGNESS AVOIDS ADULT ETHICAL CONCERNS ABOUT SEXUAL BEHAVIOR

Rind et al. suggested that "[a] willing encounter between an adolescent and an adult with positive reactions on the part of the adolescent . . . be labeled scientifically as *adult-adolescent sex,* while an unwanted encounter with negative reactions . . . be labeled *adolescent sexual abuse*" (1998, p. 46). Such a criterion is an extremely poor one because it totally ignores the vast power differential between adults and children (Meyer, 1996). Psychologically and cognitively immature children cannot possibly have developed the ability to either willingly or consensually participate in an activity they cannot yet fully understand. Nevertheless, the belief that children desire and fantasize adult-like sex has become so entrenched in our societal belief system, as well as in formal sexology circles (Meyer, 1996), that it has even become part of the denial system of pedophiles (Hanson, Gizzarelli, & Scott, 1994; Pollock & Hashmall, 1991). Indeed, because both ignored the undifferentiated nature of childhood sexuality, the continuing abuse of children may have been supported ideologically by the Freudian and Kinseyan theories (Meyer, 1996).

The historical record of adult-child sexual relations reveals that such relations have been sustained not by the choices of children but rather by the tendency of adults to attribute their sexual needs, wants, desires, and motives to children. Not surprisingly, even when society has had strict legal and religious prohibitions against them (Lascaratos & Poulakou-Rebelakou, 2000), such relations have been largely exploitative and assaultive (deMause, 1991).

An enormous literature documents forced or coercive sexual relations to be unhealthy. This includes such relations between children (e.g., Adler & Schutz, 1995; De Jong, 1989), between adolescents (e.g., Biglan et al., 1995; Shrier, Pierce, Emans, & DuRant, 1998), and between adults and children (e.g., Conte, Wolf, & Smith, 1989; Elliott, Browne, & Kilcoyne, 1995), as well as between young adults (e.g., Biglan et al., 1995; Struckman-Johnson & Struckman-Johnson, 1994) and between adults (e.g., Busby & Compton, 1997; Coxell, King, Mezey, & Gordon, 1999).

Even the Sexuality Information and Education Council of the United States (SIECUS), considered to be the nation's foremost proponent of human sexuality education, declares the problem of such relations in its position statement on sexual exploitation:

> Sexual relationships should be consensual between partners who are developmentally, physically, and emotionally capable of understanding the interaction. Coerced and exploitative sexual acts and behaviors such as rape, incest, sexual relations between adults and children, sexual abuse,

and sexual harassment are always reprehensible. There should be information and education programs to prevent such acts, laws to punish them, treatment programs to help survivors and offenders, and research to increase understanding of the causes and effects of sexual exploitation. (SIECUS, 2001, p. e3)

Attitudinal factors undoubtedly play a role in some of the coercive sexual relations among adolescents and young adults; acceptance of rape myths, a predominant factor, is a key example (e.g., Abbey et al., 1998; Marciniak, 1998). Regardless of what factors are involved, however, sexual relations in childhood, even those perceived to be consensual, may be predictive of high-risk sexual behaviors in adolescence and in young adulthood (e.g., Biglan et al., 1995; Fergusson et al., 1997; Shrier et al., 1998). Conversely, men and women who contract a sexually transmitted disease are more likely to have had earlier adverse sexual experiences, in childhood, in adolescence, and even in adulthood (Hillis, Anda, Felitti, Nordenberg, & Marchbanks, 2000; Pitzner, McGarry-Long, & Drummond, 2000).

As noted earlier in the section on psychological and behavioral harm, having sex as a child appears to be predictive of coerciveness in later sexual relations. In addition, having abusive sexual relations might predispose both girls and boys to revictimization both in adolescence and in adulthood, as well as predisposing some boys to reenactment of the abuse and repetition of sexually aggressive behaviors, including such crimes as rape.

STATISTICS ON CHILD SEXUAL ABUSE AND ITS OUTCOMES REMAIN QUITE INCOMPLETE

Rind et al., as noted at the beginning of this article, excluded the more severe clinical and legal cases from their meta-analysis. Their rationale was that research on child sexual abuse that has relied primarily on such nonrepresentative samples has led to an overestimation of negative outcomes of adult-child sexual relations. Based on the extant literature, as we have stated, we believe the opposite to be true. In fact, it appears that their exclusion has led to an underestimation of negative outcomes.

Other investigators have identified numerous problems that lead to underestimation, including: the numbers of undetected crimes, some of which might be ignored simply as sexual-initiation experiences (e.g., Smith et al., 2000; Weber, Gearing, Davis, & Conlon, 1992); delayed disclosure of abuse, and then primarily to nonauthority figures (Smith et al., 2000); ethnic and socioeconomic factors that affect entry into psychotherapy (Haskett, Nowlan,

Hutcheson, & Whitworth, 1991; Tingus, Heger, Foy, & Leskin, 1996); unsubstantiated cases of abuse, primarily those involving male victims (Besharov, 1997; Dersch & Munsch, 1999); refusal to participate in study interviews, with the most dysfunctional families usually not participating (deMause, 1991; Lynch, Stern, Oates, & O'Toole, 1993); and the role of traumatic amnesia in survival following child sexual abuse (Scheflin & Brown, 1996; Whitfield, 1997).

DeMause (1991) believes that more accurate incident results can be achieved by interviewing groups of individuals who are more likely to have been sexually molested as children. Yet these people (i.e., institutionalized criminals, prostitutes, juveniles in shelters, and psychotics) are the very types of individuals whom Rind et al. excluded from their meta-analysis. It is important to note that deMause's belief is being given credence, for example, by recent studies of incarcerated youths and adults (e.g., Browne, Miller, & Maguin, 1999; Greenfeld, 1997; Mason, Zimmerman, & Evans, 1998).

Still other investigators have been concerned with substantial underreporting of the details of child sexual abuse experiences. Lack of information regarding childhood STDs acquired through sexual abuse, for example, was discussed earlier. Overlooking pornography and prostitution as forms of sexual abuse among children and adolescents (Lemmey & Tice, 2000) also contributes to the problem of underreporting, because the only records maintained on these criminal activities are arrest records (U. S. Bureau of Justice Statistics, 1998), and those records identify children only as offenders (i.e., as prostitutes) and never as victims. Furthermore, there are no official records of how many homeless and runaway adolescents engage in survival sex, which is another form of exploitation. While none of the factors considered to be contributing to the underreporting of child sexual abuse are particularly surprising, Finkelhor (1995) explained that "[t]he victimization of children has only recently come to merit academic concern, due in part to the insight that childhood victimization may, in fact, be a prime cause of delinquency" (p. 177).

The absence of males from maltreatment research—as both perpetrators and victims—results in a lack of critical information concerning them (Haskett, Marziano, & Dover, 1996; Holmes et al., 1997; Holmes & Slap, 1998). The specific concern of Holmes et al. (1997) regarding the lack of male victim information was recently corroborated in a study of the attitudes and practices of mental health professionals toward male childhood sexual abuse (Lab, Feigenbaum, & De Silva, 2000). As Haskett et al. (1996) pointed out, "[E]ven when males are included in samples of abusive parents and individuals abused in childhood, there is an insufficient representation of males to conduct analyses that might highlight important gender differences" (p. 1181). Consequently, our current knowledge of gender differences is sketchy at best concerning sexual abuse characteristics (Gold, Elhai, Lucenko, Swingle, & Hughes, 1998), victim characteristics (Faller, 1989; Rudin, Zalewski, & Bodmer-Turner, 1995), victim post-abuse attitudes about adult-child sexual relations (Briere, Henschel, & Smiljanich, 1992; Wellman, 1993), victim post-abuse coping strategies (Sigmon et al., 1996), and victim post-abuse behaviors (Garnefski & Arends, 1998; Garnefski & Diekstra, 1997; Shrier et al., 1998), which include prostitution and other sexually criminal behaviors (Burgess et al., 1988; Widom & Ames, 1994).

Obtaining such information continues to be hampered by several factors: a reluctance in Western cultures to fully acknowledge that males can be sexually coerced or assaulted (Coxell et al., 1999; Isely, 1998; King & Woollett, 1997), which might explain why some mental health professionals have blaming attitudes toward adult-male sexual-abuse survivors (Richey-Suttles & Remer, 1997); a prejudicial viewpoint that few females perpetrate incest, sexual coercion, or sexual assaults (Fiebert & Tucci, 1998; Hetherton, 1999); the denial of father-son sexual abuse (Watkins & Bentovim, 1992); and the repressed albeit real belief in male sexual entitlement (i.e., that all sexual experiences are desirable and favorable for boys and for men). Such a belief about male sexual experiences might explain why many fewer men with court-documented histories of sexual abuse in childhood do not recall or report that experience (Widom & Morris, 1997), why others may consider their past sexual abuse to be a normal part of childhood development (Briggs & Hawkins, 1996), and why still others report having liked their abuse (Fischer, 1991). All of these factors may well contribute to the general nondetection of the mental health problems of men (Borowsky et al., 2000).

What is known about the sexual abuse of male children and adolescents, however, does indicate that both the immediate and the long-term effects are deleterious and many (Watkins & Bentovim, 1992). Anecdotal evidence of beneficial effects (Brongersma, 1990), therefore, must be carefully weighed against opposing evidence (Garnefski & Diekstra, 1997; Lisak, 1994; Myers, 1989), some of which suggests that the aftermath for boys might be far worse or more complex than for girls (Garnefski & Diekstra, 1997). It should be noted that Rind et al. failed to discuss the incompleteness of the data available for males with regard to the very question they purported to address: whether the experience of child sexual abuse "cause[s] intense psychological harm on a widespread basis for both genders" (1998, p. 22).

Data on child sexual abuse remain incomplete because their acquisition is often fragmented by the age of the abused, by the type of abuse, and by the characteristics of the offender. As Green (1993) pointed out, significant gaps remain in our knowledge of the outcomes of child sexual abuse, especially among children who never enter a mental health system. Because of the significance of the problem, virtually all investigators in the United States emphasize the need for far better national statistics to establish the true incidence and nature of child sexual abuse.

CONCLUSION

Despite all of the medical and legal evidence that child sexual abuse is harmful, Rind et al. appear instead to have expressly selected individuals who seemingly had been least affected by such abuse for inclusion in their meta-analytic review. Focusing solely on the identification of individuals who have been least harmed by adult-child sexual relations is problematic, distorting both the magnitude and complexity of the problem among children and adolescents and disregarding the myriad underlying broad-based social and cultural factors. Any study that involves those least harmed by adult-child sexual relations without recognizing the reality of those who are most harmed is a questionable, and perhaps even deceptive, scientific effort. Moreover, by reducing the behavioral dynamic of sexual abuse to a single factor, the willingness of a child to be a participant, the need for any ethical debate regarding adult-child sexual relations is essentially negated.

After several decades of cross-sectional research, our knowledge of child sexual abuse, particularly with regard to male children and adolescents, remains incomplete. Consequently, the conclusion that Rind et al. draw from their meta-analysis, that "[b]asic beliefs about CSA [child sexual abuse] in the general population were not supported" (1998, p. 22, Abstract), is invalid because their meta-analysis is conceptually and methodologically flawed. More specifically, their attempt to establish gender differences in sexual abuse outcomes and their seeming attempt to identify the subset of adolescent males as not adversely affected by sexual experiences with adults are extremely misguided. By criticizing the use of samples of more severe cases to assess child sexual abuse outcomes, Rind et al. have dismissed the proven value of collaborative research efforts. The sociocultural phenomenon that is child sexual abuse cannot be fully understood until all possible evidence is obtained, from school and community samples, as well as from clinical and legal samples, and preferably in protracted longitudinal studies of at least 10 years duration. The public health approach to child sexual abuse provides the best infrastructure, both for coordinating current research efforts toward identifying all potential outcomes and for delineating the influence of familial, social, and cultural factors on those outcomes. Without a broader viewpoint among child sexual abuse investigators than that advanced by Rind et al. and without a coordinated effort among health-care professionals, psychologists, social workers, lawyers, and law enforcement professionals, the rampant and far-reaching problem of child sexual abuse will remain the enigma it has been for many more generations to come.

NOTE

1. Much of the child sexual abuse literature we reviewed was not cited in this paper because of page limitations. Anyone interested in receiving a complete list of the reviewed articles should contact Gail L. Baker, MA, by e-mail at: <sstarinc@wt.net>.

REFERENCES

Abbey, A., McAuslan, P., & Ross, L. T. (1998). Sexual assault perpetration by college men: The role of alcohol, misperception of sexual intent, and sexual beliefs and experiences. *Journal of Social and Clinical Psychology, 17*(2), 167-195.

Abel, G. G., Becker, J. V., Cunningham-Rathner, J., Mittelman, M., & Rouleau, J.-L. (1988). Multiple paraphilic diagnoses among sex offenders. *Bulletin of the American Academy of Psychiatry and the Law, 16*(2), 153-168.

Adler, N. A., & Schutz, J. (1995). Sibling incest offenders. *Child Abuse & Neglect, 19*(7), 811-819.

Alpert, E. J., Cohen, S., & Sege, R. D. (1997). Family violence: An overview. *Academic Medicine, 72*(1 Suppl), S3-S6.

Bachmann, K. M., Moggi, F., & Stirnemann-Lewis, F. (1994). Mother-son incest and its long-term consequences: A neglected phenomenon in psychiatric practice. *Journal of Nervous and Mental Disease, 182*(12), 723-725.

Banaschak, S., & Brinkmann, B. (1999). The role of clinical forensic medicine in cases of sexual child abuse. *Forensic Science International, 99*(2), 85-91.

Basta, S. M., & Peterson, R. F. (1990). Perpetrator status and the personality characteristics of molested children. *Child Abuse & Neglect, 14*(4), 555-566.

Beck-Sague, C. M., & Solomon, F. (1999). Sexually transmitted diseases in abused children and adolescent and adult victims of rape: Review of selected literature. *Clinical Infectious Diseases, 28*(Suppl 1), S74-S83.

Benthall, J. (1991). Invisible wounds: Corporal punishment in British schools as a form of ritual. *Child Abuse & Neglect, 15*(4), 377-388.

Besharov, D. J. (1997). Overreporting and underreporting are twin problems. In R. J. Gelles & D. R. Loseke (Eds.), *Current controversies in family violence* (pp. 257-272). Newbury Park, CA: Sage Publications.

Biglan, A., Noell, J., Ochs, L., Smolkowski, K., & Metzler, C. (1995). Does sexual coercion play a role in the high-risk sexual behavior of adolescent and young adult women? *Journal of Behavioral Medicine, 18*(6), 549-568.

Borowsky, S. J., Rubenstein, L. V., Meredith, L. S., Camp, P., Jackson-Triche, M., & Wells, K. B. (2000). Who is at risk of nondetection of mental health problems in primary care? *Journal of General Internal Medicine, 15*(6), 381-388.

Bowen, K. (2000). Child abuse and domestic violence in families of children seen for suspected sexual abuse. *Clinical Pediatrics (Philadelphia), 39*(1), 33-40.

Bremner, J. D., Randall, P., Vermetten, E., Staib, L., Bronen, R. A., Mazure, C., Capelli, S., McCarthy, G., Innis, R. B., & Charney, D. S. (1997). Magnetic resonance imaging-based measurement of hippocampal volume in posttraumatic stress disorder related to childhood physical and sexual abuse–a preliminary report. *Biological Psychiatry, 41*, 23-32.

Brener, N. D., McMahon, P. M., Warren, C. W., & Douglas, K. A. (1999). Forced sexual intercourse and associated health-risk behaviors among female college students in the United States. *Journal of Consulting and Clinical Psychology, 67*(2), 252-259.

Briere, J. (1992). Methodological issues in the study of sexual abuse effects. *Journal of Consulting and Clinical Psychology, 60*(2), 196-203.

Briere, J., & Gil, E. (1998). Self-mutilation in clinical and general population samples: Prevalence, correlates, and functions. *American Journal of Orthopsychiatry, 68*(4), 609-620.

Briere, J., Henschel, D., & Smiljanich, K. (1992). Attitudes toward sexual abuse: Sex differences and construct validity. *Journal of Research in Personality, 26*, 398-406.

Briggs, F., & Hawkins, R. M. (1996). A comparison of the childhood experiences of convicted male child molesters and men who were sexually abused in childhood and claimed to be nonoffenders. *Child Abuse & Neglect, 20*(3), 221-233.

Brongersma, E. (1990). Boy-lovers and their influence on boys: Distorted research and anecdotal observations. *Journal of Homosexuality, 20*(1-2), 145-173.

Broussard, S., Wagner, W. G., & Kazelskis, R. (1991). Undergraduate students' perceptions of child sexual abuse: The impact of victim sex, perpetrator sex, respondent sex, and victim response. *Journal of Family Violence, 6*(3), 267-278.

Brown, E. J. (1998). College students' AIDS risk perception. *Journal of Psychosocial Nursing and Mental Health Services, 36*(9), 25-30.

Brown, J., Cohen, P., Johnson, J. G., & Smailes, E. M. (1999). Childhood abuse and neglect: Specificity and effects on adolescent and young adult depression and suicidality. *Journal of the American Academy of Child and Adolescent Psychiatry, 38*(12), 1490-1496.

Browne, A., Miller, B., & Maguin, E. (1999). Prevalence and severity of lifetime physical and sexual victimization among incarcerated women. *International Journal of Law and Psychiatry, 22*(3-4), 301-322.

Burgess, A. W., Hazelwood, R. R., Rokous, F. E., Hartman, C. R., & Burgess, A. G. (1988). Serial rapists and their victims: Reenactment and repetition. *Annals of the New York Academy of Sciences, 528*, 277-295.

Busby, D. M., & Compton, S. V. (1997). Patterns of sexual coercion in adult heterosexual relationships: An exploration of male victimization. *Family Process, 36*(1), 81-94.

Centers for Disease Control and Prevention. (1998a). Summary of notifiable diseases, United States, 1997. *MMWR, 46*(54), 1-87.

Centers for Disease Control and Prevention, Division of STD and TB Prevention. (1998b). *Sexually transmitted disease surveillance, 1997.* Atlanta, GA: Centers for Disease Control and Prevention.

Cohen, M. (1987). *Identifying and combating juvenile prostitution.* Washington, DC: National Association of Counties Research.

Conte, J. R., Wolf, S., & Smith, T. (1989). What sexual offenders tell us about prevention strategies. *Child Abuse & Neglect, 13*(2), 293-301.

Council on Scientific Affairs, American Medical Association. (1989). Health care needs of homeless and runaway youths. *Journal of the American Medical Association, 262,* 1358-1361.

Council on Scientific Affairs, American Medical Association. (1993). Adolescents as victims of family violence. *Journal of the American Medical Association, 270*(15), 1850-1856.

Coxell, A., King, M., Mezey, G., & Gordon, D. (1999). Lifetime prevalence, characteristics, and associated problems of non-consensual sex in men: Cross-sectional survey. *British Medical Journal, 318*(7187), 846-850.

De Jong, A. R. (1989). Sexual interactions among siblings and cousins: Experimentation or exploitation? *Child Abuse & Neglect, 13*(2), 271-279.

De Jong, A. R. (1992). Medical detection and effects of the sexual abuse of children. In W. O'Donohue & J. H. Geer (Eds.), *The sexual abuse of children: Vol. 2: Clinical Issues,* (pp. 71-99). Hillsdale, NJ: Lawrence Erlbaum Associates, Inc.

deMause, L. (1991). The universality of incest. *Journal of Psychohistory, 19*(2), 123-164.

Dersch, C. A., & Munsch, J. (1999). Male victims of sexual abuse: An analysis of substantiation of Child Protective Services reports. *Journal of Child Sexual Abuse, 8*(1), 27-48.

de Young, M. (1988). The indignant page: Techniques of neutralization in the publications of pedophile organization. *Child Abuse & Neglect, 12*(4), 583-591.

Elliott, M., Browne, K., & Kilcoyne, J. (1995). Child sexual abuse prevention: What offenders tell us. *Child Abuse & Neglect, 19*(5), 579-594.

Emmert, C., & Kohler, U. (1998). Data about 154 children and adolescents reporting sexual assault. *Archives of Gynecology and Obstetrics, 261*(2), 61-70.

Eng, T. R., & Butler, W. T. (Eds.). (1997). *The hidden epidemic: Confronting sexually transmitted diseases.* Washington, DC: National Academy Press.

Faller, K. C. (1989). Characteristics of a clinical sample of sexually abused children: How boy and girl victims differ. *Child Abuse & Neglect, 13*(2), 281-291.

Farley, M., & Barkan, H. (1998). Prostitution, violence, and posttraumatic stress disorder. *Women and Health, 27*(3), 37-49.

Feigenbaum, R., Weinstein, E., & Rosen, E. (1995). College students' sexual attitudes and behaviors: Implications for sexuality education. *Journal of American College Health, 44*(3), 112-118.

Feiring, C., Taska, L., & Lewis, M. (1999). Age and gender differences in children's and adolescents' adaptation to sexual abuse. *Child Abuse & Neglect, 23*(2), 115-128.

Fergusson, D. M., Horwood, L. J., & Lynskey, M. T. (1997). Childhood sexual abuse, adolescent sexual behaviors and sexual revictimization. *Child Abuse & Neglect, 21*(8), 789-803.

Fiebert, M. S., & Tucci, L. M. (1998). Sexual coercion: Men victimized by women. *Journal of Men's Studies, 6*(2), 127-133.

Finkelhor, D. (1993). Epidemiological factors in the clinical identification of child sexual abuse. *Child Abuse & Neglect, 17*(1), 67-70.

Finkelhor, D. (1995). The victimization of children: A developmental perspective. *American Journal of Orthopsychiatry, 65*(2), 117-193.

Finkelhor, D., & Browne, A. (1985). The traumatic impact of child sexual abuse: A conceptualization. *American Journal of Orthopsychiatry, 55*(4), 530-541.

Finkelhor, D., & Dziuba-Leatherman, J. (1994). Children as victims of violence: A national survey. *Pediatrics, 94*(4), 413-420.

Finkelhor, D., Hotaling, G. T., & Sedlak, A. J. (1992). The abduction of children by strangers and nonfamily members: Estimating the incidence using multiple methods. *Journal of Interpersonal Violence, 7*(2), 226-243.

Fischer, D. G., & McDonald, W. L. (1998). Characteristics of intrafamilial and extrafamilial child sexual abuse. *Child Abuse & Neglect, 22*(9), 915-929.

Fischer, G. J. (1991). Is lesser severity of child sexual abuse a reason more males report having liked it? *Annals of Sex Research, 4*(2), 131-139.

Follette, V. M., Polusny, M. A., Bechtle, A. E., & Naugle, A. E. (1996). Cumulative trauma: The impact of child sexual abuse, adult sexual assault, and spouse abuse. *Journal of Traumatic Stress, 9*(1), 25-35.

Gardner, J. J., & Cabral, D. A. (1990). Sexually abused adolescents: A distinct group among sexually abused children presenting to a children's hospital. *Journal of Paediatrics and Child Health, 26*(1), 22-24.

Garnefski, N., & Arends, E. (1998). Sexual abuse and adolescent maladjustment: Differences between male and female victims. *Journal of Adolescence, 21*(1), 99-107.

Garnefski, N., & Diekstra, R. F. (1997). Child sexual abuse and emotional and behavioral problems in adolescence: Gender differences. *Journal of the American Academy of Child and Adolescent Psychiatry, 36*(3), 323-329.

Gold, S. N., Elhai, J. D., Lucenko, B. A., Swingle, J. M., & Hughes, D. M. (1998). Abuse characteristics among childhood sexual abuse survivors in therapy: A gender comparison. *Child Abuse & Neglect, 22*(10), 1005-1012.

Gray, A., Pithers, W. D., Busconi, A., & Houchens, P. (1999). Developmental and etiological characteristics of children with sexual behavior problems: Treatment implications. *Child Abuse & Neglect, 23*(6), 601-621.

Green, A. H. (1993). Child sexual abuse: Immediate and long-term effects and intervention. *Journal of the American Academy of Child and Adolescent Psychology, 32*(5), 890-902.

Greene, J. M., Ennett, S. T., & Ringwalt, C. L. (1999). Prevalence and correlates of survival sex among runaway and homeless youth. *American Journal of Public Health, 89*(9), 1406-1409.

Greenfeld, L. A. (1997). *Sex offenses and offenders: An analysis of data on rape and sexual assault.* U.S. Department of Justice, Office of Justice Programs, Bureau of

Justice Statistics (NCJRS Publication No. 16392). Washington, DC: U.S. Department of Justice.

Greig, E., & Betts, T. (1992). Epileptic seizures induced by sexual abuse: Pathogenic and pathoplastic factors. *Seizure, 1*, 269-274.

Hall, D. K., Mathews, F., & Pearce, J. (1998). Factors associated with sexual behavior problems in young sexually abused children. *Child Abuse & Neglect, 22*(10), 1045-1063.

Hanson, R. K., Gizzarelli, R., & Scott, H. (1994). The attitudes of incest offenders: Sexual entitlement and acceptance of sex with children. *Criminal Justice and Behavior, 21*(2), 187-202.

Haskett, M. E., Marziano, B., & Dover, E. R. (1996). Absence of males in maltreatment research: A survey of recent literature. *Child Abuse & Neglect, 20*(12), 1175-1182.

Haskett, M. E., Nowlan, N. P., Hutcheson, J. S., & Whitworth, J. M. (1991). Factors associated with successful entry into therapy in child sexual abuse cases. *Child Abuse & Neglect, 15*(4), 467-476.

Heller, S. S., Larrieu, J. A., D'Imperio, R., & Boris, N. W. (1999). Research on resilience to child maltreatment: Empirical considerations. *Child Abuse & Neglect, 23*(4), 321-338.

Herrenkohl, E. C., Herrenkohl, R. C., & Egolf, B. (1994). Resilient early school-age children from maltreating homes: Outcomes in late adolescence. *American Journal of Orthopsychiatry, 64*(2), 301-309.

Hetherton, J. (1999). The idealization of women: Its role in the minimization of child sexual abuse by females. *Child Abuse & Neglect, 23*(2), 161-174.

Hillis, S. D., Anda, R. F., Felitti, V. J., Nordenberg, D., & Marchbanks, P. A. (2000). Adverse childhood experiences and sexually transmitted diseases in men and women: A retrospective study [electronic]. *Pediatrics, 106*(1), E11.

Holmes, G. R., Offen, L., & Waller, G. (1997). See no evil, hear no evil, speak no evil: Why do relatively few male victims of childhood sexual abuse receive help for abuse-related issues in adulthood? *Clinical Psychology Review, 17*(1), 69-88.

Holmes, K. K., Mårdh, P.-A., Sparling, P. F., Lemon, S. M., Stamm, W. E., Piot, P., & Wasserheit, J. N. (Eds.). (1999). *Sexually transmitted diseases* (3rd ed.). New York: McGraw-Hill.

Holmes, W. C., & Slap, G. B. (1998). Sexual abuse of boys: Definition, prevalence, correlates, sequelae, and management. *Journal of the American Medical Association, 280*(21), 1855-1862.

Isely, P. J. (1998). Sexual assault of men: American research supports studies from the UK. *Medicine, Science and the Law, 38*(1), 74-80.

Ito, Y., Teicher, M. H., Glod, C. A., & Ackerman, E. (1998). Preliminary evidence for aberrant cortical development in abused children: A quantitative EEG study. *The Journal of Neuropsychiatry and Clinical Neurosciences, 10*, 298-307.

Itzin, C. (1997). Pornography and the organization of intra- and extrafamilial child sexual abuse: A conceptual model. In G. K. Kantor & J. L. Jasinski (Eds.), *Out of darkness: Contemporary perspectives on family violence* (pp. 58-79). Thousand Oaks, CA: Sage Publications, Inc.

Johnson, B. K., & Kenkel, M. B. (1991). Stress, coping, and adjustment in female adolescent incest victims. *Child Abuse & Neglect, 15*(3), 293-305.

Kadish, H. A., Schunk, J. E., & Britton, H. (1998). Pediatric male rectal and genital trauma: Accidental and nonaccidental injuries. *Pediatric Emergency Care, 14*(2), 95-98.

Kaplan, S. J. (2000). Family violence. *New Directions in Mental Health Services, 86,* 49-62.

Kaufman, J., Jones, B., Stieglitz, E., Vitulano, L., & Mannarino, A. P. (1994). The use of multiple informants to assess children's maltreatment experiences. *Journal of Family Violence, 9*(3), 227-248.

Kendall-Tackett, K. A., Williams, L. M., & Finkelhor, D. (1993). Impact of sexual abuse on children: A review and synthesis of empirical studies. *Psychological Bulletin, 113*(1), 164-180.

Kerns, D. L. (Ed.). (1998). Establishing a medical research agenda for child sexual abuse [Special issue]. *Child Abuse & Neglect, 22*(6), 453-660.

King, M., & Woollett, E. (1997). Sexually assaulted males: 115 men consulting a counseling service. *Archives of Sexual Behavior, 26*(6), 579-588.

Kinsey, A. C., Pomeroy, W. B., & Martin, C. E. (1948). *Sexual behavior in the human male*. Philadelphia: W. B. Saunders Company.

Koop, C. E. (1989). *The Surgeon General's letter on child sexual abuse*. Washington, DC: U.S. Department of Health & Human Services.

Koss, M. P., & Dinero, T. E. (1988). Predictors of sexual aggression among a national sample of male college students. *Annals of the New York Academy of Sciences, 528,* 133-147.

Kral, A. H., Molnar, B. E., Booth, R. E., & Watters, J. K. (1997). Prevalence of sexual risk behavior and substance use among runaway and homeless adolescents in San Francisco, Denver and New York City. *International Journal of STD and AIDS, 8*(2), 109-117.

Lab, D. D., Feigenbaum, J. D., & De Silva, P. (2000). Mental health professionals' attitudes and practices towards male childhood sexual abuse. *Child Abuse & Neglect, 24*(3), 391-409.

Lascaratos, J., & Poulakou-Rebelakou, E. (2000). Child sexual abuse: Historical cases in the Byzantine Empire (324-1453 A.D.). *Child Abuse & Neglect, 24*(8), 1085-1090.

Lemmey, D. E., & Tice, P. P. (2000). Two tragic forms of child sexual abuse: Are they often overlooked? *Journal of Child Sexual Abuse, 9*(2), 87-106.

Liem, J. H., James, J. B., O'Toole, J. G., & Boudewyn, A. C. (1997). Assessing resilience in adults with histories of childhood sexual abuse. *American Journal of Orthopsychiatry, 67*(4), 594-606.

Lisak, D. (1994). The psychological impact of sexual abuse: Content analysis of interviews with male survivors. *Journal of Traumatic Stress, 7*(4), 525-548.

Lodico, M. A., Gruber, E., & DiClemente, R. J. (1996). Childhood sexual abuse and coercive sex among school-based adolescents in a midwestern state. *Journal of Adolescent Health, 18*(3), 211-217.

Luthar, S. S., & Zigler, E. (1991). Vulnerability and competence: A review of research on resilience in childhood. *American Journal of Orthopsychiatry, 61*(1), 6-22.

Lynch, D. L., Stern, A. E., Oates, R. K., & O'Toole, B. I. (1993). Who participates in child sexual abuse research? *Journal of Child Psychology and Psychiatry, 34*(6), 935-944.

Marciniak, L. M. (1998). Adolescent attitudes toward victim precipitation of rape. *Violence and Victims, 13*(3), 287-300.

Mason, W. A., Zimmerman, L., & Evans, W. (1998). Sexual and physical abuse among incarcerated youth: Implications for sexual behavior, contraceptive use, and teenage pregnancy. *Child Abuse & Neglect, 22*(10), 987-995.

Maynard, C., & Wiederman, M. (1997). Undergraduate students' perceptions of child sexual abuse: Effects of age, sex, and gender-role attitudes. *Child Abuse & Neglect, 21*(9), 833-844.

McCann, J., Reay, D., Siebert, J., Stephens, B. G., & Wirtz, S. (1996). Postmortem perianal findings in children. *American Journal of Forensic Medicine and Pathology, 17*(4), 289-298.

McMahon, P. M., & Puett, R. C. (1999). Child sexual abuse as a public health issue: Recommendations of an expert panel. *Sex Abuse: A Journal of Research and Treatment, 11*(4), 257-266.

McMillen, C., Zuravin, S., & Rideout, G. (1995). Perceived benefit from child sexual abuse. *Journal of Consulting and Clinical Psychology, 63*(6), 1037-1043.

Melbye, M., Rabkin, C., Frisch, M., & Biggar, R. J. (1994). Changing patterns of anal cancer incidence in the United States, 1940-1989. *American Journal of Epidemiology, 139*(8), 772-780.

Meyer, J. (1996). Sexuality and power: Perspectives for the less powerful. *Theory & Psychology, 6*(1), 93-119.

Moscicki, A.-B., Winkler, B., Irwin, C. E. Jr., & Schachter, J. (1989). Differences in biologic maturation, sexual behavior, and sexually transmitted disease between adolescents with and without cervical intraepithelial neoplasia. *Journal of Pediatrics, 115*(3), 487-49.

Mraovich, L. R., & Wilson, J. F. (1999). Patterns of child abuse and neglect associated with chronological age of children living in a midwestern county. *Child Abuse & Neglect, 23*(9), 899-903.

Muehlenhard, C. L., Highby, B. J., Lee, R. S., Bryan, T. S., & Dodrill, W. A. (1998). The sexual revictimization of women and men sexually abused as children: A review of the literature. *Annual Review of Sex Research, 9*, 177-223.

Myers, M. F. (1989). Men sexually assaulted as adults and sexually abused as boys. *Archives of Sexual Behavior, 18*(3), 203-215.

Netting, N. S. (1992). Sexuality in youth culture: Identity and change. *Adolescence, 27*(108), 961-976.

Perry, B. D., Pollard, R. A., Blakley, T. L., Baker, W. L., & Vigilante, D. (1995). Childhood trauma, the neurobiology of adaptation, and "use-dependent" development of the brain: How "states" become "traits." *Infant Mental Health Journal, 16*(4), 271-289.

Pitzner, J. K., McGarry-Long, J., & Drummond, P. D. (2000). A history of abuse and negative life events in patients with a sexually transmitted disease and in a community sample. *Child Abuse & Neglect, 24*(5), 715-731.

Pokorny, S. F., Pokorny, W. J., & Kramer, W. (1992). Acute genital injury in the prepubertal girl. *American Journal of Obstetrics and Gynecology, 166*(5), 1461-1466.

Pollock, N. L., & Hashmall, J. M. (1991). The excuses of child molesters. *Behavioral Sciences & the Law, 9*(1), 53-59.

Putnam, F. W., & Trickett, P. K. (1993). Child sexual abuse: A model of chronic trauma. *Psychiatry, 56*(1), 82-95.

Reinhart, M. A. (1987). Sexual abuse of battered young children. *Pediatric Emergency Care, 3*(1), 36-38.

Richey-Suttles, S., & Remer, R. (1997). Psychologists' attitudes toward adult male survivors of sexual abuse. *Journal of Child Sexual Abuse, 6*(2), 43-61.

Rickert, V. I., & Wiemann, C. M. (1998). Date rape among adolescents and young adults. *Journal of Pediatric and Adolescent Gynecology, 11*(4), 167-175.

Rind, B., & Bauserman, R. (1993). Biased terminology effects and biased information processing in research on adult-nonadult sexual interactions: An empirical investigation. *Journal of Sex Research, 30*(3), 260-269.

Rind, B., Tromovitch, P., & Bauserman, R. (1998). A meta-analytic examination of assumed properties of child sexual abuse using college samples. *Psychological Bulletin, 124*(1): 22-53.

Risin, L. I., & Koss, M. P. (1987). The sexual abuse of boys: Prevalence and descriptive characteristics of childhood victimization. *Journal of Interpersonal Violence, 2*(3), 309-323.

Robertson, J. M. (1992). Homeless and runaway youths: A review of the literature. In J. M. Robertson & M. Greenblatt (Eds.), *Homelessness: A national perspective* (pp. 287-297). New York: Plenum Press.

Rodreguez, R. D. Jr., Nahirny, C., Burgess, A. W., & Burgess, A. G. (1998). Missing children found dead. *Journal of Psychosocial Nursing and Mental Health Services, 36*(6), 11-16.

Roesler, T. A., & McKenzie, N. (1994). Effects of childhood trauma on psychological functioning in adults sexually abused as children. *Journal of Nervous and Mental Disease, 182*(3), 145-150.

Rudd, J. M., & Herzberger, S. D. (1999). Brother-sister incest–father-daughter incest: A comparison of characteristics and consequences. *Child Abuse & Neglect, 23*(9), 915-928.

Rudin, M. M., Zalewski, C., & Bodmer-Turner, J. (1995). Characteristics of child sexual abuse victims according to perpetrator gender. *Child Abuse & Neglect, 19*(8), 963-973.

Sanders, S. A., & Reinisch, J. M. (1999). Would you say you "had sex" if . . . ? *Journal of the American Medical Association, 281*(3), 275-277.

Santa Mina, E. E., & Gallop, R. M. (1998). Childhood sexual and physical abuse and adult self-harm and suicidal behavior: A literature review. *Canadian Journal of Psychiatry, 43*(8), 793-800.

Schaaf, K. K., & McCanne, T. R. (1998). Relationship of childhood sexual, physical, and combined sexual and physical abuse to adult victimization and posttraumatic stress disorder. *Child Abuse & Neglect, 22*(11), 1119-1133.

Scheflin, A. W., & Brown, D. (1996). Repressed memory or dissociative amnesia: What the science says. *The Journal of Psychiatry and Law, Summer*, 143-188.

Sears, D. O. (1986). College sophomores in the laboratory: Influences of a narrow data base on social psychology's view of human nature. *Journal of Personality and Social Psychology, 51*(3), 515-530.

Sexuality Information and Education Council of the United States. (2001). Position statements. Available: http://www.siecus.org/about/abou0001.html.

Shapiro, D. L., & Levendosky, A. A. (1999). Adolescent survivors of childhood sexual abuse: The mediating role of attachment style and coping in psychological and interpersonal functioning. *Child Abuse & Neglect, 23*(11), 1175-1191.

Shrier, L. A., Pierce, J. D., Emans, S. J., & DuRant, R. H. (1998). Gender differences in risk behaviors associated with forced or pressured sex. *Archives of Pediatric and Adolescent Medicine, 152*(1), 57-63.

Sigmon, S. T., Greene, M. P., Rohan, K. J., & Nichols, J. E. (1996). Coping and adjustment in male and female survivors of childhood sexual abuse. *Journal of Child Sexual Abuse, 5*(3), 57-76.

Singer, M. I., Hussey, D., & Strom, K. J. (1992). Grooming the victim: An analysis of a perpetrator's seduction letter. *Child Abuse & Neglect, 16*(6), 877-886.

Skuse, D., Bentovim, A., Hodges, J., Stevenson, J., Andreou, C., Lanyado, M., New, M., Williams, B., & McMillan, D. (1998). Risk factors for development of sexually abusive behaviour in sexually victimised adolescent boys: Cross-sectional study. *British Medical Journal 317*, 175-179.

Smiljanich, K., & Briere, J. (1996). Self-reported sexual interest in children: Sex differences and psychosocial correlates in a university sample. *Violence and Victims, 11*(1), 39-50.

Smith, H. D., Fromuth, M. E., & Morris, C. C. (1997). Effects of gender on perceptions of child sexual abuse. *Journal of Child Sexual Abuse, 6*(4), 51-63.

Smith, D. W., Letourneau, E. J., Saunders, B. E., Kilpatrick, D. G., Resnick, H. S., & Best, C. L. (2000). Delay in disclosure of childhood rape: Results from a national survey. *Child Abuse & Neglect, 24*(2), 273-287.

Spaccarelli, S., & Kim, S. (1995). Resilience criteria and factors associated with resilience in sexually abused girls. *Child Abuse & Neglect, 19*(9), 1171-1182.

Stein, M. B., Koverola, C., Hanna, C., Torchia, M. G., & McClarty, B. (1997). Hippocampal volume in women victimized by childhood sexual abuse. *Psychological Medicine, 27*, 951-959.

Strassberg, D. S., & Lowe, K. (1995). Volunteer bias in sexuality research. *Archives of Sexual Behavior, 24*(4), 369-382.

Struckman-Johnson, C., & Struckman-Johnson, D. (1994). Men pressured and forced into sexual experience. *Archives of Sexual Behavior, 23*(1), 93-114.

Teicher, M. H., Ito, Y., Glod, C. A., Andersen, S. L., Dumont, N., & Ackerman, E. (1997). Preliminary evidence for abnormal cortical development in physically and sexually abused children using EEG coherence and MRI. *Annals of the New York Academy of Sciences, 821*, 160-175.

Tingus, K. D., Heger, A. H., Foy, D. W., & Leskin, G. A. (1996). Factors associated with entry into therapy in children evaluated for sexual abuse. *Child Abuse & Neglect, 20*(1), 63-68.

U.S. Bureau of Justice Statistics. (1998). *Sourcebook of criminal justice statistics* [On-line]. Available: http://www.albany.edu/sourcebook/.

Watkins, B., & Bentovim, A. (1992). The sexual abuse of male children and adolescents: A review of current research. *Journal of Child Psychology and Psychiatry, 33*(1), 197-248.

Weber, F. T., Gearing, J., Davis, A., & Conlon, M. (1992). Prepubertal initiation of sexual experiences and older first partner predict promiscuous sexual behavior of delinquent adolescent males: Unrecognized child abuse? *Journal of Adolescent Health, 13*(7), 600-605.

Wellman, M. M. (1993). Child sexual abuse and gender differences: Attitudes and prevalence. *Child Abuse & Neglect, 17*(4), 539-547.

Whitfield, C. L. (1997). Traumatic amnesia: The evolution of our understanding from a clinical and legal perspective. *Sexual Addiction & Compulsivity, 4*(2), 107-135.

Widom, C. P., & Ames, M. A. (1994). Criminal consequences of childhood sexual victimization. *Child Abuse & Neglect, 18*(4), 303-318.

Widom, C. S., & Morris, S. (1997). Accuracy of adult recollections of childhood victimization: Part 2. Childhood sexual abuse. *Psychological Assessment, 9*(1), 34-46.

Williams, L. M. (1994). Recall of childhood trauma: A prospective study of women's memories of child sexual abuse. *Journal of Consulting and Clinical Psychology, 62*(6), 1167-1176.

Implications of the Memory Controversy for Clinical Practice: An Overview of Treatment Recommendations and Guidelines

Christine A. Courtois

SUMMARY. The controversy surrounding delayed and recovered memories of incest/child sexual abuse has had a profound impact on clinical practice. This article first provides an overview of the positions taken by both sides in the dispute, the "false memory" proponents and the traumatic stress proponents. It then presents the major findings of several of the professional task forces charged with reviewing the controversy and arriving at recommendations for research, clinical practice, and forensic practice regarding delayed recall of memories for sexual abuse. The current status of scientific and clinical knowledge is discussed, especially in terms of its implications for therapists and clinical

Christine Courtois, PhD, is a psychologist in private practice in Washington DC. She is also clinical and training director, as well as co-founder of The CENTER: Posttraumatic Disorders Program, The Psychiatric Institute of Washington, DC (in-patient and partial hospitalization programs). Dr. Courtois is also the author of *Recollections of Sexual Abuse: Treatment Principles and Guidelines* and *Healing the Incest Wound: Adult Survivors in Therapy*.

Address correspondence to: Christine A. Courtois, PhD & Associates, PLC, 3 Washington Circle, Suite 205, Washington, DC 20037 (E-mail: CACourtois PhD@aol.com).

[Haworth co-indexing entry note]: "Implications of the Memory Controversy for Clinical Practice: An Overview of Treatment Recommendations and Guidelines." Courtois, Christine A. Co-published simultaneously in *Journal of Child Sexual Abuse* (The Haworth Maltreatment & Trauma Press, an imprint of The Haworth Press, Inc.) Vol. 9, No. 3/4, 2001, pp. 183-210; and: *Misinformation Concerning Child Sexual Abuse and Adult Survivors* (ed: Charles L. Whitfield, Joyanna Silberg, and Paul Jay Fink) The Haworth Maltreatment & Trauma Press, an imprint of The Haworth Press, Inc., 2001, pp. 183-210. Single or multiple copies of this article are available for a fee from The Haworth Document Delivery Service [1-800-HAWORTH, 9:00 a.m. - 5:00 p.m. (EST). E-mail address: getinfo@haworthpressinc.com].

practice. Nineteen recommendations and practice guidelines are presented for therapists working with individuals who report or suspect childhood sexual abuse on the basis of continuous and/or recovered memory. *[Article copies available for a fee from The Haworth Document Delivery Service: 1-800-HAWORTH. E-mail address: <getinfo@haworthpressinc.com> Website: <http://www.HaworthPress.com> © 2001 by The Haworth Press, Inc. All rights reserved.]*

KEYWORDS. Trauma, memory, traumatic memory, traumatic amnesia, recovered/false memory controversy, clinical practice, treatment guidelines

INTRODUCTION

At present, the controversy regarding delayed and recovered memories of incest/child sexual abuse and other forms of trauma is in its eighth year. During the mid-1990s when the controversy was at its height and at its most contentious, it generated considerable media coverage that galvanized public attention. The press extensively reported allegations that false memories of abuse were widespread, largely as the result of being implanted by psychotherapists. Although these reports were informative to some members of the public, they had the unfortunate effect of creating widespread confusion and misunderstanding regarding child abuse, adult survivors, and psychotherapy. Abused children and formerly abused adults once again came under suspicion of fantasizing about, lying, or exaggerating reports of abuse, a perspective that had only begun to change in the late 1970s when the contemporary study of child abuse began. The public's confidence in the mental health professions and psychotherapy was seriously eroded, and therapists found that they were viewed with suspicion in some quarters.

As the controversy intensified, it moved from the treatment setting to the courtroom. Civil lawsuits were filed in increasing numbers charging therapists with malpractice for suggesting or implanting false memories of: (a) current abuse in children through flawed and repetitive assessment interviews, and (b) past abuse in adults based upon unsound theory about recovered memory and the use of faulty technique and inappropriate influence. Most lawsuits involving adults were filed by disgruntled former patients, but some were filed by third parties (such as parents) who claimed to be falsely accused based on these false memories and to be emotionally damaged as a result (Brown, Scheflin, & Hammond, 1998). A "false memory" defense became quite routine in civil cases such as these, and also in criminal cases involving charges of contemporaneous child sexual abuse. In cases of either type, a false memory defense was likely even when recovered memory was not an issue. In addition to lawsuits, false memory critics encouraged the filing of ethics charges and licensing board complaints against therapists who were suspected of having used improper, suggestive, and in some cases, experimental/unproven techniques.

The controversy also entered the legislative arena. Attempts were made to eliminate child abuse reporting statutes with respect to current abuse (Brown et al., 1998; Courtois, 1999). Where past abuse was at issue, bills were introduced (but not passed as of this writing) in a number of state legislatures that would have placed restrictions on the practice of psychotherapy. The bills would have set extremely conservative criteria regarding what constituted a credible memory of past abuse, acceptable conditions and settings for the initial disclosure of such information, and acceptable versus prohibited therapeutic techniques and areas of inquiry (Hinnifeld & Newman, 1997). A number of professional associations countered that these attempts would be damaging to the public, even though the bills were introduced under such headings as "The Mental Health Consumer Protection Act," "The Consumer Fraud Protection Act" and "The Truth and Responsibility in Mental Health Practice Acts" (APA, 1996a; Hinnifeld & Newman, 1997). Additionally, attempts were made to mandate that psychotherapists have a formal duty to third parties. In effect, this would mean that the interests of third parties (which might differ from those of the primary client) would need to be formally considered by the therapist. This would be a radical departure from current professional practice, where the therapist's duty is owed formally only to the primary client. This effort also failed, although a duty has been allowed in some cases and in some jurisdictions; the Ramona case is the most well-known and regarded by many observers as a bellweather for future cases, but even this case was not the classic third party situation (*Ramona v. Isabella,* California Superior Court, Napa, C61898).

As a result of these accumulated, legal, licensure, and legislative initiatives and the negative press coverage that surrounded them, many mental health professionals became quite apprehensive when treating patients for current or past child sexual abuse or other forms of trauma (whether recovered memories were involved or not). Some refused to treat traumatized patients and/or left mental health practice altogether. This exodus is a cause for alarm. Child abuse, along with its pervasive personal, relational, and societal effects, has been identified as a major public health issue (Bloom, 1997). Ongoing prevention and intervention on the part of professionals and the public at large are required to interrupt what has been identified as an intergenerational cycle of abuse and violence.

In the early days of the controversy, extremists on both sides of the issue held sway, garnering the most press and public reaction. At present, a more moderate tone is evident and media reports are less frequent and alarmist. This moderation is largely in response to calls for restraint issued by the leaders of a number of mental health organizations and to the recommendations of professional task forces charged with studying the most pressing issues of the controversy. Leaders and task force members advised that fixed and rigid professional positions are premature because much research remains to be conducted regarding memories for traumatic events and other issues pertinent to the controversy. They also urged a move away from unsupported charges and *ad hominem* accusations (often made in the media or at professional meetings and common in the early years of the controversy) as unscientific as well as unprofessional. These leaders and experts further called for increased efforts to support front line providers of mental health services through better training in the treatment of all forms of interpersonal violence and trauma (including attention to professional, ethical and legal responsibilities) and through the development and ongoing evolution of treatment guidelines on such topics as the assessment of allegations of contemporaneous abuse (including those that occur in child custody disputes) and the management of delayed and recovered memories of past abuse as they present in clinical practice (Brown et al., 1998; Courtois, 1999).

The purpose of this article is to first provide a brief synopsis of the main points of the controversy, then to present an overview of the main findings and recommendations of several representative professional task forces. These findings are then discussed in terms of their implications for clinical practice and with respect to available recommendations and guidelines regarding the treatment of adults who report delayed memories or suspicions of past abuse.

AN OVERVIEW OF THE CONTROVERSY

The gist of the controversy is as follows: Proponents of what has come to be known as the "false memory position" charge that a substantial number of therapists (especially those who are young, female, inexperienced, possibly ill-trained and with a bias against men) have caused naive patients with no previous recollection or suspicion to recover memories of child abuse that never occurred (i.e., false memories) (Loftus, 1993; Loftus & Ketcham, 1994; Ofshe & Waters, 1994; Underwager & Wakefield, 1990; Wakefield & Underwager, 1992; Yapko, 1994). The critics charge that therapists (advertently or inadvertently) propose abuse on the basis of mistaken notions about the workings of human memory and inaccurate theory regarding repressed and recovered memory for trauma (especially incest and child sexual abuse) that has developed over the past two decades. These therapists supposedly instill illusory memories through the extensive use of therapeutic techniques that the critics have highlighted as suggestive and which, in aggregate, they have labeled Recovered Memory Therapy (RMT). These techniques include hypnosis, sodium amytal interviews, guided imagery, dream interpretation, journaling, art therapy, "body therapy," referral to self-help literature (especially the book *The Courage to Heal* [Bass & Davis, 1988, 1994]), and participation in abuse survivor groups. Critics also contend that abuse is the default option of many therapists who believe that a majority of individuals seeking mental health treatment harbor repressed memories of childhood sexual abuse that must be exhumed for the individual to get well. They further argue that many therapists have come to overinterpret such presenting problems as eating disorders, depression, and panic attacks and/or to over rely on checklists of symptoms (often found in the lay literature on abuse and alcoholic/dysfunctional families) to make their assessment and diagnosis of repressed or unrecalled abuse, and then to erroneously diagnose the patient with Posttraumatic Stress Disorder (PTSD) or Dissociative Identity Disorder (DID).

False memory proponents assert that patients who repeatedly experience this type of suggestive treatment develop a set of symptoms characterized as "false memory syndrome" (FMS),[1] whereby they regress from previously high levels of functioning and become enmeshed with and overly dependent upon their therapists. According to these critics, in a typical course of recovering memories, patients initially unearth memories of incest (first by one relative and then by many, alone and in groups) followed by memories of more bizarre and improbable forms of abuse (such as Satanic Ritual Abuse, other forms of group or cult-related abuse, alien abductions, etc.). On the basis of these recovered memories and encouraged by their therapists, a number of these patients then accuse their parents and others of horrific abuses, in the process causing enormous distress and emotional upheaval. Additionally, at the suggestion of their therapists, many sever contact with their families and even initiate civil lawsuits seeking redress for the abuse.

Proponents of what has become known as the "traumatic stress position" argue that alterations in memory (including the loss and later retrieval of memories) have long been identified as an aftermath of severe traumatization; therefore, it is not unusual for traumatized individuals to have variable recollections of past abuse and trauma, some of which might emerge within or outside of psychotherapy, often in response to cues or triggers in the environment and not solely the result of suggestive influence in psychotherapy (Bass & Davis, 1994; Brown et al., 1998; Freyd, 1994; Terr, 1991, 1994; van der Kolk & van der Hart, 1995). Moreover, delayed and recovered memories are not always false and therefore should not be assumed *a priori* to be false.

Traumatic stress commentators charge that, to date, inadequate documentation has been provided to substantiate the serious charges regarding psychotherapists, the ostensible implantation of false memories, and even the existence of "false memory syndrome" (Pope, 1996). They assert that the critics have overgeneralized their critique to include all therapists (lay and professional alike) who work with traumatized individuals and, furthermore, that they have irresponsibly labeled many standard therapeutic techniques as suggestive without data to support the claim. Since they are not trained as therapists and have no expertise in trauma (many of them are cognitive psychologists who are memory researchers), they are seen as operating outside of their field of expertise in critiquing psychotherapy practice and techniques.

False memory critics are also charged with having only a limited understanding of human traumatization and its effects (in general but especially with regard to incest/sexual abuse and other forms of child maltreatment and domestic violence), and additionally with having confounded the work and writing of professional therapists with those of lay counselors and self-help authors. Traumatic stress proponents assert that false memory critics have not yet adequately studied trauma and traumatic memory in children and adults in either laboratory or field conditions to determine whether it does, in fact, differ from memory for normal events. Memory experts have relied upon and prematurely generalized from the findings of memory studies of normal events conducted in the laboratory on non-traumatized subjects (mostly college students).

Additionally, many traumatic stress proponents question the politics of the controversy and believe it constitutes a backlash against contemporary gains in the identification and treatment of child abuse and domestic violence. They see it as a return to the Freudian repudiation of the reality of incest and other forms of abuse, and the discrediting of female therapists and female patients in particular. They question the critics' tendency to disbelieve the memories of victims (most of whom are female) who allege abuse while uncritically accepting the denials of the accused (most of whom are male) despite considerable research on abusers that documents their tendency to lie, deny, and minimize their abusive activity. The writings of some of the critics routinely assume that memories of victims are false (especially those that were recovered after a period of absence) while those of alleged perpetrators are true (even without evidence), an unbalanced and unscientific position (for example, see Cheit's article in this volume).

PROFESSIONAL TASK FORCES:
MODERATION AND COMMON GROUND

The controversy has been so adversarial that it has been described as "the memory war." A rational common ground that acknowledges the complexity of the issues involved while incorporating the legitimate issues and critiques of each side has been lacking but is now beginning to emerge and solidify (Lindsay & Briere, 1997). Several teams of memory and trauma researchers are engaging in collaborative research and have recently found some points of common agreement (Read & Lindsay, 1997) and a middle ground in clinical practice that incorporates information on memory processes and offers practice guidelines for psychotherapists is also emerging and growing (Briere, 1997b; Brown et al., 1998; Chu, 1998; Courtois, 1997a, 1997b, 1999; Gold & Brown, 1997; Knapp & VandeCreek, 1997; Mollon, 1998; Pope & Brown, 1996: Whitfield, 1995; Brown, Scheflin & Whitfield, 1999).

Collaborative efforts between memory and trauma experts have been encouraged by many of the major mental health organizations. A number of them impaneled task forces (composed of experts in human memory processes and in traumatic stress) with the charge of reviewing pertinent issues and making recommendations to professionals regarding research, clinical, and forensic practice and to consumers regarding the controversy and psychotherapy services.[2] A comparison of these reports shows that they arrived at similar conclusions and made many parallel recommendations; however, as would be expected, some of the findings were influenced by the allegiances and biases of the members and to the philosophy espoused by their particular discipline. Despite some shortcomings, the reports have helped define preliminary points of agreement and delineate important scientific and clinical issues. A comparative analysis of the categories of recommendations of the various reports can be found in Grunberg and Ney (1997), and in an updated version in Courtois (1999).

The findings of four representative task forces, those of the American Psychiatric Association, the American Psychological Association, The British Psychological Association, and The Royal College of Psychiatry in Great Britain, are highlighted here as they identify the current status of scientific and clinical issues and as they inform the development of treatment recommendations and guidelines, discussed in the final section of this article.

The American Psychiatric Association

"The Statement on Memories of Sexual Abuse" (American Psychiatric Association Board of Directors, 1993) was the first published report and a forerunner of the others. The statement begins: " . . . The American Psychiatric Association has been concerned that the passionate debates about these issues have obscured the recognition of a body of scientific evidence that underlies widespread agreement among psychiatrists regarding psychiatric treatment in this area. We are especially concerned that the public confusion and dismay over this issue and the possibility of false accusations not discredit the reports of patients who have indeed been traumatized by actual previous abuse." Regarding working from a position of neutrality with delayed memory issues brought to treatment, the statement's authors cautioned: "It is not known how to distinguish, with complete accuracy, memories based on true events from those derived from other sources." The report's authors were clear in extending sensitivity to abused patients and cautioned clinicians against automatically disbelieving reports of abuse, yet they additionally cautioned against pressuring patients to believe in events that may not have occurred. Psychiatrists as well as other mental health professionals were reminded that treatment plans should address the range of the patient's clinical concerns (not just memory issues) and should be based upon a comprehensive assessment. Therapists were advised to caution patients and help them to assess the impact of any extra-therapeutic action and life decisions and to help those patients with unclear memories that do not clarify or resolve to tolerate and adapt to the uncertainty.

The American Psychological Association

The American Psychological Association Working Group on the Investigation of Memories of Childhood Abuse[3] was composed of three clinicians with expertise in trauma treatment and three memory researchers, one of whom (Elizabeth Loftus), as a leading spokesperson for the False Memory Syndrome Foundation Professional and Scientific Advisory Board, was strongly identified with the false memory position. This group's composition made consensus difficult and resulted in the split of the professional reports, one that illuminated the starkly different perspectives of both sides. The Working Group first issued an interim report that listed key points of agreement among members (American Psychological Association, 1994). These were:

- Controversies regarding adult recollections should not be allowed to obscure the fact that child sexual abuse is a complex and pervasive problem in America, which has historically gone unacknowledged.
- Most people who were sexually abused as children remember all or part of what happened to them.

However, it is possible for memories of abuse that have been forgotten for a long time to be remembered. The mechanism(s) by which such delayed recall occur(s) is/are not currently well understood.

• It is also possible to construct convincing pseudo-memories for events that never occurred. The mechanism(s) by which these pseudo-memories occur(s) is/are not currently well understood.
• There are gaps in our knowledge about the processes that lead to accurate and inaccurate recollections of childhood abuse.

The APA Board of Directors supplemented the interim report with the following guidance to the public and the profession:

• There is no single set of symptoms that automatically means that a person was a victim of childhood abuse.
• All therapists must approach questions of childhood abuse from a neutral position.
• The public should be wary of two kinds of therapists: those who offer instant childhood abuse diagnoses, and those who dismiss claims or reports of sexual abuse without exploration.
• When seeking psychotherapy, the public is advised to see a licensed practitioner with training and experience in the issues for which treatment is sought.

More extensive conclusions and recommendations incorporating and expanding upon these interim points were offered in the final report (American Psychological Association, 1996b).

The British Psychological Society

Members of The Working Party of the British Psychological Society reviewed the scientific literature, carried out a survey of selected members of The British Psychological Society and scrutinized the records of the British False Memory Society. The Working Party report contained the following conclusions (British Psychological Society, 1995):

• Complete or partial memory loss is a frequently reported consequence of experiencing certain kinds of psychological traumas including childhood sexual abuse. These memories are sometimes fully or partially recovered after a gap of many years.

- Memories may be recovered within or independent of therapy. Memory recovery is reported by highly experienced and well-qualified therapists who are well aware of the dangers of inappropriate suggestion and interpretation.
- In general, the clarity and detail of event memories depends on a number of factors, including the age at which the event occurred. Although clear memories are likely to be broadly accurate, they may contain significant errors. It seems likely that recovered memories have the same properties.
- Sustained pressure or persuasion by an authority figure could lead to the retrieval or elaboration of "memories" of events that never actually happened. The possibility of therapists creating in their clients false memories of having been sexually abused in childhood warrants careful consideration, and guidelines for therapists are suggested here to minimize the risk of this happening. There is no reliable evidence at present that this is a widespread phenomenon in the United Kingdom.
- In a recent review of the literature on recovered memories, Lindsay and Read (1994) commented that "the ground for debate has shifted from the question of the possibility of therapy-induced false beliefs to the question of the prevalence of therapy-induced false beliefs." We agree with this comment but add to it that the ground for debate has also shifted from the question of the possibility of recovery of memory from total amnesia to the question of the prevalence of recovery of memory from total amnesia.

The following were the overall conclusions of the Working Party:

- Normal event memory is largely accurate but may contain distortions and elaborations.
- With certain exceptions, such as where there has been extensive rehearsal of an imagined event, the source of our memories is generally perceived accurately.
- Nothing can be recalled accurately from before the first birthday and little from before the second. Poor memory from before the fourth birthday is normal.
- Forgetting of certain kinds of trauma is often reported, although the nature of the mechanism or mechanisms involved remains unclear.
- Although there is a great deal of evidence for incorrect memories, there is currently much less evidence on the creation of false memories.
- Hypnosis makes memory more confident and less reliable. It can also be used to create amnesia for events.

- There are a number of significant differences between false confessions and false (recovered) memories which preclude generalizing from one to the other.
- There are high levels of belief in the essential accuracy of recovered memories of child sexual abuse among qualified psychologists. These beliefs appear to be fueled by the high levels of experience of recovered memories both for CSA and for non-CSA traumatic events. The nondoctrinaire nature of these beliefs is indicated by the high level of acceptance of the possibility of false memories.
- There is not a lot of evidence that accusers fit a single profile. From the British records, at least, there is no good evidence that accusers have invariably recovered memories from total amnesia. Further documentation of the phenomenon is needed by the False Memory societies in order to obtain a more reliable picture. It appears that only in a small minority of instances do the accusations concern abuse that ended before the age of 5.
- Guidelines can be laid down for good practice in therapy.

The Working Party made a number of additional recommendations: that clinical training courses include appropriate attention to the properties of human memory, that increased priority be given to research in the areas covered in the report, that the findings of the report be taken into consideration when psychotherapy services are reviewed as to the quality of services and training, that appropriate parts of the report be brought to the attention of the general public, and that psychologists who conduct therapy practice within the following guidelines:

1. It may be necessary clinically for the therapists to be open to the emergence of memories of trauma that are not immediately available to the client's consciousness.
2. It is important for the therapist to be alert to the dangers of suggestion.
3. Although it is important always to take the client seriously, the therapist should avoid drawing premature conclusions about the truth of a recovered memory.
4. The therapist needs to tolerate uncertainty and ambiguity regarding the client's early experience.
5. Although it may be part of the therapists' work to help their clients to think about their early experiences, they should avoid imposing their own conclusions about what took place in childhood.
6. The therapist should be alert to a range of possibilities, for example, that a recovered memory may be literally true, metaphorically true, or may derive from fantasy or dream material.
7. If the role of the professional is to obtain evidence that is reliable in forensic terms, they need to restrict themselves to procedures that enhance

reliability (e.g., use of the cognitive interview and avoidance of hypnosis or suggestion and leading questions).

8. CSA (child sexual abuse) should not be diagnosed on the basis of presenting symptoms, such as eating disorder, alone–there is a high probability of false positives, as there are other possible explanations for psychological problems.

The Royal College of Psychiatrists

In 1994, the Royal College of Psychiatrists in Great Britain convened The Working Group on Reported Recovered Memories of Child Abuse. Controversy also surrounded the proceedings and findings of this group, with the result that the College decided not to publish the report[4] and instead published consensus recommendations for good practice (Royal College of Psychiatrists' Working Group on Reported Recovered Memories of Child Sexual Abuse, 1997). These include:

(a) The welfare of the patient is the first concern of the psychiatrist. Concern for the needs of family members and other may also be necessary, within the constraints imposed by the need for confidentiality.

(b) In children and adolescents, symptoms and behavior patterns may alert the clinician to the possibility of current sexual abuse, but these are no more than indicators for suspicion. Previous sexual abuse in the absence of memories of these events cannot be diagnosed through a checklist of symptoms.

(c) Psychiatrists are advised to avoid engaging in an "memory recovery techniques" which are intended to reveal evidence of past sexual abuse of which the patient has not memory and should regard with extreme caution memories of this kind whenever they appear. There is not evidence that the use of consciousness-altering techniques, such as drug-mediated interviews or hypnosis, can reveal or elaborate evidence of childhood sexual abuse. Techniques of "regression therapy," (age regression, guided imagery, "body memories," journaling, or literal dream interpretation, where this is used as evidence of fact) are of dubious provenance.

(d) Forceful or persuasive interviewing techniques are not acceptable in psychiatric practice. Doctors should be aware that patients are susceptible to subtle suggestions and reinforcements, whether or not these communications are intended.

(e) The psychiatrist should alert the patient to any doubts about the historical accuracy of recovered memories of previously unknown sexual abuse. This is particularly important if the patient intends to take action outside the therapeutic situation. Memories however emotionally intense and significant to the individual, may not necessarily represent historical truth. Memories may be historically true, metaphorical representations, caused by the psychological state of the patient or be the result of unintentional suggestion by the practitioner.

(f) It may be legitimate not to question the validity of a recovered memory while it remains within the privacy of the consulting room, although this introduces the risk of colluding in the creation of a life history based upon a false belief.

(g) Action taken outside the consulting room, including the revelation of accusations to any third party, must depend on circumstances and the wishes of the patient, but the full implications of such actions must always be considered. Adults who report previously forgotten childhood abuse may wish to confront the alleged abuser. Such action should not be mandated by the psychiatrist and it is rarely, if ever, justifiable to discourage or forbid the patient from having contact with the alleged abuser or other family members. The psychiatrist should help the patient think through the consequences of any confrontation. In these circumstances it is important to encourage a search for corroborative evidence before any action is taken. The truth or falsity of the underlying memories cannot be known in the absence of such evidence.

(h) Once an accusation is taken outside the consulting room, especially where any question of confrontation or public accusation arises, there is rarely any justification for refusal to allow a member of the therapeutic team to meet family members.

(i) Where an alleged abuser is still in touch with children, serious consideration must be given to informing the appropriate social services. This must be done where there are reasonable grounds for believing the alleged assault took place and that children may still be at risk. The psychiatrist must also be prepared to state clearly whether he or she believes that the grounds for any accusation are unlikely or impossible.

(j) The patient may wish to take legal advice with a view to the prosecution of, or litigation against, the alleged abuser. It is inappropriate to make any decision about this as a condition of continuing treatment.

(k) Alongside reports of recovered memories of sexual abuse there have been growing numbers of cases of multiple personality disorder (also known as dissociative identity disorder). There seems to be little doubt that many of these cases are iatrogenically determined. Any spontaneous presentation of multiple personality disorder should be sympathetically considered but should not be made subject of undue attention nor should the patient be encouraged to develop "alter personalities" in whom to invest aspects of their personality, their fantasies or their current life problems. Psychiatrists should be particularly aware of the unreliability of the memories reported in these cases and of the close association both with prolonged therapy and with recovered memories of sexual abuse, particularly alleged satanic abuse. Since there is not settled view of the validity of multiple personality disorder, and because of the very strong correlation with recovered memories of sexual abuse which is itself a disputed concept, there is a strong case for a consensus paper on multiple personality disorder based upon a substantial review of the literature.

CURRENT STATUS OF SCIENTIFIC AND CLINICAL ISSUES

The conclusions and recommendations of these four representative task forces, contribute to a more balanced viewpoint and recognize fundamental scientific and clinical issues and unanswered questions in need of continued research. Several of the core scientific issues include the following: The actuality and possibility of recovered memory and false memory (both within and outside of the context of psychotherapy) has been substantiated by research; however, the relative prevalence of these occurrences and the mechanisms by which they occur have not yet been identified. Evidence documenting memory loss (or traumatic amnesia) in the aftermath of different types of trauma has accumulated; yet, much remains to be learned about the mechanisms of forgetting and recovering memories of trauma, especially trauma that is complex and occurs repeatedly over an extended period of time and/or over the course of childhood (Brown et al., 1999). The formal scientific study of memory in the aftermath of trauma in both adults and children is relatively new and much additional research is needed in order to determine similarities to and differences from normal event memory. It is clear that memory is malleable but that conditions of encoding, storage, and retrieval might differ during an event that is traumatic versus one that is neutral or moderately stressful.

It is also apparent that recovered memory is not veridical (that is, not always an exact representation of an event) and that memory can be influenced in a number of different ways. It is as yet unclear how frequently genuine false memories (versus false beliefs) can be created and by what other sources of ongoing influence besides psychotherapy. On another matter, preliminary research findings suggest that many cues to remembering occur quite naturalistically outside of therapy and that individuals who report recovered memories of abuse have not reported psychotherapy as the major cue or trigger to remembering (Briere & Elliott, 1994). Issues of suggestibility, particularly concerning conditions related to the acceptance of suggestion and whether whole, complex memories and associated psychiatric conditions can be suggested or implanted, are as yet unproven and need more investigation. Additionally, the issue of whether research conducted in a laboratory setting on non-traumatized subjects is applicable in a wholesale way to traumatized individuals and to the conditions of psychotherapy remains open. The complexities of working with recovered memory issues in clinical practice have also been acknowledged. Therapists have the demanding task of increasing (or not suppressing) disclosure of genuine abuse while simultaneously decreasing the risk of false memory production and not unduly influencing the patient. Put another way, therapists must operate with caution with awareness of the possibility of both false positives and false negatives. Research is needed to determine with more specificity what conditions and procedures are more likely rather than less to be suggestive and ways to control for them in clinical practice. Studies are also needed that provide data about memory recovery per se. How often does it occur and under what conditions? What gives rise to the spontaneous emergence of memories? Finally, are there specific benefits associated with the recovery and processing of previously unavailable memories? At present, some personal testimonies are available regarding both the perceived benefits and the perceived harm. Preliminary outcome studies have been conducted that support the utility of encouraging patients to address issues (including memories) of childhood trauma in individual and group treatment; however, more investigation is needed.

IMPLICATIONS FOR THERAPISTS AND CLINICAL PRACTICE

In summarizing their analysis of the practice recommendations of nine of the task force reports, Grunberg and Ney (1997) wrote: "Generally, as the guidelines indicate, there is developing concern (albeit with increasing consensus) among clinicians about how memory works and how clinicians should conduct themselves in their work with trauma survivors and with clients who may or may not be trauma survivors" (p. 543). These reviewers further recognized that consensus was not achieved in all nine categories across the reports of the different professions, possibly due to the need for different perspectives by different disciplines. This suggests that, at a minimum, the practitioner should be familiar with and follow the recommendations made by his/her respective profession. Grunberg and Ney provided the following additional perspective and guidance:

> In many cases there is no "right" or "wrong" way to act; aspects of the situation must be weighed and a combination of sensitivity and realism must be considered in all clinical practice. We anticipate that guidelines will evolve in conjunction with developments in clinical practice and research in this area. There is still much that is not yet understood, and

guidelines which are overly prescriptive will not likely survive the test of time; however, without sufficient detail and rationale in the guidelines, the clinician is left without adequate reason for acting in particular ways. (p. 543)

By the mid to late 1990s, in the absence of clear definition and as a way of reassuring clinicians and ensuring that they continue to treat traumatized individuals, a number of clinical researchers articulated principles and guidelines of practice for working with recollections of abuse and other forms of trauma (Briere, 1997a, 1997b; Brown, 1995; Brown et al., 1998; Chu, 1998; Courtois, 1997a, 1997b, 1999; Enns, Campbell, Courtois, Gottlieb, Lese, Gilbert, & Forrest (1998); Gold & Brown, 1997; Knapp & VandeCreek, 1997; London, 1994; Mollon, 1998; Pope & Brown, 1996; Whitfield, 1995). By and large, they anticipated and incorporated many of the recommendations made by the professional task forces. Courtois (1997a, 1997b) summarized and consolidated these recommendations into a set of 19 guidelines for treatment that outlined several general principles for posttrauma treatment of abuse along with cautions and recommendations for working with delayed/recovered memories and suspicions of abuse when they emerge during the course of therapy. She noted (in keeping with Grunberg and Ney) that these guidelines are not absolute nor are they intended to be prescriptive, that they must be modified and applied with attention to the needs of the individual patient and with clinical judgment, and that they are expected to evolve in response to more sophisticated clinical and research data. Clinicians are therefore advised to keep abreast of developing and newly published research and literature relevant to this treatment. Additionally, these guidelines are intended to be overarching and general and do not address detailed technical or process issues, specific transference and countertransference-based issues, or other, more specialized concerns that are discussed elsewhere in the literature.[5]

The 19 guidelines, which have been updated for this article, are as follows:

I. GENERAL TREATMENT ISSUES AND RECOMMENDATIONS

1. Practice within the established professional code of ethics and practice standards.

Mental health professionals are advised to work within existing codes and standards for his/her discipline since, as yet, there are no formal practice standards for posttrauma treatment (in general or for post-abuse and delayed/recovered memory issues). Clinicians must avoid what is often a countertransference-driven belief that abused/traumatized patients are so unique or special as to require special forms of treatment or special techniques that do not conform to accepted professional standards.

2. Develop specialized knowledge and competence.

The clinician who works with abuse/trauma-related cases has responsibility for developing specialized knowledge in issues of abuse, trauma, memory, and posttrauma treatment as well as developing both intellectual and emotional competence in providing this treatment. Although no formal standard of care is as yet available for the treatment of posttraumatic conditions, several sets of treatment guidelines pertaining to the treatment of Posttraumatic Stress Disorder are now available (Foa, Davidson, & Frances, 1999; Ballenger et al., 2000) or are soon to be published (Foa, Keane, & Freidman, 2000) as are guidelines for the treatment of Dissociative Identitity Disorder (International Society for the Study of Dissociation, 1997) with which the clinician should be familiar.

3. Maintain an awareness of transference, countertransference, secondary traumatization, and self-care issues.

It is well recognized that individuals who have been repeatedly traumatized over the course of childhood often suffer significant developmental consequences, including emotional dysregulation and interpersonal difficulties (Herman, 1992). They can therefore have complex clinical presentations and be difficult for the clinician to treat. Traumatized patients are notorious for the transference and countertransference challenges they present. Therapists can also have strong personal reactions as a consequence of both listening to the traumatic material and experiencing the relational challenges of treating the traumatized, a process now labeled vicarious traumatization. Therapists can be additionally stressed by patients who suspect but don't know abuse and/or those whose memories are recovered or spotty. Therapists must become aware of these various relational issues in order to be able to identify and work with them therapeutically. Failure to manage them can cause the treatment to fail or can result in a variety of misalliances, some of which (i.e., overidentification with the patient and overdependence on the part of the patient) have been highlighted within the definition of "false memory syndrome."

4. Provide information about treatment and establish a therapeutic contract with the prospective and ongoing patient.

Informed consent and informed refusal are especially important with this treatment population. The patient should be informed about the treatment ahead of time and should maintain an ongoing awareness of the goals of treatment. S/he should be invited into a collaborative relationship with the therapist, a strategy that is designed to encourage empowerment and decision sharing on the part of the patient. Concerning recovered/delayed/repressed memory, the patient should be given information about professional recommendations for working with these issues. Informed consent issues should be offered in writing and can be supplemented with material about memory (i.e., the American Psychiatric Association statement is succinct and informative and is in a form that is easily provided to a prospective or ongoing patient).

> 5. Begin with a comprehensive psychosocial assessment including questions about past abuse/trauma and use psychological testing and ancillary assessments as warranted.

The clinician begins treatment by conducting a comprehensive psychosocial inquiry. This should include questions about past abuse, trauma, and other life crises embedded within more standard psychiatric/psychological assessment (i.e., the patient is queried about whether s/he has memories, knowledge of, or suspicions of having been abused or otherwise traumatized across the lifespan). The patient's responses to these questions make up the baseline of the therapist's knowledge base, information that is supplemented over the course of treatment. Therapists should be aware that inquiry does not always lead to disclosure and that, in many cases, a positive abuse/trauma history may not be disclosed due to a number of factors, among them resistance, shame, disbelief, and lack of memory. A number of specialized instruments for trauma and dissociative symptoms are now available (Briere, 1997c; Carlson, 1997; Stamm, 1996; Wilson & Keane, 1997) and can be utilized as necessary. It is also recommended that therapists seek information from previous treatment providers with attention to the methods used in treatment and the emergence of recovered memories during the course of past treatment. Finally, ancillary sources of information and consultation should be utilized as needed.

> 6. Develop a diagnostic formulation over time and after considering a range of information.

The therapist should avoid making "instant diagnoses" and should instead make a preliminary diagnosis with careful consideration of the individual and his/her presenting information, symptoms, and level of functioning. When past abuse/trauma is in question and is suspected by the patient rather than known, a diagnosis of PTSD cannot be formally made because all of the diagnostic criteria are not met (Criterion A has to do with the objective nature of the trauma). A posttrauma or postabuse treatment model (see item 7 for a description) is adopted when PTSD is formally or provisionally diagnosed. For patients who suspect abuse yet do not have posttraumatic symptoms, a more generic treatment strategy is recommended.

7. In providing posttrauma treatment, follow the consensus model of sequenced treatment.

The practitioner is advised to establish a treatment plan that conforms with the consensus model of posttrauma treatment (that is, a treatment that is sequenced and progressive). A number of experts in trauma treatment have identified three loosely organized stages of treatment (these are not lock-step and often overlap as patients move back and forth between the various tasks and issues that make up each stage): Stage 1, generally directed towards personal safety, stabilization, self-management and skill-building, stable or improved functioning, the resolution of immediate problems and crises, the improvement of current personal and interpersonal functioning, and the development of the treatment alliance; Stage 2, work with the traumatic content and emotions, titrated to the individual's capacities and motivation, and undertaken only after the individual has been stabilized and has skills to manage intense emotional stimulation; Stage 3, involving personal and interpersonal issues that remain after the formal trauma resolution and processing work of the second stage.

As noted in item 6, when no trauma history is known or determined from available information, a more generic model of treatment is advisable. The initial emphasis of Stage 1 on present-day issues and personal functioning resembles more generic treatment. Thus, its adoption provides for an adequate course of treatment for a patient with uncertainty about an abuse/trauma history, whether or not such a history is later determined.

II. ISSUES PERTAINING TO MEMORY

8. Ascertain personal and professional assumptions and biases and work for a stance of supportive neutrality.

The therapist must monitor personal and professional assumptions and biases and avoid leading questions, specific suggestions, undue influence, premature closure of exploration, and/or overly accepting the individual's recollections as historical truth. The therapist must be able to personally tolerate uncertainty about the past and be able to encourage the patient to do the same. Open-ended questions eliciting free recall on the part of the patient and a nonauthoritarian stance on the part of the therapist, is generally important but especially so with patients who are highly dependent, suggestible, or hypnotizable. As stated so cogently by Judith Herman, MD, therapists must be technically neutral but morally cognizant of the prevalence and possibility of abuse. This does not mean that the therapist is in denial about abuse as a serious and common occurrence or about its possibility in the patient's past; rather, it is the patient who must come to an understanding of and comfort with his/her personal history, especially when memories are fragmentary, hazy, uncertain, etc.

9. Watch assumptions about incomplete and spotty memory for childhood.

When a patient reports incomplete and spotty memory for childhood, the therapist should not automatically assume abuse/trauma as its cause. Normal memory for childhood is uneven. Other findings regarding childhood memory should also be taken into consideration: Early childhood is characterized by the inability to remember much (infantile amnesia). On average, children begin to cognitively remember at approximately 2 to 3 years, as they mature physically and develop a sense of self. Young children are able to remember events, but often remember the gist more than peripheral details and may need to be directly questioned about details before they remember or report them. Older children remember better, on average, than very young children.

10. Do not automatically assume sexual abuse from a set of symptoms.

No one symptom or set of symptoms (either initially or long-term) is pathognomic of childhood abuse/trauma, so the therapist should not automatically and conclusively assume an abuse history based on particular symptoms, especially when the patient does not report or even suspect abuse.

11. Be open to the possibility of other childhood trauma besides sexual abuse.

The therapist should be aware that a variety of individual and family crises may be traumatizing to a child and lead to posttraumatic reactions; thus, sexual abuse should not be assumed as the sole possible cause of symptoms.

12. Keep adequate records.

The therapist should keep records in sufficient detail to document the primary issues and events in the treatment, to articulate and track symptoms and the treatment plan, and to chronicle all major communications with the patient. Records should be neutral in tone and should be based on fact and behavior rather than on the therapist's speculations. The chart should include mention of any erroneous expectations and misinformation regarding abuse and memory held by the patient and should document the provision of more factual and accurate information and the discussion of process issues regarding memory retrieval. Additionally, notes should document memories and events as reported by the patient rather than as historical reality.

13. When using any method of memory retrieval, including hypnosis, in the treatment of trauma survivors, it is important to follow existing guidelines, and to be careful to avoid undue suggestion.

At present, available research suggests that memories that emerge as a result of any therapeutic technique, including hypnosis, can be compelling yet may also be inaccurate. The veridicality of these memories should not be assumed (although some may very well be accurate). The nature of hypnosis (or any specialized technique) requires specialized training according to the guidelines recommended by the various professional organizations that focus on these issues and methods. Moreover, hypnosis should not be used if the patient is involved in a legal proceeding of any type or has the likelihood of taking any future legal action (whether related to past abuse or not) since its use may result in the inadmissibility of material in such a proceeding.

14. Ascertain the individual's understanding and expectations about memory, therapy, and any sources of influence and social compliance. Correct misinformation.

The therapist should attempt to ascertain the patient's understanding and expectations about therapy as they pertain to abuse/trauma and memory and should further ascertain sources of influence and social compliance. Any misinformation should be noted along with the therapist's provision of corrective or counterbalancing information. It is recommended that the therapist engage in and model open-ended inquiry and a scientific attitude over time, especially regarding memories that are fragmentary and unclear. It is crucially important that the therapist not "fill in," "confirm," or "disconfirm" reported suspicions of an unrecalled abuse history but rather help the patient explore the content and its possible meaning while guarding against suggestion, pro and con. Individuals with positive histories of abuse/trauma often struggle with differentiating what is real and what is not, experience ambivalent emotions, and require a supportive context in which to consider various perspectives. Similarly, individuals with suspicions but no memories or corroboration must have the latitude to explore without constraint.

15. Recommend self-help books and groups judiciously and only when familiar with their content and perspective.

The therapist should be cautious in recommending self-help books and should be familiar with the content of any book that is suggested. In the case of suspected abuse, a generic book that discusses the many possible effects of a painful childhood is preferable to a book that is specifically oriented to abuse survivors or one that seeks to help the reader find his/her missing memories. A related issue is involvement in self-help or therapy groups. The patient with absent memory for abuse is best referred to a heterogeneous group for general mental health concerns rather than a homogeneous abuse focused one.

16. Support the patient's search for corroboration after adequate exploration and preparation in therapy.

The therapist can support a search for outside sources of information and possible corroboration (e.g., medical and school records, witnesses, other victims, etc.) as a means of gaining potential material to be assessed during the course of therapy. It is advisable that the patient explore the ramifications of a search before undertaking one and take action only after having achieved a relative degree of life and symptom stability and after adequate preparation. The patient should also consider the possible consequences of a search, ranging from confirmation to disconfirmation of his/her suspicions and beliefs, before initiating an investigation.

17. Do not recommend family cut-offs on the basis of recovered memory.

In the absence of clear cut information about ongoing danger when the therapist might be mandated to take action or suggest distancing, the therapist should be cautious in suggesting that the patient cut off contact with family. This is especially the case when recovered memories form the basis for abuse suspicions or beliefs.

18. Contract for no unplanned/impulsive disclosures, confrontations, or legal initiatives.

The therapist should have a collaborative agreement in place that unplanned/impulsive disclosures, confrontations, or legal initiatives not be undertaken without extensive discussion in therapy. These actions are risky even for the patient who has clear memory and/or corroboration; when abuse is suspected or believed on the basis of recovered memory without corroboration, they are even riskier (for both patient and therapist). Ideally, initial disclosures should be made to individuals who have the greatest likelihood of being supportive and should be undertaken after the patient is relatively stabilized. Like the search for corroboration (item 16) the results of disclosure, confrontation, and legal action can range from highly positive to highly negative; all possible options ought to be considered as to their likelihood and prepared for accordingly.

19. Do not encourage or suggest a lawsuit.

It is not the therapist's role to suggest a lawsuit. Litigation is enormously stressful and requires an extensive time commitment as well as the allocation of significant personal and financial resources. The plaintiff in a lawsuit must meet a standard of proof that is not required in a clinical setting. Lawsuits have become even more difficult since the advent of the memory controversy and the routine use of a false memory defense. The patient needs to understand the mechanics of a lawsuit and the potential difficulties that will be encountered in the process. Should the patient opt to initiate a lawsuit in spite of the deterrents, the therapist must avoid the dual relationship of being a treating therapist and a psychological expert.

CONCLUSION

The aim of this article was to provide a general overview of major positions in the recovered/false memory controversy and to review recommendations made by professional task forces as they suggest guidelines for the treatment of adult survivors reporting delayed memories or suspicions of past abuse. Clinicians must strive to neither suggest nor suppress reports of remembered or suspected abuse and trauma; instead, they must practice from a stance of supportive neutrality regarding the historical accuracy of memories of abuse, especially when memories have been recovered after a period of unavailability and/or are unclear. Therapists are advised to not equate recovery of memories of abuse with recovery of the patient, to seek to improve the client's overall clinical status and functionality, and to work with the retrieval and processing of traumatic memories judiciously and as needed.

NOTES

1. "False memory syndrome" (FMS), a term coined by an advocacy organization by the same name, The False Memory Syndrome Foundation (FMSF), is defined as: "condition in which a person's identity and interpersonal relationships are centered around a memory of traumatic experience which is objectively false but in which the person strongly believes. *Note that the syndrome is not characterized by false memories as such* . . . Rather, the syndrome may be diagnosed when the memory is so deeply ingrained that it orients the individual's entire personality and lifestyle, in turn disrupting all sort of other adaptive behaviors" (definition attributed to Dr. John F. Kihlstrom, False Memory Syndrome Foundation brochure, 1993, italics added). It is important to note that FMS is not an officially codified and accepted diagnosis, as it is not included in the *Diagnostic and Statistical Manual* published periodically by the American Psychiatric Association or in other official diagnostic manuals; therefore, individuals cannot be formally *diagnosed* as suffering from a condition called "FMS."

2. Professional task forces and working groups and the date of publication of their reports are as follows: American Medical Association (1994); American Psychological Association (1994, 1996, 1998); American Psychiatric Association (1993); Australian Psychological Society (1994), American Society of Clinical Hypnosis (1994); British Association of Counseling (1997); British Psychological Society (1995); Canadian Psychological Association (1996); National Association of Social Workers (1996); New Zealand Psychological Association (1995); The Royal Australian and New Zealand College of Psychiatrists (1996); The Royal College of Psychiatry–Great Britain (1997); and The International Society for Traumatic Stress Studies (1998). Two additional documents having to do with the treatment of interpersonal violence were published in 1996 by the American Psychological Association, *Professional, Ethical and Legal Issues Concerning Interpersonal Violence, Maltreatment and Related Trauma* and *Potential Problems for Psychologists Working with Areas of Interpersonal Violence.*

3. The author was one of the clinician members of this Working Group.

4. A paper entitled "Recovered memories of childhood sexual abuse: Implications for clinical practice," a revised version of the report originally submitted to the Royal College, was recently published in the *British Journal of Psychiatry,* not as a College document but as a paper by individual authors (Brandon, Boakes, Glaser, & Green, 1998). It includes a summary of the evidence on recovered memories of childhood sexual abuse in addition to the previously released recommendations.

5. Since Courtois' publication of this summary set of guidelines, a number of additional books on clinical practice (Chu, 1998; Courtois, 1999; Gold, 2000; Mollon, 1998) and on research findings and clinical practice (Applebaum, Uyehara, & Elin, 1997; Brown, et al., 1998; Lynn & McConkey, 1999; Williams & Banyard, 1999) have been published.

REFERENCES

American Medical Association Council on Scientific Affairs. (1994). *Memories of childhood abuse, CSA Report 5-A-94.* Chicago: Author.

American Psychiatric Association Board of Directors. (1993). *Statement on Memories of Sexual Abuse.* Washington, DC: Author.

American Psychological Association. (1994). *Interim report of the Working Group on Investigation of Memories of Childhood Abuse.* Washington, DC: Author.

American Psychological Association. (1996a). Analysis of the "Truth and Responsibility in Mental Health Practices Act" and similar proposals. Washington, DC: Author.

American Psychological Association. (1996b). *Final report of the Working Group on Investigation of Memories of Childhood Abuse.* Washington, DC: Author.

American Psychological Association ad hoc Committee on Legal and Ethical Issues in the Treatment of Interpersonal Violence. (1996c). *Potential problems for psychologists working with the area of interpersonal violence.* [Brochure]. Washington, DC: Author.

American Psychological Association ad hoc Committee on Legal and Ethical Issues in the Treatment of Interpersonal Violence. (1996d). *Professional, ethical, and legal issues concerning interpersonal violence, maltreatment and related trauma.* [Brochure]. Washington, DC: Author.

American Society of Clinical Hypnosis. (1994). *Clinical hypnosis and memory: Guidelines for clinicians for forensic hypnosis.* Des Plaines, IL: American Society for Clinical Hypnosis Press.

Appelbaum, P. S., Uyehara, L. A., & Elin, M. R. (Eds.). (1997). *Trauma and memory: Clinical and legal controversies.* New York: Oxford University Press.

Australian Psychological Society Limited Board of Directors. (1994). *Guidelines related to the reporting of recovered memories.* Sydney, New South Wales, Australia: Author.

Ballenger, J. C., Davidson, J. R. T., Lecrubier, Y., Nutt, D. J., Foa, E. G., Kessler, R. C., McFarland, A. C., & Shalev, A. Y. (2000). Consensus statement on posttraumatic stress disorder from the International Consensus Group on Depression and Anxiety. *The Journal of Clinical Psychiatry, 61* (Supp 5), 60-66.

Bass, E., & Davis, L. (1988). *The courage to heal: A guide for women survivors of child sexual abuse.* New York: Harper & Row.

Bass, E., & Davis, L. (1994). *The courage to heal: A guide for women survivors of child sexual abuse.* New York: Harper & Row.

Bloom, S. (1997). *Creating sanctuary: Toward the evolution of sane societies.* New York: Routledge.

Brandon, S., Boakes, J., Glaser, D., & Green, R. (1998). Recovered memories of childhood sexual abuse: Implications for clinical practice. *British Journal of Psychiatry, 172,* 296-307.

Briere, J. (1997a). *Therapy for adults molested as children: Beyond survival* (2nd ed.). New York: Springer Publishing Co.

Briere, J. (1997b). An integrated approach to treating adults abused as children with specific reference to self-reported recovered memories. In J. D. Read & D. S. Lindsay (Eds.). *Recollections of trauma: Scientific evidence and clinical practice* (pp. 25-48). New York: Plenum Press.

Briere, J. (1997c). *Psychological assessment of adult posttraumatic states.* Washington, DC: American Psychological Association.

Briere, J. & Elliott, D. M. (1994). Immediate and long-term impacts of child sexual abuse. *The Future of Children, 4,* 54-69.

British Association of Counseling. (1997). *False memory syndrome: A statement.* Rugby, Warwickshire, England: Author.

British Psychological Society. (1995). *Recovered memories: The Report of the Working Party of the British Psychological Society.* London: Author.

Brown, D. (1995). Pseudomemories, the standard of science, and the standard of care in trauma treatment. *American Journal of Clinical Hypnosis, 37,* 1-24.

Brown, D., Scheflin, A. W., & Hammond, D. C. (1998). *Memory, trauma treatment, and the law.* New York: W. W. Norton & Company.

Brown, D., Scheflin, A., & Whitfield, C. L. (Spring, 1999). Recovered memories: The current weight of the evidence in science and in the courts. *The Journal of Psychiatry and Law, 26:5-156.*

Brown, L. S. (1996). Politics of memory, politics of incest: Doing therapy and politics that really matter. In S. Contratto & M. J. Gutfreund (Eds.), *A feminist clinician's guide to the memory debate* (pp. 5-18). New York: The Haworth Press, Inc.

Canadian Psychological Association (1996). *Position statement: Adult recovered memories of childhood sexual abuse.* Toronto, Canada: Author.

Chu, J. A. (1998). *Rebuilding shattered lives: The responsible treatment of complex posttraumatic and dissociative disorders.* New York: Wiley.

Courtois, C. A. (1997a). Guidelines for the treatment of adults abused or possibly abused as children (with attention to issues of delayed/recovered memory). *American Journal of Psychotherapy, 53,* 497-510.

Courtois, C. A. (1997b). Informed clinical practice and the standard of care: Proposed guidelines for the treatment of adults who report delayed memories of childhood trauma. In J. D. Read & D. S. Lindsay (Eds.). *Recollections of trauma: Scientific evidence and clinical practice* (pp. 137-361). New York: Plenum Press.

Courtois, C. A. (1999). *Recollections of sexual abuse: Treatment principles and guidelines.* New York: W. W. Norton & Company.

Elliott, D. M. & Briere, J. (1995). Posttraumatic stress associated with delayed recall of sexual abuse: A general population study. *Journal of Traumatic Stress, 3,* 629-648.

Foa, E. B., Keane, T. M., & Friedman, M. J. (2000). *Effective treatments for PTSD: Practice guidelines from the International Society for Traumatic Stress Studies.* New York: Guilford Publications.

Foa, E. B., Davidson, J. R. T., & Frances, A. (1999). The Expert Consensus Guideline Series: Treatment of Posttraumatic Stress Disorder. *The Journal of Clinical Psychiatry, 60,* Supp. 16, 1-76.

Freyd, J. J. (1996). *Betrayal trauma: The logic of forgetting childhood abuse.* Cambridge, MA: Harvard University Press.

Gold, S. N. (2000). *Not trauma alone: Therapy for child abuse survivors in family and social context.* Philadelphia: Brunner-Routledge: Taylor & Francis Group.

Gold, S. N. & Brown, L. S. (1997). Therapeutic responses to delayed recall: Beyond recovered memory. *Psychotherapy, 34*(2), 182-191.

Grunberg, F., & Ney, T. (1997). Professional guidelines on clinical practice for recovered memory: A comparative analysis. In J. D. Read & D. S. Lindsay (Eds.), *Recollections of trauma: Scientific evidence and clinical practice* (pp. 541-556). New York: Plenum Press.

Herman, J. (1992). *Trauma and recovery.* New York: Basic Books.

Hinnefeld, B. & Newman, R. (1997). Analysis of the Truth and Responsibility in Mental Health Practices Act and similar proposals. *Professional Psychology: Research and Practice, 28*(6), 537-543.

International Society for Traumatic Stress Studies. (1998). *Childhood trauma remembered: A report on the current scientific knowledge base and its applications.* [Brochure]. Northbrook, IL: Author.

Knapp, S. J., & VandeCreek, L. (1997). *Treating patients with memories of abuse: Legal risk management.* Washington, DC: American Psychological Association.

Lindsay, D. S., & Briere, J. (1997). The controversy regarding recovered memories of childhood sexual abuse: Pitfalls, bridges, and future directions. *Journal of Interpersonal Violence, 12*(5), 631-647.

Loftus, E. F. (1993). The reality of repressed memories. *American Psychologist, 48,* 518-537.

Loftus, E. F., & Ketcham, K. (1994). *The myth of repressed memory: False memories and allegations of sexual abuse.* New York: St. Martin's Press.

Lynn, S. J. & McConkey, K. M. (1998). *Truth in memory.* New York: Guilford Press.

Mollon, P. (1998). *Remembering trauma: A psychotherapist's guide to memory and illusion.* New York: John Wiley & Sons.

National Association of Social Work National Council on the Practice of Clinical Social Work. (1996). *Evaluation and treatment of adults with the possibility of recovered memories of childhood sexual abuse.* Washington, DC: Author.

New Zealand Psychological Society. (1995). *Memory of traumatic childhood events.* New Zealand: Author.

Ofshe, R., & Watters, E. (1994). *Making monsters: False memories, psychotherapy, and hysteria.* New York: Charles Scribner's Sons.

Pezdek, K., & Banks, W. (1996). *The recovered memory/false memory debate.* New York: Academic Press.

Pope, K. (1996). Memory, abuse, and science: Questioning claims about the false memory syndrome epidemic. *American Psychologist, 51,* 957-974.

Pope, K., & Brown, L. S. (1996). *Recovered memories of abuse: Assessment, therapy, forensics.* Washington, DC: American Psychological Association Press.

Read, J. D., & Lindsay, D. S. (Eds.). (1997). *Recollections of trauma: Scientific evidence and clinical practice* (pp. 541-556). New York: Plenum Press.

Royal Australian and New Zealand College of Psychiatrists. (1996). *Guidelines for psychiatrists dealing with repressed traumatic memories.* (Clinical Memorandum No. 17).

Royal College of Psychiatrists' Working Group on Reported Recovered Memories of Child Sexual Abuse. (1997). Recommendation for good practice and implications for training, continuing professional development and research. *Psychiatric Bulletin, 21,* 663-665.

Stamm, H. (1996). *Measurement of stress, trauma, and adaptation.* Lutherville, MD: Sidran Press.

Terr, L. (1991). Childhood traumas: An outline and overview. *American Journal of Psychiatry, 148,* 10-20.

Terr, L. (1994). *Unchained memories: True stories of traumatic memories, lost and found.* New York: Basic Books.

Underwager, R., & Wakefield, H. (1990). *The real world of child interrogations.* Springfield, IL: Thomas.

van der Kolk, B., & van der Hart, O. (1995). The intrusive past: The flexibility of memory and the engraving of trauma. In C. Caruth (Ed.), *Trauma: Explorations in memory* (pp. 158-182). Baltimore, MD: The Johns Hopkins University Press.

Wakefield, H. & Underwager, R. (1992). Recovered memories of alleged sexual abuse: Lawsuits against parents. *Behavioral Sciences and the Law, 10,* 483-507.

Whitfield, C. L., (1995). *Memory and abuse: Remembering and healing the effects of trauma.* Deerfield Beach, FL: Health Communications.

Williams, L., & Banyard, V. (Eds.). (1999). *Trauma & memory.* Thousand Oaks, CA: Sage.

Wilson, J. P., & Keane, T. M. (1997). *Assessing psychological trauma and PTSD.* New York: Guilford.

Yapko, M. (1994). *Suggestions of abuse.* New York: Simon & Schuster.

Index

Numbers followed by an "f" indicate figures; "t" following a page number indicates tabular material.